Strategic advice to help businesses grow.

We have more than 100 years' experience in providing intellectual property advice and offer specialist expertise in: biotechnology and pharmacology, brand protection and designs, chemical engineering, chemistry, electronics and engineering, energy and environmental technology, ionic liquids, IT and communications, medical devices, and nanotechnology.

For a free initial consultation on how we can assist you in using your IP to gain competitive advantage, contact us now.

A straight talking intellectual property firm that's committed to giving clients a competitive edge.

Marks&Clerk

You Predict the Future, We Protect it

Whether your business leads on brand identity or technology value, Intellectual Property is a key element in establishing your position in the marketplace. It is vital that you work with advisers who have the right experience and expertise to protect your IP – and help you to exploit its full potential.

At Marks & Clerk, our unrivalled resources in Europe, Asia and North America, and long-standing relationships with leading IP firms worldwide, allow us to give you access to a wide range of services worldwide.

Our commercial approach combined with local knowledge and expertise enables us to tailor our services to create the most effective IP strategy for your business.

From the smallest inventive step to the largest commercial leap, from information technology to biotechnology, we are here to ensure that you get the maximum value and benefit from your IP.

www.marks-clerk.com

FOREWORD

Innovation, the successful exploitation of new ideas, is key to economic growth. As governments and businesses focus on innovation capability, processes and support are evolving rapidly. One example of this was the creation of the Technology Strategy Board, the UK's innovation agency, in 2007. More generally, for all those in the chain of creating new value from innovation, assumptions are being revised and conventions rewritten. The search for ideas with potential is becoming more open and people are working together to resolve challenges swiftly and explore new paths to market.

Knowledge is flowing more freely. Big players in business and government are looking outside for inspiration. Academic researchers are becoming more commercial. Entrepreneurial ventures are bringing disruptive thinking, and users are becoming an integral part of the creative process.

For those who can collaborate to apply the right idea to the right model at the right time, the rewards can be high. In the UK, I see many examples of businesses experiencing dramatic growth in spite of the dark economic clouds that have hung over us for the last four or five years.

But there are many obstacles, and failure can occur anywhere on the path from concept to commercialization. It can be difficult for large companies to accept the investment risk, or for small companies to persuade external investors. It can be hard to spot the long-term trends that bring opportunity, or to be ready for the disruption in supply chains and markets that innovation causes. And it may not be easy for companies to navigate the complex landscape of resources available.

To address these problems in the UK and reduce innovation risk, new approaches, tools and techniques have been developed by the Technology Strategy Board and others. Networks make connections and spark new ideas. Funding programmes such as innovation vouchers, Smart awards and SBRI (the Small Business Research Initiative) encourage new ideas and solutions to flourish. Business-focused researchers work inside companies to commercialize ideas, intellectual property is managed more flexibly as an asset, and templates are being created to help the exchange of knowledge.

One important development is the Catapult centres which the Technology Strategy Board is setting up. This is a large-scale, long-term investment, and each Catapult will bring together the very best UK businesses, scientists and engineers in its field, working together to transform ideas into new products and services that will generate economic growth.

This is both a major initiative and a powerful symbol of the new directions that innovation is taking. This book explores many more.

Iain Gray
Chief Executive, Technology Strategy Board
For further details: www.innovateuk.org

PART ONE
New innovation

systematically working back from customer definition and needs to an outline programme of work designed to meet those needs. Clear articulation of the journey (with an acknowledgement that things may need to change along the way) will help secure partners and backing.

4. Present a full package

Some corporate investors still claim that they are only interested in the quality of the science. This can be misleading, as corporate investors take a very rounded view of investment. It is fundamental to present a complete package of information. The commercialization plan for the technology should aim to gather or create all of the necessary information during its execution.

The Cell Therapy Catapult works with collaborators towards an investible package which includes:

- clinical data;
- clinical trial access;
- manufacturing processes;
- regulatory pathway;
- intellectual property;
- market data;
- viable business model;
- reimbursement information;
- accessible clinical delivery partners (ie customers);
- skills and leadership;
- analytical tools.

5. Create or be part of a portfolio

A further way to make a project seem more attractive to investors is for it to be part of an actual or virtual portfolio. Investors need to invest certain quantities of money, but also seek diversification. At the same time, investors are limited in their ability to analyse diverse technologies. The innovation markets are very heterogeneous, with a great diversity of technologies, and within a defined space such as cell therapies, investors may lack the resources to make fully informed decisions. However, grouping technologies in actual or virtual portfolios allows groups of investors to share due diligence resources and achieve a high enough absolute level of investment.

Some innovation centres can act as the coordination or gathering point for such portfolios.

6. Help investors make educated decisions on whether to invest

If there is access to relevant expertise, investors may perceive the risks to be lower. A Catapult can help with due diligence and increase investor confidence. Perception of risk is further reduced by the belief that appropriate expertise will be available for the lifetime of the investment.

7. De-risk for management and talent

New ventures don't just need to be de-risked for investors. They need to be de-risked to attract capable managers. Managers are often asked to come into SMEs with high-risk profiles. Capable management, with other options, may opt for lower-risk companies, leaving only those who often have less experience.

8. Truly align investors and management

Reducing the risk as described can help attract talent. In the traditional SME model there is an additional risk. Good management operating as a true team is a precious resource that takes time to build. In a single technology company nobody knows more about what is going on than the management, and they are the conduit of information to investors. Investors will often withdraw resources as a product appears to face technological difficulty. The blame for failure is usually placed on management, without reference to the scale of the technological challenge they were asked to undertake. This means that managers may delay disclosing bad news in order to be able to continue product development. Maintaining a strong incentive for success and focus should not require the management to also take all of the downside of technological failure. Investors in SMEs (which includes the management) may be able to avoid throwing good money after bad by providing alternatives for management where there is technological rather than management failure. Technology portfolio companies are one way of offering this. Another is linkage with innovation centres where new opportunities can be found, maintaining a valuable team.

9. 'Seek the truth'

In the development and commercialization of technologies it is crucial for entrepreneurs and stakeholders to be evidence based in their decisions. An enthusiastic entrepreneur can drive a mediocre product a long way before it eventually fails. By this point often entrepreneur and investor are exhausted and a lot of money has been wasted. Making early decisions to opt out of technologies can save managers their reputation and investors' money. An example of this is in the biotech industry, where products are occasionally pushed through to Phase II based on inadequate data, only to fail after much more expense has been incurred in subsequent trials. Rigorous early testing, and in the case of cell therapy a stronger Phase II trial design, can help avoid this waste, bringing down the development costs of the whole industry.

Conclusion

These thoughts arose during the strategic planning of the Cell Therapy Catapult, one of a number of elite innovation centres in the UK. It has been set up to close the gap between concept and commercialization, as have the other Catapults which cover a range of industries. Engaging closely with these centres will help speed the success of individual technologies and industry as a whole.

Jessica Griffiths is a business analyst at the Cell Therapy Catapult and Matthew Durdy is its Chief Business Officer. The Cell Therapy Catapult is focused on the needs of the industry, spanning capabilities from commercialization planning to manufacturing process development and regulatory and clinical execution. It is a national centre in a global location at Guy's Hospital in London and is developing 1,200m^2 of laboratories and offices containing the equipment and expertise needed to help SMEs innovate in cell therapy.

E-mail: Jessie.Griffiths@ct.catapult.org.uk; Matthew.Durdy@ct.catapult.org.uk; web: https://ct.catapult.org.uk

The
University
Of
Sheffield.

Innovate with the University of Sheffield

Get connected with the University of Sheffield to enhance your market competitiveness and secure the long-term skills and innovation demands for your business.

The University of Sheffield is a multi-disciplinary research intensive university with a long history of industrial collaboration. Operating across the full range of Technology Readiness levels, from basic research up to product manufacturing and support, we can assist you in your drive to push innovative technology out into the marketplace.

Our experience in collaborating and translating research to solve real-world problems makes the University the ideal supply chain partner for industry. Organisations such as Rolls-Royce, Boeing, E.ON, Tata Steel, Jaguar, Nissan, Messier Dowty and Siemens already work with the University as well as a multitude of SME's in the UK and worldwide.

Our approach to collaborative ways of working and open innovation can connect you with funding, new IP, R&D resources, consortiums, key supply chains, talented employees as well as support you with your innovation goals.

Find out more

For examples of how companies in the energy, renewables, medical and nuclear sectors have benefited from partnering with us, visit **www.researchatsheffield.co.uk.**

Contact our dedicated business gateway to discuss your needs with staff that have both commercial and research experience in key industry sectors.

gateway@sheffield.ac.uk
0114 222 9735
www.sheffield.ac.uk/seg

Strategic partnerships

Developing a single innovative collaboration with a university is the first step in what can prove to be a long-term and mutually beneficial strategic relationship, where both parties invest in each other's future. Over the years, Rolls-Royce has grown its relationships with key university partners through its University Technology Centres (UTCs), which give access to a wealth of talent and creativity to help protect their capability into the future. At the University of Sheffield we have several Rolls-Royce UTCs with a continuous flow of staff between the two organizations, embedding the relationship at a very deep level.

Innovation hubs

Universities sit at the centre of a national innovation hub and can connect companies to expertise, funding and networking opportunities. The independence of universities allows us to bring together competing organizations to work collaboratively as a consortium. Typically, this might encompass bringing an underpinning technology to several market sectors, or a shared industry endeavour to bring about a step-change in the market environment.

Universities can work across the whole supply chain and regularly bring diverse businesses together. Recently, the University of Sheffield acted as an innovation catalyst, introducing Smith & Nephew to an innovative SME, MicroLab Devices. This new industry–university partnership applied for TSB Collaborative R&D funding and received £600k to develop novel new polymer gels for wound dressings to quickly detect and control infection.

An innovation opportunity

This is a unique period for collaborative open innovation with universities in the UK, with cultural, structural and funding changes all coming together to create an ideal climate for innovation to strengthen the UK's global market competitiveness.

Accessing the university innovation toolkit

Nationally it's a complex picture

A key challenge for any university's business development teams is to map their university's capabilities. When you consider the vast range of research activities undertaken, staff turnover and evolving research interests, it is easy to see how difficult it is to track what is actually taking place. Multiply this across the UK and you have a complex, changing environment of knowledge creation. In order to resolve this issue, the TSB has implemented a range of mechanisms to help industry access this expertise, by placing leading universities at the hubs of the UK innovation network.

What is going on in a given technology sector?

To understand how a particular sector is developing in terms of technology, markets, government policy, EU policy, funding and economics, the KTNs are a great place to start and they cover all the main areas of innovation in the UK. Through regular reports, newsletters and events, members can keep up to date with the latest developments. In addition, there are many other independent networks focusing upon specific technologies.

Where do I find specific expertise?

The TSB has set up a national platform to simplify collaboration and networking called _connect; this allows members to search for potential collaborators and partners. This is a great starting point, but it can still be difficult to determine which universities have the depth of capability in a specific area. The more research-intensive Russell Group universities have a broad scope of expertise, but it is also worth considering your local universities who may have expertise in the required area and, owing to their proximity, may be easier to work with for general technical assistance.

Working with universities

Most large universities have business development teams who are ideally placed to help you navigate the complex environment of who does what, and which activities or funding mechanisms would be most appropriate to employ. Before talking to them, it is useful to define your business requirements and project timescales clearly, in order to ascertain the most beneficial method of collaboration.

The breadth of universities allows access to ideas and expertise outside the technical area a company may think it's involved in. Quite often we find that the solution may not be technical but a business one, for example access to management school expertise may help provide an innovative way of working.

Examples of how industry can work with universities include:

- Solving an immediate challenge: Where you require a fast response to a pressing business problem, asking an academic to offer consultancy advice can give you fast access to expertise. Various specialist business centres can also help. For example, FaraPack Polymers at the University of Sheffield can solve polymer-specific issues through a dedicated team of specialists.

- Exploring new ideas: Engaging with students is an excellent way to investigate longer-term business ideas, giving students placements or projects to evaluate a range of scenarios. This provides the students with invaluable industry experience and gives companies visibility at the university and access to potential future employees.

- Testing or analysis: Universities have major state-of-the-art equipment assets which can be made available to industry. Many universities also have spin-out companies which can provide responsive services; for example, a University of Sheffield spin-out company, Blastech Ltd, operates large-scale facilities for hazardous experimental testing by industry. Innovation vouchers can sometimes be used to help fund smaller projects.

- Acquiring new technologies: Knowledge Transfer Projects (KTPs) are a very successful tool for transferring and embedding knowledge or technology from a university into a company. These subsidized projects favour SMEs, typically last for 18 months and employ an associate who works between the company and the university. For example, the University of Sheffield collaborated via a KTP with Sarantel to introduce new metamaterial technology into its production process of a smaller, higher-gain antenna for mobile radio applications.

- Research & Development: There is a wide range of options, from industrially relevant research carried out through the sponsorship of a PhD to collaboration on TSB-funded projects or the development of a whole research centre. Collaboration with universities may enable external funding to be leveraged for larger projects.

- Graduates: Employing graduates can bring fresh ideas and technologies into your business and help foster innovation. Within universities, there is an increasing trend for alumni to be used as a knowledge bridge between industry and their former university; this is seen to be beneficial to their personal development, their employer and their former university.

Experience has shown that the simple process of networking more widely and developing relationships with academics creates opportunities and fosters greater innovation within your organization.

Neale Daniel played a key role in creating the Engineering Gateway team at the University of Sheffield in 2009 as a resource for developing partnerships between industry and academia in the Faculty of Engineering. Prior to this he spent almost 30 years as a professional engineer and R&D manager, developing innovative electronic and software products for a wide variety of markets.

Sheffield Engineering Gateway website: www.sheffield.ac.uk/seg; e-mail: gateway@sheffield.ac.uk; tel: 0114 222 9735; LinkedIn: uk.linkedin.com/in/nealedaniel/linkedin

The IP framework

Rosa Wilkinson, Director of Innovation at the Intellectual Property Office (IPO), discusses how the IP system is adapting to rapid changes in technology and trade

In trying economic times, the wise innovate. They understand that innovation generates a new capacity to generate wealth which, over time, fuels prosperity for all. Over recent years governments around the world have recognized that great innovation demands a supportive business and creative environment. In a top innovating nation like Britain, with its world-leading research base, its creative flair and its determined inventiveness has fuelled a significant programme of legislative reform and service development to the intellectual property (IP) landscape.

Rapid changes in technology and the creative force of free-flowing information will continue to put a premium on the creation and use of IP. Our companies need an IP environment that encourages ease of access, sharing of information and collaborative partnerships, but provides the effective protection which allows the translation of ideas into value not just at home but in markets around the world, supporting the global ambitions of today's businesses.

In developing a plan to capture the potential of 21st-century technologies and ideas, the IPO is actively looking to support high-growth ventures, push through international barriers and build confidence in the protection of IP rights.

High growth

IP can act as a powerful stimulant to growth, acting as a channel for commercializing ideas and attracting investment. We know that small firms perform better when they manage the commercial rights in their ideas and improvements. By using IP to create, transfer and exploit their knowledge they see improved productivity and increase their growth potential and likelihood. Research tells us that such innovative firms grow twice as fast as everyone else. The worry is that too often smaller firms are failing to gain fully from their capacity for creativity and innovation through poor management of their IP.

At the IPO, our goal is to find ways of engaging and supporting those with the potential for high growth by making sure that they can access high-quality advice, guidance and the tools they need to maximize the value of their innovation. Our approach begins at home. We want to be confident that the services we deliver meet your needs by keeping watch on your experience of contacting us, understanding how you use our services and making sure that the comments you make drive continuous improvements in how we deliver them. The UK IPO is already regarded by many as the best in the world. In the coming year, users will see further improvements in our services with the launch of a faster patents application service and faster trade marks and Tribunal services. You will also see continued transformation of the patent service provision as we modernize our IT infrastructure to make sure it reflects 21st-century business methods and complete the roll-out of our new trade mark publication processing system. Increasingly our services will be made available online. If you have thoughts and ideas about how we might develop our services so that your business can flourish, we want to hear about them.

In parallel, we are reaching out more to help businesses to make the most of their ideas, both directly through guidance, seminars, workshops and simple tools, and indirectly by making sure that other advisers you talk to are equipped to talk about IP issues.

International reach

Looking to international markets, the IPO will continue its work to influence the development of an international IP infrastructure which supports collaboration across borders and international trade. UK companies with significant IP assets need to be confident that those assets will be protected wherever they trade, so the IPO will continue to develop strong relationships with emerging markets, particularly high-growth markets such as China, India, Brazil and the East Asian markets. In the past year we have posted attachés to our embassies in these key markets to support the development of strong national IP regimes and to work alongside UK Trade & Investment (UKTI) in supporting UK exporters and investors. In the coming year, we will complement the support they provide with a refresh of guidance for businesses seeking to protect their IP in the markets where they have the greatest concerns.

We will also continue to play a strong role in improving the multilateral framework of IP rules, both to strengthen protection where necessary and to reduce the costs and bureaucracy experienced by businesses trading internationally. We will continue to maximize our influence in key international institutions such as the World Intellectual Property Organization (WIPO), the European Patent Office and others to provide a global business environment that delivers for our businesses and creators. Our work will include pushing forward implementation of the agreement to create a Europe-wide patent and patent court, part of which will be based in London. This should put EU businesses on a more equal footing with businesses from our global competitors, such as the United States and China, which already enjoy a single patent environment.

Enforcement

Many SMEs are concerned about the potential cost of enforcing their IP rights, or defending themselves against a claim of IP infringement. For those with limited resources, litigation can be expensive and the impact can be significant. Examples of our efforts to secure better outcomes for SMEs include:

- Extensive reform of the Patents County Court, to improve access to justice, particularly for SMEs, by reducing costs, streamlining procedures and increasing clarity and certainty around fees and jurisdiction. Changes have included a fixed scale of recoverable costs limited to £50,000, a cap on damages of £500,000 and a new Small Claims Track, with informal procedures, for uncomplicated claims of under £10,000. These changes ensure that court costs are proportionate to what is at stake and that lower-value and less complex cases which would typically involve SMEs will fall within the jurisdiction of the lower and now cheaper court.

- Support for alternative mechanisms for resolving disputes before they reach the courts. Our mediation service has been re-launched to help businesses and individuals resolve IP disputes quickly and effectively. We will continue to facilitate coordination between the multiple actors involved in tackling IP crime, and a coordinated response to IP crime can now be made through our intelligence hub and the IP Crime Group. As part of our ongoing efforts, we also provide a training module for trading standards offices, which are able to take action on the ground.

Summary

The IPO's vision is to create an environment in which the full potential of ideas, knowledge and creativity can be realized for the benefit of our economy and society. Our role in delivering that vision is to promote innovation by providing a clear, accessible and widely understood IP system which promotes UK growth, delivers high-quality rights-granting services and enables businesses to understand, use and protect their IP. This brief introduction gives some highlights from the programme of action we are taking to deliver on those goals. If you have views or comments that can help us, we're keen to hear them; get in touch at information@ipo.gov.uk.

Rosa Wilkinson has been innovation director at the Intellectual Property Office for the past two years. Previously, she was with UK Trade and Investment where she held a number of roles, including work to market the UK internationally. Until 2009, Rosa was Director of Public Policy and Regulation of one of the UK's largest banks through the financial crisis. This role followed a 20-year civil service career encompassing roles leading enterprise and manufacturing policy, stimulating change in approaches to public procurement, implementing legislation within the energy sector and shaping European policy issues.

Further details: www.ipo.gov.uk

PART TWO
Innovation premium

FIND OUT MORE
www.industrialsustainability.org

EPSRC Centre
for Innovative
Manufacturing in
INDUSTRIAL
SUSTAINABILITY

"These days, CEOs don't just get judged by how well their share prices are doing, but by what impact they are having on society".
Paul Polman CEO Unilever 2012

The Centre for Industrial Sustainability, can unlock the benefits of sustainable business.

RESILIENCE   PRODUCTIVITY   MARKET LEADERSHIP COST REDUCTION

Eco-efficiency
Reducing resource use (water, energy, materials)
Improvements without radical changes
to product or process

Eco-factory
Technology to add value and improve
production capability and responsiveness
Decreasing consumption of natural resources

Sustainable Industrial System
Exploring future configurations of the industrial
system and their implications
Improve understanding of the long term
challenges facing industry

50+ Researchers   New tools
4 Universities   Shared Experiences
Research   Grounded in Practice

 UNIVERSITY OF CAMBRIDGE    Imperial College London    Loughborough University

Steve Evans, Centre Director   Ian Bamford, Commercial Director
email - se321@cam.ac.uk   email – imb31@cam.ac.uk
tel – 01223 339815   tel – 0771 851 7946

Some of our Industry partners

Unilever

M&S

TOYOTA
eef The manufacturers' organisation

wrap

VITSŒ

GM

Finding new value

The pace of innovation can be punishing. Steve Evans at the Centre for
Industrial Sustainability describes five characteristics that keep you ahead

The drumbeat of innovation is becoming faster and faster. Companies strive ever harder to deliver new value in an increasingly competitive and demanding environment. Product development lead times are becoming ever more challenging and yet the products being offered are also becoming increasingly complex. This brings pressure across the value chain and demands that companies become increasingly expert in coordination and cooperation across functional *and* organizational boundaries.

Mastery of such skills and competences can result in a leadership position, while failure to embrace the changing environment for innovation can lead to the loss of market share at a phenomenal rate. One need only look at the journey of Nokia and the desperate battle it faces to regain a leadership position in the mobile phone market. Once a clear leader, Nokia has slipped back into the pack and now strives for its very survival while the smartphone leaders chase hard development cycles which must deliver the must-have features and benefits on a seemingly ever-shortening six-monthly cycle.

This chapter seeks to explore some of the characteristics that are becoming increasingly commonly observed among leading innovators. An additional pressure is brought to bear, however – the search for ever-cheaper production. In a race to the bottom everyone loses, as quality and flexibility become ever more compromised. Against this backdrop, signals from key stakeholders indicate that considerations beyond economic return should be considered, not just as a nice-to-have corporate social responsibility (CSR) story but as a core element of the way business is done, helping both to mitigate business risk and to create new opportunities. We choose to highlight two case studies that bring to bear elements of these wider considerations which make up the notion of industrial sustainability, and in which we observe some of the key innovation characteristics that will be key to success in manufacturing in the 21st century.

Open innovation

Open innovation seeks to maximize the domain in which innovation may be done by drawing on ideas from without the organization as well as those found within. By taking advantage of a wider set of knowledge than could ever be held within one corporate culture, companies can gain an important edge. However, it is not as simple as looking over the garden fence and asking the neighbour; identifying sources of knowledge and appropriate partners, being able to filter the noise and pick the winners are all important capabilities which can deliver competitive advantage. The ability to reach beyond organizational boundaries and engage meaningfully in the search for new ideas is an increasingly sought-after capability.

Responsible innovation

The reach of new technologies has never been wider and the speed of dissemination has never been faster. When a new technology finds application, the ability to scale up and out to deliver to consumers worldwide has never been greater. The need for careful consideration of responsibility in the product pipeline has simultaneously grown. Looking forward at the role of innovation in the company and society can help in the identification of opportunities, the mitigation of key impacts and the avoidance of potential pitfalls and time-bombs.

Provenance

The ability to demonstrate the origins of the goods supplied to you is no longer the preserve of high-end goods or local supply chains. Even highly complex global supply chains are required to demonstrate an understanding of the origins of materials, with heavy punishments from consumers, NGOs and governments alike for those who neglect their product and service origins. During the horsemeat crisis, the shock of the public when they realized that what they were getting wasn't what the list of ingredients suggested was matched only by the surprise when they saw the length and complexity of the relationships that delivered the food to their plate. This applies when very complex supply chains span many actors and cross many inter-national boundaries.

Resilience

Global supply chains are becoming increasingly lean, with stock levels at an all-time low and just-in-time delivery enabled by sophisticated networks. At this level of stretch, however, unexpected events can cause significant disruptions to the supply chain. The ripple effect of events like Fukushima and the floods in Thailand have disrupted global production and affected the value of companies. The ability to resist, respond to and recover from disruptions is becoming an ever-greater part of firm planning.

Five key lessons

1 *Kissing frogs* – many of these capabilities require an element of experimentation and you may expect to fail more times than you succeed, and so you may need to kiss many frogs without reward. Don't be afraid to try new things in small ways in an attempt to find something that works. Innovation is inherently risky, so start small and build quickly when you do find your prince!

2 *Collaboration* – you may wish to engage with partners with whom you may not have worked before but who can give you access to knowledge or capabilities that have previously been beyond you. Do you want to understand your consumers better? Are there organizations that are non-competitive but have the same values as your customers? These strangers may be able to help you deliver more value to your customers; what value can you offer them in return?

3 *Adaptation* – with rapid incremental innovation and increasing product churn you may find that the factory you built just a few years ago is now being used for products with a very different production characteristic. Cars are now nearly 40 per cent electronics by value – a transition which has happened in just 15 years. You may not be operating your plant in the most effective way for your very latest business proposition and so the ability to adjust to changing markets needs to be built into manufacturing operations as well as product development cycles. This flexibility needs to be built into production systems on day one and, where legacy systems are in place, remember to challenge the assumptions behind the system, where practical – what were sensible design choices five years ago may be limiting the quality of decisions today.

4 *Trust* – as branding becomes ever more sophisticated and companies seek to build more intimate relationships with customers, remember that this is a door that swings both ways. Recent events in the European meat supply chain highlight this better than any other. It's not enough to say that a distant supplier or merchant cheated you – it's your name on the label. If we have learnt anything from the horsemeat crisis, it is that ignorance is not only no defence, but is in fact a red rag to both customers and regulators.

5 *New science and new models* – fundamentally different chemistries and processing routes are being developed. Graphene, for example, is generating much excitement as an opportunity for product and process innovation. These new chemistries and routes will create new opportunities for product innovation but may feature unusual and disruptive processes. Developments such as these may be embraced as an opportunity to explore alternative supply chain configurations and revisit the design of industrial systems. Interest in concepts such as the circular economy and closed-loop business models is growing; these challenge not only the science and technology of recovery, reuse and recycling, but also the infrastructure and the way we do business. To realize these goals we need to close the physical loops and also share the knowledge and capabilities that help us to build the relationships that allow these systems to flourish.

Final thoughts

There are opportunities aplenty for those who choose to engage beyond their traditional boundaries, and at the same time risks for those who fail to recognize the connectedness of the system in which they operate. Innovation of both product and the process of manufacture is changing the technologies we use and the practices that use those technologies. The number of pioneers who are supplying and using these new methods is growing, forming a sound base for further experimentation and development. Finally, the mechanisms for identifying and sharing this knowledge in an increasingly connected world have never been greater. These conditions create a near-perfect storm of opportunity to seek to scan more widely, engage in experimentation more readily and cooperate more fully to deliver the sustainable innovations that will take your business forward.

British Sugar

Farmers in the region who currently supply AB Sugar could conceivably be using their fields to deliver any crop. With the European Union's complex and changing set of agricultural subsidies creating a challenging and uncertain environment, AB Sugar has moved to work in partnership with its farmers and ensure that it has the best chance of profiting from and with their beet. Beet is sampled on arrival at the plant, with data about sugar levels and nutrient content fed back within 24 hours to help farmers plan their future crops. The company also collaborates on and funds long-term industry research initiatives conducted by the British Beet Research Organization. This has played a part in the industry reducing nitrogen use by 40 per cent and phosphor use by 70 per cent since 1982, and in the same period pesticide usage has reduced by 60 per cent, all helping reduce the unit cost for the company's farmers. Meanwhile, average beet yields have increased by 60 per cent and have been rising faster than those of any other UK arable crop.

The company has sought to increase the flexibility and diversity of the Wissington-based plant by extending its operations beyond its core business to now include generating its own electricity, using spare heat and CO_2 to grow tomatoes and engaging with other firms in partnerships to maximize the revenues from other non-sugar goods. AB Sugar is now even producing bio-ethanol in conjunction with BP and capturing industry-grade CO_2 in partnership with BOC. Thanks to these innovations (among others), the plant in Wissington is now the most economically efficient beet processor in Europe. These efforts have been inspired by a deep understanding of the long-term policy environment and have been enabled by a willingness to seek new opportunities. This is all underpinned by business processes that help the company understand when to develop new businesses internally, when to seek partnerships and how to make them work.

Toyota Motor Europe

The famed Toyota production system has long been delivering more economically efficient car production; however, the same tools and techniques and culture are now tackling environmental key performance indicators (KPIs).

Toyota Europe's manufacturing operations have drawn inspiration from their innovative product platform strategy, which is striving towards the goal of producing the ultimate eco-car with zero emissions. As such, Toyota also strives for the ultimate eco-factory.

This vision was based upon a strong foundation of legal compliance and risk reduction, with special focus on four major KPIs: energy/CO_2, water, waste, and air emissions (Volatile Organic Compounds – VOC). These represent the most significant manufacturing-plant environmental impacts.

As an example, through a practical programme of continuous innovation Toyota UK has achieved between 60 and 75 per cent reductions in its key environmental KPIs, achieved zero waste to landfill in 2003 and achieved the rare feat of decoupling CO_2 emissions from increasing production volumes since 2003.

Toyota UK and its sister plant in France were selected as two of five global Toyota 'sustainable plants' which serve as best practice development models for the wider Toyota organization. These plants focus on achieving leading environmental performance, increasing the use of renewable energies and ensuring that the plants are in harmony with their local surroundings.

This radical incrementalism helps Toyota stay ahead of legislation and drives down costs by keeping improvement activities at the centre of the business.

Steve Evans is the Director and Principal Investigator of the Centre for Industrial Sustainability, University of Cambridge. The Centre carries out research into areas that are critical to enabling the transformation of businesses to sustainable practices and operations. It has over 50 researchers and staff working at doctoral and post-doctoral levels. Research is grounded in practical business operations by working with both large and small companies and testing results in operational environments. The Centre is based at the University of Cambridge and encompasses Imperial College London, Cranfield and Loughborough Universities. It operates a membership model for businesses. If you are interesting in participating in research or gaining access to our latest tools and methods, please contact us.

Tel: 44 (0)1223 766141; e-mail: Steve Evans – se321@cam.ac.uk or Ian Bamford (Commercial Director) – imb31@cam.ac.uk; web: www.industrialsustainability.org

FIS Food Innovation SOLUTIONS

INNOVATION IS THE ABILITY TO SEE CHANGE AS AN OPPORTUNITY

WHO ARE FIS?

FIS are a leading food consultancy at the forefront of strategic innovation, management, food and concept development for retailers, manufacturers and restaurants. Our food experts have a stellar record of working with start ups through to global brands, adding value by offering such services as:

- Innovation thought leadership and business building strategies

- Consumer insight, trends and research

- NPD and innovation models – development and training

- Implementing innovation into organisations, range development and processes

- Innovative restaurant concepts & development.

WHAT OUR CLIENTS SAY

"The experienced background of the team at FIS meant they were able to contribute with an abundance of relevant examples through the course. I feel that it was time worthwhile spen out of the day job, which it most wholeheartedly and that I got something practical to take away w would make a real change. Not only did we creat category change plan but we also had a re-energ team focused on change for the better, that will n a real difference to our customers every day."

Leading International Retailer

Contact us for your free copy of our recent food trends report.

Call +44 (0) 1284 705787 www.foodinnovationsolutions.com

Innovation that pays off

In a recession, how do you maximize the results of what you spend on innovation and cut out any waste? The choices you make can lead to creation of fresh value or the danger of being left on the shelf, says Mike Faers at Food Innovation Solutions

One of the first questions to ask the top management of any organization is: how do you define innovation within your business? Very rarely do you get an aligned response from the team – this is understandable, as each department is impacted differently by innovation and therefore they seek to influence its direction in different ways. However, this is an indicator of a business culture that is unlikely to be maximizing the returns on their innovation investment and is likely to be wasting a good percentage of their scarce budget and resources on the wrong activity.

So what are the ways to reduce spending on innovation and improve your returns? In a recession as deep as this one, it is a vital question. While all businesses have uniquely different solutions, we can generalize with a degree of certainty on the key drivers of success.

Innovation can be defined in two ways:

- consumer innovation – a product, service or market positioning that meets consumers' emerging or unmet needs and is differentiated from the current solutions;
- business innovation – activity that delivers incremental benefit across the organization's value chain.

Why do the rules change in a recession?

After five years of recession, all types of consumers are looking to buy products more for the longer term than ever before and are moving away from a throw-away society and back to wanting real value for money – this being measured not just in free product but expecting more in terms of improved service, product guarantees or genuinely new products.

In the boom times when average innovations may have worked, they now fail. With consumers having fewer pounds in their pocket they are more careful about what they spend them on, and they are less likely to take the risk on a new product they are not certain they will be satisfied with. Innovation can differentiate, create new markets and increase value in a competitive marketplace but during a recession the consumer must clearly perceive a genuine additional value or benefit.

Innovate or fail

Let's be clear: the only way to grow in a flat or declining market is to increase share, and how you do that is through:

- new products or services;
- marketing more aggressively;
- building more outlets.

We are not the first food industry to go through such a deep recession; there are plenty of examples of companies that have been here before and survived, and we can learn from their experiences.

In the 1920s, there were two choices of packaged cereal in the United States, Kellogg's or Post. When the depression hit, Post decided to cut spending across the board, but Kellogg's invested heavily to develop and launch a new product, Rice Krispies, and by 1933 Kellogg's profits had risen nearly 30 per cent and it had become the undeniable number one brand in the cereals market.

In the 1930s, Brazilian coffee makers, faced with a surplus of coffee, approached Nestlé and asked it to develop a new coffee product that was soluble in hot water and retained its flavour. Nescafé was born and quickly became the favourite of coffee drinkers around the world. Even though the technology for this product was invented in 1901 at the pan-American world fair in Buffalo, it required the coffee surplus and the drive in consumer demand for more convenience post war to give the push required to develop and launch this product. We should never confuse innovation with invention.

In the 1980s, Lucozade repositioned itself from a tonic for sick children to a sports brand, as the former was no longer relevant to its 1930s origins and Lucozade realized that there was a far bigger market targeting well, rather than sick, people. It tripled its sales in three years by repositioning its product.

Apple is frequently cited as an innovative product, but it has consistently put the consumer, together with innovation and design, at the heart of its business and has delivered huge sales growth as a result. Apple's P&L for the most recent financial year gave results of:

- annual turnover €108bn – a 65 per cent increase year on year;
- gross margin of 40% – a 1-point increase year on year;
- 300% increase in iPad sales, with sales now $20bn;
- annual earnings per share growth of 80 per cent.

There are not many other businesses that in these financial times are rapidly expanding at such a rate, despite charging a considerable premium for its products, not discounting, and improving its margin. This demonstrates that consumers are still prepared to pay for true innovation even in a recession.

Value innovation, not value engineering

In recent years when consumers had less time and more money, if you bought an iron and it lasted only 12 months, the chances are that you would just have bought another one as you didn't have the time to complain and seek a replacement. Now, however, consumers are far more likely to shop for a company rather than a product they trust and for a product with a guarantee of satisfaction, quite often through a product warranty or customer reviews. If you want to sell, you need to show customers that you care intensely about your product and what it stands for. You need to demonstrate that your motivation is not just financial but a desire to help improve your customers' lives.

The point here is that businesses tend to look to value engineers in times of raw material inflation and recession to maintain margin. Consumers have noticed and rejected this strategy and want more genuine product for their investment – it's a race to the bottom and we must seek, through innovation, to race to the top.

For example, within the meat industry, we have seen the price of mince rise dramatically as cheaper dishes such as shepherd's pie are in greater demand, with premium burgers replacing the steak occasion. So let's look at a different way of innovating by using the retro and forgotten cuts such as pig and ox cheeks, which can be bought very cheaply compared to lean mince yet are a far superior cut and used frequently in trendy Michelin-starred restaurants. We will have to tell consumers what to do with them, but they will reward us with their loyalty in the longer term. This is a good example of where we can use value innovation in the supply chain to deliver against consumers' needs.

Tomatoes are another example of an innovative approach to delivering growth. How many times have you heard a friend say 'I only eat tomatoes when I'm abroad' or 'they don't taste like they do when I'm on holiday' – this is insight and actually consumers were right. UK tomatoes 10 years ago were poor in quality and range, and there was no real differentiation between retailers; if your only benchmark is beating the industry norm, you have no reason to change.

If you listen to the consumer, there is a white-space opportunity to leapfrog the competition and demonstrate bold leadership that's relevant to consumers and will halo back to your brand. This in turn will drive trust and loyalty through an improved experience in-store and at the point of consumption.

Now, if you look at the tomato fixture, there are at least 20 varieties: on the vine, different colours and unique varieties positioned for different usage occasions. Interestingly, the Brix ratio has shifted significantly over the past 10 years, meeting the taste expectations of consumers for a sweeter eat – this has delivered real value to the category when you look at the relative retail sales prices (RSPs).

Packaging is another area that can add dramatically to product innovation. Look at the wine glass with the rip-off seal that appeared on *Dragons' Den* (unsuccessfully) – how many times do you see these being consumed on trains, at events, picnics etc? This is an example of invention that led to innovation, and is now available in the high street and growing because it meets consumers' needs for certain occasions, and delivers convenience with it.

Intelligent packaging will be a real differentiator in the next decade, with food waste already a government issue that is rapidly becoming a consumer one. Microbial films that inhibit food spoilage organisms combined with laser edge sealing and cutting is an example of business innovation that will reduce wastage in the supply chain and deliver manufacturing flexibility – reducing costs etc. While the consumer won't see a difference, it will give them benefits with the extended shelf life of their fresh food purchases. The new strawberry punnet, with a patented mix of minerals that remove ethylene, a hormone that makes fruit ripen and go mouldy, will add two days to the shelf life.

Finally, augmented reality – an emerging technology that will hit packaging design and consumers over the next decade – is also one to watch, with the increased opportunities it gives to communicate with customers at point of purchase and consumption.

What this demonstrates is that if you look to innovate across all elements of the marketing mix, you will deliver a more sustainable return on investment and build trust with your consumers.

Lean innovation

Identifying new ways of reducing costs is critical for any business to survive but it is important this is not done to the detriment of your innovation process. There is clearly enough evidence to substantiate the claim that innovating in a recession is the right decision and, if you think about it, it makes perfect sense: there is less competition as companies cut innovation and marketing budgets, meaning less noise in the market, and so good innovations can stand head and shoulders above the competition. Also, there are far more skilled people becoming available to recruit as companies divest skills in the short term.

To achieve lean innovation within any business calls for a combination of consumer insight, creativity, category expertise and process discipline. The following programme of tools (Figure 2.2.1) uses best practice from several industries to structure and guide the management of innovation activity within a recession, and challenges and enables organizations of any size to:

- define and align innovation within their business;
- create organizational plans and recruit and train mentors to develop industry-leading teams;
- stop non-relevant or non-aligned activity and speed up time to market;
- follow metrics that deliver fact-based decision making and measurement;
- use consumer-led thinking with an operationally smart execution;
- deliver more bang for your innovation buck by working across the entire value chain.

FIGURE 2.2.1 Lean innovation – a blueprint for successfully innovating in a recession

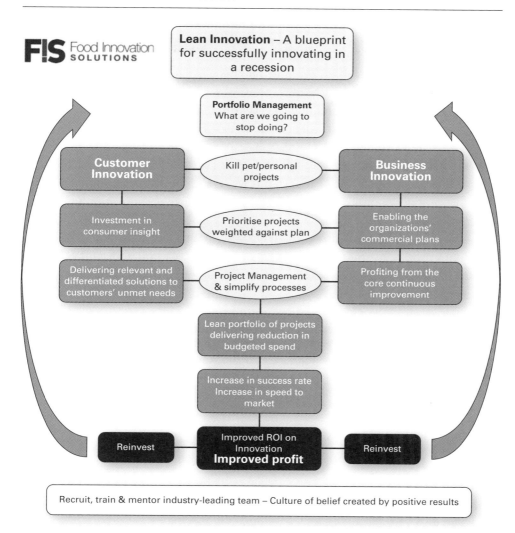

This will create a virtuous circle of profitable relevant and sustainable innovation across the entire spectrum, from 'big shifts' to continuous improvements.

A business that manages its portfolio across the entire innovation spectrum will have a balanced return. It's like playing roulette: if you place all your chips on 13 red, the returns will be impressive if it lands. However, a spread bet on all red is likely to be safer and include some lower returns, but is more likely to succeed. Remember, however, that a journey like this can take two years; it's as much about hearts and minds and internal alignment as it is about a new product or service.

Ten golden rules for successfully innovating in a recession

- Get your core offer relevant and optimized with continuous improvement programmes, ensuring you profit from the core.
- Be ruthless with your resource/portfolio management – decide what you are going to stop doing.
- Weight your resources and budgets according to the corporate plan.
- Over-invest in consumer insights and needs – be operationally smart, look for the synergies and make the most of what you already know.
- Over-invest in training, up-skilling and recruiting the best people.
- Create the burning platform – what if we don't innovate successfully?
- Measure the success – socialize the fiscal importance of innovation to the organization.
- Remove from the organization any process, system and cultural blockages.
- Innovation is a commercial function and should be accountable at P&L level.
- Manage the portfolio across the spectrum and look forward a minimum of five years.

One thing is certain: innovation will continue to be critical in creating market value within the food industry, which means that new product development must continue to adapt to meet changing consumer trends. Hopefully, by raising the importance of innovation on the business agenda and ensuring the continued focus on delivering products that meet a real consumer need, the future is positive for the food industry and we will see some truly innovative new products being developed as a result.

Mike Faers is the MD of Food Innovation Solutions, the international food innovation consultancy. FIS works with some of the largest international food retailers and manufacturers building innovation capability and brands through strategy and delivery: setting direction, realigning the team, mobilizing resources through training and development, and managing programmes of innovation and new product development (NPD) change.

Tel: 01284 705787; e-mail: mike@foodinnovationsolutions.com

Harnessing technology

The history of innovation is rich in spectacular successes and disappointing failures. What lessons can be drawn today, ask Professor Richard Brook and Dr Jane Gate at AIRTO?

Harnessing technology, from the invention of the steam engine to creation of the internet, has driven economic development relentlessly for the past two and a half centuries. Fortunes have been made and lost in the process, by individuals and corporations of all shapes and sizes. There are clearly many, many ways to exploit technological development in order to build new businesses and no shortage of entrepreneurs wanting to take up the challenge. But, in a highly competitive world, in order to be successful, innovators need to take advantage of all the help, advice, experience and knowledge that they can lay their hands on, plus there is an element of serendipity in terms of being in the right place, with the right offering, at the right time.

Many aspiring entrepreneurs and investors will look for the 'next big thing' to build their success upon. In recent times the list has included new semiconductors, microcomputers, nanotechnology, biotechnology, the internet and internet-enabled social media businesses, to name just a few. Each time such a potentially disruptive technology emerges, there is a rush of entrepreneurial enthusiasm to exploit the technology for competitive advantage, building on existing businesses or starting new ones. Many of these efforts result in 'me-too' propositions and there will inevitably be a high mortality rate as the dynamics of the competitive economy weeds out the weak in order to focus on the best.

These 'next big things' attract a lot of attention and then some eventually fade while others become well established. In the process there is the well-known cycle of (over)enthusiasm, then some disillusion as applications are slow to take off, followed by eventual renewed confidence and then maturity in day-to-day applications. It is important to understand where a technologically driven proposition is positioned in this sequence of development; this positioning conditions the attitudes of financiers and funders as well as, to some extent, end users and eventual customers. This cycle also drives the dynamics of mergers and acquisitions in the industries affected, where ownership and competence in the relevant technologies start to be perceived as key to future competitiveness and markets. A current example is to be seen in the scramble to extend web services to mobile platforms.

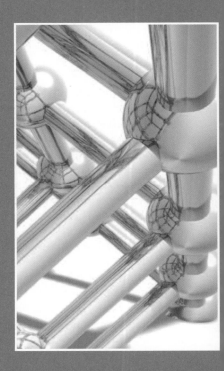

Predicting what will be a 'big thing' is notoriously difficult, as history shows. The cinema and computers were both thought by those close to the inventions at the time to have very limited application. Other equally successful inventions and the associated innovations have taken widely varying lengths of time to 'make it' into widespread application. The length of time from invention to uptake, known as the diffusion rate and measured in this instance by the time taken for half the population of the United States to start using the invention, ranges from 10 years for the internet to 19 years for the PC to 28 years for radio and 71 years for the telephone. Many factors affect the diffusion rate, including the extent of commitment to existing alternatives, user reaction to and understanding of new technologies, and the payback on the cost of acquiring new products and processes. Diffusion rates for individual innovations vary widely, but arguably the pace is accelerating and diffusion rates are shortening.

Predicting the potential and likelihood of success for individual innovations remains very difficult, though, and most plans for exploitation don't anticipate, in one way or another, all of the circumstances that are encountered in practice. Inventors frequently succeed through perseverance and by sticking tenaciously to their ultimate goals. Entrepreneurs (individuals or companies) usually succeed in exploiting inventions by picking up further incremental innovations, remaining flexible and adapting plans and actions according to the circumstances encountered. One only has to look at the stories behind the introduction of the steam engine and the invention and adoption of the jet engine to see this in practice.

Having succeeded, it is then necessary to keep on innovating. Complacency and slow reactions to new technology and changes in the market provide opportunities for competitors to supplant hitherto successful enterprises. Look at IBM being supplanted by DEC in the field of minicomputers or, today, the struggle of the established players such as Google, Microsoft and Facebook to adapt their products to perform on mobile platforms. Just how do the best Formula 1 motor racing teams stay ahead of the game? How do they organize themselves to come up with original ideas for continuous incremental innovation under intense pressure of time?

This pressure to stay ahead of the competition in virtually all areas of business provides a very varied landscape of continuous innovation for entrepreneurs to attack, driven by relentless advances in technology and anticipation of the opportunities that such advances may create.

Becoming the best at innovation

There are many things to get right in seeking to harness technology successfully to drive innovation. Perhaps the most critical pre-condition for success is to ensure that there is going to be a market for the innovative product, process or business model being proposed.

Sometimes, if technology is driving the vision, it takes an act of faith to believe that the market will emerge when the product or process has been developed. Taking the emergence of market demand on trust is not something that appeals to investors and it is perhaps preferable to look first for an unfulfilled market demand, even if latent, and then search for a technological innovation capable of delivering a solution.

Where a new technology (the internet for example) is being used as the basis for delivering new services, successful commercialization may rely on innovation in the business model as opposed to the technology. The technology is key in this instance but everyone has access to it, creating immense competition. This has a tendency to attract 'me-too' propositions; and the ability to publish more or less anything readily and quickly can expose innovators to some poorly appreciated risks.

The particular example of internet technology has created major opportunities and successes but also failure and disappointment for many who have attempted to build new web-based businesses without adequate market understanding, finance or experience. Others have succeeded spectacularly, as exemplified by the famous success of Facebook, founded by students at Harvard University in 2004, and which by 2012 had amassed over one billion users worldwide.[1] Another recent example is the success of UK-based Nick D'Aloisio, who became the youngest-ever person to receive venture capital investment aged 15. His creation, Summly, is a smartphone app launched in 2011 and now sold to Yahoo for around $30m in 2013.[2]

So, is there a formula for successful innovation? In all cases, the key skill for innovation is the ability to put together the concept for the product or process (ideally based on market need) and the technology needed to realize it.

For major corporations this has become an exercise in global coordination, seeking out the best technological design expertise from across the globe. GE's global development of wind turbines is an example, using teams from upstate New York, Shanghai, Bangalore and Munich to design and integrate various aspects of the system components required.[3]

Successful innovation, particularly in business, also relies on coming up with a workable business model for making money and on developing the pitch which will sell it to others. For entrepreneurs and new businesses this means being able to convince financial and other backers. For innovators in the corporate environment this means making the case for investment to the finance director and others on the company board. This needs an all-round credible pitch and the ability to convey technological concepts easily to a non-technological audience. This can be a difficult process for some technically minded innovators. But such encounters with adversity can also stimulate innovative ways of stimulating innovation, including the 'skunk works' model for which 3M was famous.

Those with experience clearly have an advantage in terms of knowing what to expect, how to tackle problems and whom to seek out for help and advice. For newcomers, the challenge is to find these people and solicit their assistance.

Notes

1 Facebook tops billion-user mark, *The Wall Street Journal* (Dow Jones), 4 October 2012.

2 Nick D'Aloisio, Britain's 17-year-old app entrepreneur, *The Telegraph*, 27 March 2013.

3 Managing global innovation, Yves Doz, as reviewed in *Engineering and Technology*, April 2013.

Professor Richard Brook is President of AIRTO. His expertise as a technology specialist lies in the field of measurement, instrumentation and control systems, with experience extending from research and development in both public and private sectors to proving new technology and products commercially in the field. He is an experienced angel investor and company director. He co-founded early-stage venture capital company E-Synergy, where he still coaches and mentors companies preparing for financing and investment. Current directorships include NPL Management Ltd (National Physical Laboratory), The Institute for Sustainability (Trustee, Director and Deputy Chairman) and the Thames Innovation Centre.

Dr Jane Gate joined NPL in 2011, and serves as the Director of Operations for AIRTO. In addition to overseeing AIRTO, Jane has been part of the formulation and delivery team for the National Measurement System International Programme at NPL. Previously Jane held a range of management and leadership roles at King's College London, within the health schools, and within the university's research commercialization and research support division, King's Business Ltd, where she was responsible for leading engagement with business.

AIRTO (The Association for Independent Research and Technology Organizations) is the foremost membership body for organizations operating in the UK's intermediate research and technology sector. AIRTO's members deliver vital innovation and knowledge transfer services, which include applied and collaborative R&D, frequently in conjunction with universities, consultancy, technology validation and testing, incubation of commercialization opportunities and early-stage financing. AIRTO members have a combined turnover of over £2bn from clients both at home and outside the UK, and employ over 20,000 scientists, technologists and engineers. AIRTO members include commercial companies, research and technology organizations, research associations and selected research and technology exploitation offices from universities, operating at the interface between academia and industry. Most of AIRTO's members operate in the important space between pure research and the pull of the market for commoditization of knowledge into new products and services.

For further information please contact Dr Jane Gate, Director of Operations, AIRTO: tel: +44(0)20 8943 6354; e-mail: jane.gate@airto.co.uk; web: www.airto.co.uk

Taking a lead in innovation

Innovation in a knowledge economy demands a radically different style of leadership, argues John Sorsby at Sheffield Hallam University

> *A leader is best when people barely know he exists, not so good when people obey and acclaim him. Worse when they despise him. But of a good leader, who talks little, when his work is done, his aim fulfilled, they will say: We did it ourselves.*
>
> **(LAO-TZU, CHINESE PHILOSOPHER, 6TH-CENTURY BC)**

This historical view from Eastern culture provides us with an enlightening insight when framing the subject of innovation leadership, which is supported by the more up-to-date words of Hitt who in 1998 stated that 'we are on the precipice of an epoch', as the context in which today's leaders operate is radically different from that which has gone before. Today's knowledge economy is challenging the dominant thinking of leadership which has been so prominent from the industrial revolution of the early 1900s and throughout the 20th century, where highly mechanistic and regulatory control procedures were very much in vogue. The paradigm shift in economic drivers is, in turn, seeing a shift in leadership style, away from the directive and at times autocratic leaders of the bureaucracies of the industrial age to a far more distributed and democratic leadership style in the 21st-century adhocracies, based as they are on more lateral forms of interaction. This shift in leadership style is of particular relevance in the innovation arena for three reasons:

1 As the eminent leadership thinker Peter Drucker states, knowledge workers, so important in an innovation-led organization, are not subordinates, they are associates, and as such are not requiring of a leadership style predicated on unitary control.

2 We have over the past 10–15 years seen a rise in the number of companies which operate a far more open approach to innovation as they look to exploit the rich knowledge landscape created by the internet and the rise in venture capitalist funding, meaning that leaders can no longer have a monopoly of knowledge, gained from years working their way up a corporate ladder.

3 Viewing leadership not as a position of authority, but as far more emergent and based on an outcome of interactions among individuals within an organization, allows us to view organizations as complex adaptive systems, which are commonly defined as: 'A collection of agents that produce emergent and at times extreme phenomena when competing for limited resources without the need for central coordination.'

Termite mounds, swarms of bees and flocking birds are all examples of complex adaptive systems, as are the global stock markets. This approach of viewing organizations in a far more holistic and systemic way, based on the interactions of constituent members, opens up a whole new vista for modern-day leadership, because, referring back to the complex adaptive system definition, there is no explicit need for central coordination, as one of the central tenets of complex adaptive systems is self-organization. This doesn't consign the leader or the leadership role to the annals of history but it does allow us to view leadership through a different lens.

If we examine complex adaptive systems in more detail, they are made up of three states:

1 An ordered state where, adopting Boulding's law of requisite variety, the internal controls of an organization repel the variety (or complexity) in the organization's external environment.

2 If we move to the polar view where the environmental complexity overwhelms the internal controls, then a chaos state reigns – a stock market crash would serve as a timely example of such a state.

3 However, at the interface between order and chaos exists a third defined state known as the edge of chaos, for example the point at which you see the phase change from ice to water and again from water to steam. In his book *Managing on the Edge*, Pascale argues that successful leaders push their organizations to the edge of chaos, because, using complex adaptive system terminology, this is where the organization has maximum fitness or, in business speak, has optimal performance.

So what does this mean for today's leaders of innovation, who as well as having to adopt a more distributed and empowering style, meaning that their controlling grip is loosened, are also, it would seem, required to preside over organizations seemingly heading for the turbulent waters of chaos? As Ilya Prigogine identified, and indeed for which he was awarded the Nobel Prize back in 1977, in the natural world, chaos is a necessary condition for the growth of dynamic systems, but all such systems are held together by simple order-generating principles.

This link back to the natural world would seem to offer some clues as to the future role of leadership in the complex and highly competitive landscape of the knowledge economy.

Innovation leadership considerations in an age of complexity

1. A leader as a maker of meaning

Evidence of the simple order-generating principles described by Prigogine can be found in what we commonly observe on the surface as highly complex structures in nature (the infinite number of snowflake forms being a good example). These are actually based on simple self-repeating patterns based around reference points, so-called fractals. So if we apply the fractal principle to organizations, a leader can create unambiguous meaning for colleagues within an organization by clearly expressing key reference points such as the organization's values, identity and purpose; in this way the leader creates a sense of order, as distinct from the control exhibited by a more punitive leadership style. A seemingly excellent exponent of creating fractals that evoke meaning that is well understood in an organizational context is Sir David Brailsford, Head of British Cycling and Team Sky, who has a simple reference point of 'Medal or Nothing', leaving team members in no doubt of the organization's overall purpose, but still allowing and indeed encouraging freedom to explore interactions within this particular complex adaptive system.

2. A leader as a provider of information

The next leadership consideration takes into account the second law of thermodynamics, or entropy, which states that all natural systems tend to a state of disorder. So if an organization operates as a largely closed system, devoid of energy (in the form of information and ideas) from the external environment, it will eventually come into equilibrium with that environment and as such become energy-less. Imagine a ball left to bounce without any energy input: the ball operating as a closed system will eventually come to rest on the floor because all the ordered energy within it has dissipated into the environment, as entropy takes over. A leader therefore has a key role in ensuring that his or her organization operates as an open system with information and ideas flowing into it across a semi-permeable organizational structure, to ensure that the organization has a constant energy input (the equivalent of the energy input required to keep the ball bouncing) to fight the debilitating effects of entropy.

Many companies are now recognizing that they are no longer a knowledge fortress and are starting to exploit open systems thinking as a way of exploiting the rich knowledge landscape and enhancing the inputs into their innovation funnels. For example, the food manufacturing giant General Mills has a well-established open innovation platform called G-Win which allows prospective solution providers to access General Mills' innovation needs, and in 2012 the company launched a low-calorie brownie through a partnership developed through this online platform.

3. A leader as a facilitator of interactions

For many years, organizations have been designed and led based on mechanistic first-order thinking – that is, if you apply 'law-like' interventions, in turn you can propose rational solutions – the classical control and command scenarios. These solutions are largely based on suppressive negative feedback loops that ensure the system is 'order seeking', and take no account of the interactions of individuals within the organization. If we again look to the natural world for evidence of negative feedback loops, the homeostatic controls employed to regulate a constant (or ordered) body temperature serves as a useful analogy. However, when considering the leadership of complex adaptive systems, a more systemic second-order-thinking approach is required which places greater emphasis on the amplifying effects of positive feedback loops embedded in the complex interactions of organizational members; these in turn contribute to the organization being ultimately 'chaos seeking', an inevitable consequence for all innovative, dynamic organizations. The evocative butterfly effect serves to illustrate the importance of the interconnected web of interactions that exist in complex adaptive systems by observing that if 'a butterfly flaps its wings over the Amazon rain forest, it can set in motion events that leads to a storm over Chicago'.

4. A leader as a creator of agile organizational climates

The term climate is applied deliberately in this context to differentiate from that of culture so often used in business writings, as culture in an organizational sense is often hidden and fixed in espoused beliefs, whereas climate is far more visible and, to use Darwin's famous words, 'adaptable to change'. The leaders of today and indeed of the future need to develop organizational climates that favour innovation, and to do this they need to create adhocracies that are more flexible and externally focused than ever before, suggesting a new post-bureaucratic era, where the focus moves from internal control to external flexibility. This is perhaps best summed up by Sir Richard Noble, who in his ongoing attempts to secure the world land speed record identifies the directly proportional relationship between the clock speed (or agility) of his organization and the level of distributed leadership it fosters.

So in summary, the leaders of innovation both now and in the future are faced with an intriguing dilemma: the need to adopt a more distributed leadership style based on order rather than control, while heading inextricably towards chaos. However, by viewing an organization as a complex adaptive system, the leader can follow some intrinsically simple steps to ensure that in fact the organization stands astride the edge of chaos – a highly competitive place to be in the constantly evolving knowledge economy.

> I think the next century will be the century of complexity. (Stephen Hawking, speaking at the start of the millennium)

John Sorsby, a qualified biochemist, is Head of the Centre for Food Innovation at Sheffield Hallam University, prior to which he spent 15 years working in food manufacturing and retailing. He is currently studying for a Doctorate in Business Administration (DBA) at the University where he is researching the role that leadership style plays in developing an organizational climate that best suits a more open approach to innovation. John hopes that you found this contribution thought provoking and is more than happy to be contacted to discuss his work.

E-mail: j.sorsby@shu.ac.uk

Technology credits

Maximize the support for the speed and scale at which a technology can grow, argues Guy Paterson at Equinox Innovations

The technology landscape is changing at a fast and furious pace. Growing organizations need to find a compelling reason to differentiate themselves, and when time to market and intellectual property are crucial to success, companies need to take advantage of opportunities provided by government programmes to supplement their technology investment.

Growth is essential to the success of every young company. With growth comes extremely challenging financial decisions which could be pivotal to a company's survival. A balance between investment in product development, process development and creation of competitive advantage could generate the leverage companies need to secure success. Unfortunately, internal resource investment is costly and counteracts the need for sales and marketing budgets.

In the past, only those companies with deep pockets were able to spend years researching and developing innovative products providing advances in technology which attracted enough attention to generate sales without the traditional sales-driven approach. Only recently have we seen great advances in technology by unknown organizations as opposed to large multinationals. Why is this? Aside from situations where large organizations fund the endeavours of young innovative companies, we now have governments engaged in the ideology that supporting growth at early stages provides huge economic uplift in the future.

Don't miss the opportunity to claim your tax credits!

You don't need to be trying to build the next space shuttle or wearing a white lab coat in order to qualify for R&D tax credits. As long as your company's activities are technical in nature and experimentation is involved, your company may be able to obtain tax credits for innovation using this programme. Usually businesses strive to improve the overall performance, functionality or effectiveness of their technology or systems. These are the types of activities which are eligible. Many companies believe that they won't qualify and do not bother to investigate further the specific scheme guidelines. This may be a very costly error in judgement for expanding technology firms, which could naturally use the extra funds to expedite their growth.

R&D tax relief is readily available to both SMEs and large businesses alike to help minimize tax liabilities above the actual expenses on the eligible R&D costs. This programme is intended to encourage companies to invest in innovation and increase the competitiveness of UK organizations. It's a very generous programme which is regularly neglected by many organizations simply because of the intricacies associated with distinguishing eligible activities. Many businesses may be very surprised to learn just how many of their day-to-day activities are eligible for the R&D tax credit programme. It is easy to understand that most businesses are not entirely dedicated to R&D. The actual tax relief can therefore be applied to a portion of the overall daily activities which fall inside the guidelines. This makes it possible for a diverse range of companies in various markets to take advantage of the programme. Don't be fooled into thinking that only traditional R&D-related industries can apply. Even industries such as software development, food, manufacturing, chemical processing and plastics/textiles are constantly involved in innovative activities which could support a claim. Frequently, companies engaged in non-traditional R&D underestimate the magnitude of time and expense consumed in their innovation efforts.

Any field within the wide scope of science and technology will generally qualify (along with some financial consideration), as long as the following qualities are met:

- There is technological advancement.
- Uncertainties are involved in the project.
- A process to overcome those uncertainties was undertaken.
- Individuals leading the project are competent professionals in the relevant field.

The driving force behind innovation is the need to overcome problems by developing new and insightful methodologies necessary to formulate a solution

The goal to enhance innovation and boost the UK's competitiveness on the world stage is essential as the rest of the world becomes centred on information economies. Other countries such as Canada have already been very successful in carrying out similar programmes, distributing billions of dollars to Canadian organizations and boosting the existing competitiveness of the Canadian economic environment. The UK's system is in fact tightly modelled after the Canadian Scientific Research and Experimental Development (SRED) programme. With the success of the Canadian programme the UK is certainly on the right course, supporting innovation in an economic climate that needs it the most.

It is very important to use highly trained technology professionals in order to assist in processing your claims

Various providers may work on a contingency basis, meaning that if the submission is not successful there is no fee. This will reduce your financial risk, which is always important for growing companies. As a result of the numerous complexities inherent in the programme, it is difficult and time consuming for companies to make their own submissions using internal staff. Although this was not the intent, the reality is that the programme is complex, with very detailed guidelines which must be followed in order to make a successful claim. Even so, the fact is that organizations can potentially submit their own claim; however, tying up essential technology personnel is usually not cost-effective, often results in under-claiming and decreases the overall tax benefit. Additionally, you run the risk of a claim being rejected by including activities that are not eligible and missing out on others that are.

Remember that the R&D tax credits programme is 95 per cent technical

Think about it this way. If a new piece of software was created, you might describe it as a functioning application for the user. On the other hand, software engineers would break it into its base components. They would see the design, algorithms, all the relevant data mechanisms such as transfer efficiency, control, storage and encryption as well as the custom component integration to improve the overall system flow. In this scenario the engineers will be able to identify all of the components which will qualify for the R&D credits, support these activities and ensure that your company receives the maximum benefits without fear of the entire claim being disqualified.

Don't delay checking your eligibility

It is essential that you do not delay filing your R&D tax claims. You can submit claims for the past two fiscal years, so don't let your accounting period for the current year lapse. HMRC enforces strict deadlines on filing R&D tax claims. Do not miss out on your opportunity to claim. Most companies new to the scheme should be able to claim the previous two years and a third (current year) as soon as the year end is reached. Having the ability to make three claims in such a short time span could be a windfall for many companies.

Equinox Innovations has been offering R&D tax credit advisory services to fast-growing innovative organizations for over a decade, helping to maximize claims while minimizing time, effort and risk. Assessments to determine your eligibility are free. We are also happy to provide free advice on the programme if you do decide to make a claim for yourself.

Further details: Guy R Paterson, CEO, Equinox Innovations:
e-mail: Guy.Paterson@EquinoxInnovations.com;
web: www.EquinoxInnovations.com; tel: London: 0203 551 7452;
Manchester: 0161 300 1131; Brighton: 0127 343 4144;
Leeds: 0113 238 5454; Sheffield: 0114 287 0104

PART THREE
How innovation is changing

HIGHBURY
Maximising the value in your innovation

ABOUT HIGHBURY

We work with you to recognise, protect, value and commercialise your creations

What we do:
Business development & market research
Pre-partnering due diligence
Technology, product and company valuation
Technology transfer and licensing
Deal negotiation and implementation

We run workshops for entrepreneurs, transferring our IP skills to your community

Christi Mitchell
T: 01462436894
M: 07973224804
E: Christi@highburyltd.com
www.highburyltd.com

Open innovation collaboration

Free exchange of ideas across organizational walls? Christi Mitchell at Highbury takes a look at open innovation in all its different forms

What is open innovation?

Innovation is a proprietary activity conducted largely inside an organization in a series of closely managed steps.

What is open innovation[1]? It can be defined as a golden opportunity for innovators and more specifically as the forging of a close or loose partnership with those outside your company who have created or own technology or a product that meets with the searcher's definition of a product or technology need or gap. It may also be an open brief that allows the searching company to openly explore totally new ideas. The searching company is likely to have defined the level of potential risk and reward that it is prepared to experience and share by moving into the arena of a new technology or product. If correctly executed, open innovation lowers the barrier for collaborations between researchers working inside and outside an organization, facilitating free exchange of ideas between researchers across the traditional fortress of organizational walls, and providing a helping hand to the advancement of science and development. Multinational companies such as GSK, Unilever and Procter & Gamble (P&G) have created their own successful open innovation models.

Crowdsourcing has also been demonstrated to be an effective strategy to enhance the efficiency of a firm's innovation process. Tournament-based crowdsourcing, also called broadcast search, relates to the situation where the technical challenge of a 'seeker' is announced broadly to a group of external 'solvers'. Groups of potential solvers then collectively decide if it is worth investing time and effort to solve the challenge and create a solution. Little has been written about the success or failure of these different approaches to open innovation or how the termination of the 'not invented here' attitude may affect the internal structure and thinking of a company. To have to admit that the required research cannot be carried out in-house, or that external sources are more capable of this product development, must be a management challenge.

Accessing the knowledge of a variety of external agents has been shown to overcome the generally poor outcomes achieved by local search-based problem-solving approaches, which tend to result in product or process improvements rather than radical change (Jeppesen and Lakhani, 2010).

The open innovation process has been defined by a series of models specific to individual companies. This process must start with an internal audit that aims to identify gaps, looking at existing intellectual property (IP), technology and products. These gaps then have to be analysed in terms of value, market, accessibility, potential time frames etc. The required gap filler will then be defined by specific criteria.

British Technology Group (now BTG Plc) had been operating as a facilitator of open innovation for many years before the Chesbrough publication.

Who operates open innovation?

Opportunity targets will be defined by companies and scouts deployed to find these opportunities; alternatively, these companies may create websites promoting their technology needs. P&G, which opened a new website 'Connect+Develop' in February 2013, is one such example. They aim to speed and simplify external innovation connections, linking innovators to company needs, and linking P&G business executives directly to external innovation submissions. The basic programme was developed over 10 years ago and is said to have created more than 2,000 global partnerships. Unilever has a well-developed web-based model called the U-Partner Open Innovation Submission Portal, in addition to employing a vast array of employee and consultant global innovation scouts.

Eli Lilly has also created a platform for the sharing of ideas: The Open Innovation Drug Discovery Programme. It has created a network with academic and biotech researchers to provide access to proprietary, disease-relevant phenotypic assays. Compounds are submitted and Lilly uses a Material Transfer Agreement (MTA) while it evaluates the compound (an Evaluation Agreement may also be used). All IP rights remain with the originator until Lilly decides that it wants to collaborate.

In January 2013, Tate & Lyle opened an open innovation portal designed to encourage universities, start-ups and established companies specializing in food science to submit proposals which are aligned with Tate & Lyle's innovation priorities regarding speciality food ingredients.

GlaxoSmithKline (GSK) has a well-developed open innovation model: The Stevenage Bioscience Catalyst campus is a major hub for early-stage biotech companies, providing them with access to GSK expertise and facilities. It aims to create a culture of open innovation that will nurture the UK bioscience sector and deliver ground-breaking healthcare solutions. In 2011, GSK took an unusual step and entered into collaboration with the McLaren Group (motor sports). This relationship aims to develop business performance analysis, sports nutrition science and employee engagement, and to develop a new McLaren–GSK Centre for Applied Performance. Like Orange, this is a novel initiative looking for opportunities and collaboration outside of the normal box.

Orange did operate an open innovation model and took this a step further by creating 'mobile volunteering'. Orange used the crowdsourcing model to promote mobile volunteering and to collect ideas for mobile applications from which society would benefit. Crowdsourcing was used to find ideas and to vote for the ones the users would like to see developed, leaving Orange to develop them.

Essentially, many open innovation models exist – from links with specific universities, consultancy and employee scouts to web pages asking for innovation ideas – but whatever the methodology used to access these potential new products and technologies, a process of evaluation and due diligence has to follow.

Ensuring the model is successful

Normal due diligence rules must apply once a potentially useful technology or product has been identified. It would be good practice for inventors and SMEs to recognize what the 'open innovation companies' are looking for beyond the product/technology.

Companies operating open innovation models will be looking to secure specific product targets that can be fully integrated within their own portfolio. This may be achieved via in-licensing, joint-venture, acquisition, assignment, spin-out, share acquisition, R&D alliance or distribution agreement.

Initial due diligence will determine the potential product fit within the acquiring organization and will flag up potential risks that may make the product unacceptable. Strategic alignment, internal acceptance and product champions are all essential. A traffic-light due diligence process is required and will also need to include the reputation of the providing company. Companies need to avoid contamination of pre-existing internal IP, disputes over IP ownership and the potential for misunderstandings between the company and diverse open innovation participants. It is likely that the majority of the new opportunities will come from SMEs and individual inventors and that the management of these parties may prove challenging. Due diligence plays a major role in managing both the expectations gap and the cleanness of the IP.

Due diligence considerations will include:

- the current level of development of the technology;
- the status of IP;
- the regulatory framework;
- the competitive landscape;
- the potential overall financial return;
- the potential for reinvention or copying of the technology;
- the degree of technical competitiveness offered by the innovation;
- the cost of taking the technology to market;
- the take-to-market process and time frames;
- the expected business impact.

Once the decision to take the technology on has been made, the legal, financial and business terms of acquisition must be determined and again may prove to be a stumbling block. Adoption will be followed by implementation, which must be seen as a strenuous and critical hurdle. There will always be the increased challenge of working with IP created by external sources. Once the new product is fully functional it will need to be reviewed, improved and measured for success. Highly innovative companies using open innovation may also be more likely to experience cost overruns in new-product development. Balancing the effective collaboration needed to be innovative against the constraints of a cost-conscious business environment is essential. *Intellectual Asset Management* (IAM) encourages portfolio management systems – knowing when and what to disinvest and what value it carries can be as important to effective innovation portfolio management as creating new products. Often companies carry too many products, services, customers and stock. This is costly to the organization and can be a hindrance to growth.

Open innovation is not yet fully matured. Organizations are still in the experimental phase, but in a few years open innovation will probably be seen simply as another form of innovation, where internal and external collaborations have become a normal way of doing business alongside the more traditional internal creation model. Open innovation aims to increase business efficiency and effectiveness, develop brand awareness by bringing customers closer to the company, reduce costs and increase output-to-market.

Note

1 The term 'open innovation' was first coined by Henry Chesbrough, Executive Director of the Center for Open Innovation at the Haas School of Business, part of the University of California, Berkeley. In his book, published in 2003, he defined it as follows: 'Open innovation is a paradigm that assumes that firms can and should use external ideas as well as internal ideas, and internal and external paths to market, as the firms look to advance their technology.'

References

Chesbrough, H (2003) *Open Innovation: The new imperative for creating and profiting from technology*, Harvard Business School Press, Boston

Jeppesen, LB and Lakhani, KR (2010) Marginality and problem-solving effectiveness in broadcast search, *Organization Science*, **21** (September–October), 1016–33

Christi Mitchell, Intellectual Property (IP) Director, founded Highbury Ltd 14 years ago as an independent business development company specializing in international product and technology licensing and commercialization across a range of technical fields. Christi's academic background includes human genetics, molecular biology and business. She has over 25 years' worldwide IP, technology and product collaboration experience, specializing in the life sciences and healthcare sectors. Highbury Ltd also specializes in raising start-up funding, in social enterprise roll-out and replication, and in patent, trade mark and IP portfolio development, management and valuation.

Digital media

Internet RIP? Why the birth of the mobile era brings boundless opportunities to innovate, says Peter Matthews, CEO of Nucleus

We live in a digital age where the velocity of change has gathered such momentum that paradigms shatter at ever-decreasing intervals, posing challenges for established businesses, but also for entrepreneurs and venture capitalists who want to cash in before their latest and greatest idea is, well, too late.

Moore's law, first described in 1965, suggested that the number of transistors placed on an integrated circuit doubles approximately every two years, with each improvement dramatically enhancing the performance of any new digital device. Gordon E Moore's mid-sixties prediction has been surprisingly accurate and, in practice, processing speeds have doubled at an even faster rate, and over an even longer time-frame, than initially forecast.

Pixel development follows a similar path to improvements in chip technology, evidenced by today's crystal-clear tablet and smartphone screens, while network capacity expands faster still. Butters' law – named after Gerry Butters, long-serving Head of Optical Networking at Bell Labs – observes that data volumes double over the same fibre every nine months.

These advances in fundamental science underpin the increasingly rapid development cycles of digital devices, digital networks and, ultimately, our use of digital media.

Internet RIP

The great achievement of indexing the internet and turning disorder into organized data occurred between 1994 and 2004, during a period that is now referred to as Web 1.0. The social phenomenon took off in 2004 during Web 2.0, creating addictive social media behemoths, which have only in the past year or so launched themselves onto the public markets as reasonably mature corporations. By 2011, another paradigm shift emerged, with the start of the most dynamic phase to date (and the first with the capacity to touch almost everyone on the planet) – not Web 3.0, but what we at Nucleus call the mobile era. The mobile era really starts to influence our lives in 2013.

Mobile benefits from both the miniaturizing of the latest chips with their super-fast processing speeds and HD pixel technologies, but currently operates over existing mobile data networks. We get a glimpse of what is going to be possible when we use a mobile device on a broadband wi-fi network, but most of us have

Innovating for the Mobile era.

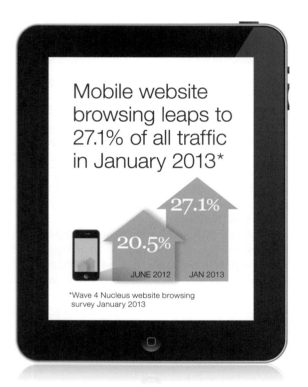

Mobile website browsing leaps to 27.1% of all traffic in January 2013*

27.1%

20.5%

JUNE 2012   JAN 2013

*Wave 4 Nucleus website browsing survey January 2013

The birth of the Mobile era creates the opportunity to look at the world through a new lens. Nucleus helps businesses adapt and innovate, turning good ideas into winning brands.

To find out more about how we create and capture value for our clients in the Mobile era, visit www.nucleus.co.uk

nucleus

Brand + Digital + IP

yet to experience the impact of mobile combined with G4 networks. These double-speed mobile networks are being rolled out across UK cities and will deliver at least twice as fast download speeds as current broadband networks and up to 130 Mbps. Even newer technology will provide speeds of 300 Mbps (more bandwidth than most business networks), which will enable mobile multitasking, such as shopping online while watching several HD video streams as well as yet unimagined high-definition content.

Even though the current mobile networks are slow, relative to what's coming next, consumers are already changing habits rapidly, shifting from PCs to mobile devices – especially iPads – not just to experience apps and downloads, but also for web browsing, booking, banking and shopping.

mCommerce – the next business frontier

According to Mary Meeker's influential Year-end Internet Trends report, mobile traffic has grown to 13 per cent of global web traffic, up from 10 per cent at mid-year. There are now 1.1bn smartphone users around the world and growth is running at 45 per cent a year, although this still only accounts for a mere 17 per cent of all mobile users on the planet. While this shows impressive growth with huge upside potential, what should take any retail or consumer brand owner's breath away is that smartphones and tablets accounted for 24 per cent of all US online shopping on Black Friday 2012 (the day after Thanksgiving), versus 6 per cent just two years before. Out of this near-quarter of online shopping comes another staggering fact: iOS devices accounted for 75 per cent of all mCommerce: that's 4× more than Android, even though Android smartphones are supposed to outnumber iOS 6:1. Clearly, Apple is not the world's most valuable company just because it sells cool devices...

Our own data support Mary Meeker's analysis, with mobile web browsing accounting for 27.1 per cent of all website traffic in our January 2013 survey, up from 20.1 per cent six months earlier, a rate of growth that should be taken very seriously by every business that makes its money online.

What's next?

So, how long will the mobile phase last? If you take Moore's law as a yardstick, perhaps not as long as some think. My hunch is that the mobile era will be super-seded by a 'connected age', by which time we won't be thinking about the web or the internet at all. Everything will be connected, everywhere. This will take bandwidth, lots of it, including spectra that haven't yet been used for two-way communication, such the now redundant analogue TV spectrum (which has the very useful benefit of travelling easily through walls).

In the connected age we will not think twice about interacting with a favourite brand on a 4.5-inch or a 60-inch screen, or possibly both at the same time – all in high definition. This poses problems for designers, who have to create compelling digital brand experiences that work across numerous screen sizes and resolutions, but that won't stop it happening.

As Eric Jackson recently conjectured on Forbes.com, the rate of change is so fast that even the greatest companies find it hard to migrate from one phase to another (think AoL, MySpace, Yahoo) and draws into question whether even today's 'super-platforms', Google and Apple, will be around in such dominant form in five years' time, let alone Facebook, which is rooted in Web 2.0 and has yet to establish itself as a revenue-generating mobile 'super-platform'. While this is hard to contemplate, it's also hard *not* to contemplate against a backdrop of history and continuing rapid change.

The web has, therefore, been entirely consistent with the converging world of computing. Hermann Hauser observed that no corporate leader has led more than one wave: with the first wave of mainframes led by IBM; the second, minicomputing, led by DEC; third came workstations, led by Sun and HP; fourth came the PC, led by Microsoft. Apple and Android lead the fifth wave of 'mobile computing'.

In this context, leadership longevity is almost a contradiction in terms, so can Apple and Android break the mould and maintain their momentum into the connected age? Will Facebook prove it's not another Yahoo by spending its new capital wisely? Will these companies' investments in innovation provide long-term reward or will new competition or patent wars destroy them? Only time will tell, albeit sooner than ever before...

What you should do to innovate effectively in the mobile era

Here are our 10 tips to help you innovate in the mobile era:

1 Put mobile first – this is where the market is going to be.
2 Recalibrate your marketing thinking from finite audiences to infinite audiences.
3 Identify where competitors, even big ones, have been slow to adapt to the mobile era, and exploit their weaknesses.
4 Re-imagine your business model to benefit from a personal, always on, location-savvy relationship with customers.
5 Redefine your customer experience to be seamless, using mobile as the core, or as a complement to a more personal experience, eg retail.
6 Simplify – if you can't do it in a few taps or swipes, it's too complicated.
7 Take security seriously – personal data must not be compromised.
8 Define and measure all your key interactions and implement a process of continuous improvement.
9 Use social media to take your brand viral.
10 Protect your intellectual property assets – both inventions and brand assets.

Peter Matthews is founder and CEO of Nucleus, the world's first brand, digital and intellectual property consultancy. He is also Chairman of Smart Transactions Group and Luxury Explorer.

For more than 30 years he has advised corporate clients on branding, digital and intellectual property matters and how best to create and protect value from investments in innovation. Peter is also expert adviser and commentator on mobile commerce and payment systems.

Follow him on Twitter @NucleusLondon or visit the Nucleus website: www.nucleus.co.uk

basck™

Creating value for your business

Are you looking for a modern approach to efficient and commercially focused Intellectual Property Rights?

We are an IP Consultancy Firm who has the best people no matter where they are in the world.

Contact:
Christian Bunke
Managing Director
christian@basck.com
Phone: +44(0)1223 654547

www.basck.com
United Kingdom, Nordics, India

The market for ideas

Christian Bunke at Basck reports on the trends that are shaping

the growth of innovative ventures

There is a need for a better working market to access new inventions and ideas. Since the global financial crisis post-2008, access to capital has dropped dramatically and hence the growth strategy through acquisition along with it. This said, the acquisition of technology companies and innovative businesses has continued to be strong as large corporates need new innovation to fuel their growth. In Europe, we have seen a number of big acquisition deals involving technology companies such as Skype, Autonomy and MYSQL. There is also new talent in Spotify, Rovio, Supercell and others that show promise. Most often, new ideas and disruptive inventions emerge from small, fast-moving technology companies which are not afraid of doing things differently and breaking a few rules, especially the 'we have always done it this way' model ingrained in established businesses.

Business models and increased intellectual property rights (IPR) filings

There is often a discussion about the correlation between patent filings and innovation. As technologies and markets converge, the business model and market acceptance are often much more powerful than technology and patents in determining what will succeed or not. This does not, however, mean that the importance of IPR will disappear as openness and collaboration increase. Even taking into account variations between industries, we are seeing a continued growth in patent filings of 7.7 per cent and for industrial design filings of 13.3 per cent globally during 2009–11.

The United States is still the dominant market for patent application filings but there is a clear shift in recent years to more patent application filings coming out of Asia. In 2011, China became the largest patent office, handling 526,412 patent filings compared to the United States handling 503,582 patent filings. Further, the main filers in Asia, namely China, Japan and South Korea, also have much a higher percentage of residents in patent filings than other regions.[1] We are likely to see an increased importance of the emerging countries in driving innovation owing to their large market size and also as local companies move up the value chain in offering more advanced products and services. This will also increase the importance of IPR, as shown by China over the past 10 years.

Europe and the UK falling behind

In a review of the top 100 most innovative multinationals in the world based on patent analysis, it was a worrying sight to see that not one UK company made the list, which was dominated by the United States, Japan and South Korea. The UK was therefore behind European countries such as France, Sweden, Switzerland and Germany when it came to different measures related to patenting activity by global companies.[2]

This type of analysis, which focuses purely on patent data, should not be used to draw too many conclusions about innovation and new ideas without further investigation. It also reinforces the need for more than just patents in a market for new ideas. Further, it highlights the need for a well-functioning market of new ideas where innovation and inspiration come from sources other than predominantly multinationals to help create economic growth in Europe.

Focus on research together with high-tech clusters

The UK is very well positioned, with nine universities in the top 100 globally,[3] coming second only to the United States. The University of Cambridge is one example that is attracting investment from around the globe and has a successful technology transfer operation through Cambridge Enterprise. In its 2012 report it was shown that 80 per cent of the companies receiving investment from Cambridge Enterprise were still in business three years later.[4] But are commercialization divisions or technology transfer offices (TTOs) the only answer?

Professor Andy Hopper, Cambridge Computer Laboratory, is advocating that innovation in the UK would benefit more if the universities were willing to release intellectual property (IP) more easily to start-ups in return for a small share in such ventures.[5]

This said, we could always do better in the UK and across Europe in licensing inventions and new ideas from the higher educational institutions and using them in existing or new companies with the right people able to commercialize them.

Finding the next big thing

Technology scouting projects are often used to identify new ideas and technologies for mergers and acquisitions (M&A), competitive landscapes, technology standards and for optimizing IP strategies. Technology scouting needs to be done with a unique combination of skills not always found in traditional IP firms or technology consultancies:

1 technical understanding;
2 patent know-how and landscaping;
3 business insight and market knowledge.

Technical understanding is vital to be able to frame the technology scouting to find the right ideas that will have a real market impact. Patent landscapes are often a useful first step to filtering out those companies that do not have inventions and ideas which are patented, defendable and with the right market impact. Finally, the most underestimated and overlooked aspect of scouting for inventions and ideas is the fit with the business model and channels to market. Just look at the business model and market position of ARM, one of the world's leading IP businesses, which has ARM-designed chips produced by its partners in over 95 per cent of smartphones and tablet computers.[6]

Patent Box and the European Patent

So are there reasons why we might see SMEs, start-ups and inventors increasing their patenting in the UK and the EU?

The Patent Box initiative by the UK government, which saw corporate tax lowered from 23 to 10 per cent (phased in over five years) from April 2013, is hopefully a step in the right direction in stimulating the patenting of new products and services. This said, it is really the SMEs and start-ups which should be planning ahead to have the right patents in place for when the profits are realized. A Patent Box due diligence, looking at a company's patent portfolio strategically, should pay off for the majority of companies within months.

Similarly, the European Common Patent which will come into force from 2014 has been widely debated in the EU. In April 2013, Spain and Italy, which were against the common patent going ahead without them, lost their appeal to stop it.[7] The fact that the common patent will allow a European-wide patent coverage at a lower cost than using the European Patent Convention (EPC) option today will benefit those who need it most to get the European economy going: universities, SMEs, start-ups and inventors.

Number of patent sales increasing

The market for buying and selling patents has always existed, but has grown rapidly in the past 15 years. Examples include The Patent & Licensing Exchange (founded in 1998), Ocean Tomo (founded in 2003) and the emergence and market entry of more sophisticated IP brokers such as GIPLG, ICAP and many others. Also, the number of non-practising entities (NPEs; some of them also called patent trolls) has increased substantially in the past decade and has played its part in more patent transactions and litigation taking place. 'We are seeing how the sophistication of both buyers and sellers is improving every year and how businesses now have a stated intent in continuously improving their IPR position' (John Pryor, Managing Director – Europe, ICAP Patent Brokering).

We might not see the big patent-related deals that took place in recent years, with the sale of the Nortel patent portfolio for $4.5bn (2011) or Google acquiring Motorola for $12.5bn (2012), for some time but the number of transactions will increase. In 2013, the Bridge Crossing LLC (including ARM) consortium is looking to acquire the MIPS patent portfolio totalling 498 patents for $350m.[8] This acquisition of the MIPS patent portfolio was put together by the Allied Security Trust (AST), known to buy up patents to counter activities of NPEs.

Emerging markets should be seen as an opportunity

The market for new ideas should not be bound by country boundaries. Open innovation, which is still rare in many companies, can help firms find the best ideas around, and many of these ideas may come from quite distant sources. Jaideep Prabhu, Professor of Marketing at the Cambridge Judge Business School and the author of *Jugaad Innovation*, explains the need for businesses and investors in the West to look to emerging markets for new ideas, different ways of innovating and commercializing options for new ideas.

Professor Prabhu says:

> The opportunity to sell to the emerging markets like India, Russia and Brazil is very large if one can find the right innovative product offering. That said, jugaad innovation, the frugal and flexible approach to innovation seen in those markets, can also show the US and Europe what can be done with limited resources and with a different approach to the market. By engaging with emerging economies Western firms and economies have a great deal to gain in the future.

Those businesses which embrace what Professor Prabhu so eloquently describes above, and also understand the importance of mixing the collaborative nature of ideas with strong business models and enforceable IPR positions, will prosper in the future.

Notes

1 WIPO – World Intellectual Property Indications 2012 Edition

2 2012 Thomson Reuters Top 100 Global Innovators, http://top100innovators.com/

3 *The Times*, March 2013, www.timeshighereducation.co.uk/world-university-rankings/2013/reputation-ranking/range/91-100,

4 Cambridge Enterprise Results 2012, http://www.enterprise.cam.ac.uk/news/2013/1/cambridge-enterprise-announces-2012-results/

5 *Computer Weekly* interview, 18 March 2013, http://www.computerweekly.com/video/Interview-with-Professor-Andy-Hopper-Cambridge-Computer-Laboratory

6 http://www.dailytech.com/Intel+ARM+Chips+Are+Propellers+We+Build+Jet+Engines/article29995.htm

7 http://www.bloomberg.com/news/2013-04-16/spain-italy-lose-eu-court-appeal-over-patent-system-adoption.html

8 http://www.eetimes.com/electronics-news/4400672/ARM-and-Imagination-divvy-up-MIPS

Reference

Raju, N, Prabhu, J and Ahuja, S (2012) *Jugaad Innovation: Think frugal, be flexible, generate breakthrough growth*, Jossey-Bass, San Francisco

Christian Bunke is the Founder and Managing Director of Basck, an IP consultancy firm with offices in the UK, Nordics and India. Basck works with some of Europe's leading start-ups and SMEs on IP strategy, patenting prosecution and brokering. The team of technical PhDs, Patent Attorneys and experienced business professionals make Basck a leading IP commercialization partner.

Tel: +44(0)7884052079; e-mail: christian@basck.com; Twitter: BasckIPR; web: www.basck.com

IP as a business asset

The commercial and financial applications of IP are evolving rapidly,

reports Simon Mounteney, Managing Partner, Marks & Clerk Consulting LLP

The term 'intellectual property' (or 'IP') defines a range of legal rights that have traditionally been used to protect the results of research, development and creative effort as well as protecting reputation and goodwill. These rights are true items of property in the sense that they can be traded or licensed in the same way as other assets. Furthermore, the rights can be exploited even more flexibly than many other assets, since rights to use them can be granted to many users simultaneously, split by territory, product or technical field, and granted for exclusive or non-exclusive use within a given field or territory.

Despite this, many boardrooms and SME owners alike have traditionally tended to think of IP as a mere defensive tool. But IP has now developed into an asset class that offers an increasing range of commercial uses and these have in turn spawned businesses, business models and arguably entire industries that are driven entirely by them.

In this chapter, we will take a look at some of these rapidly evolving uses of IP assets and consider how an ambitious business might benefit from them.

Monetization

'Monetization' refers to the use of IP as a revenue-generating asset in itself (rather than as a defensive legal tool). Revenue can be generated through selling the IP, licensing it out or litigating for infringement. Although none of these processes are new in themselves (and have been long used by universities and other businesses lacking their own production resources), the concept of using the IP purely for revenue generation is more recent, particularly where the IP is acquired (or created) by the owner specifically for these purposes.

Monetization has now developed substantially and there are substantial businesses that do nothing but monetize IP. Because such businesses tend not to sell the goods, services or technology that is the subject of the IP, they are generally known as 'non-practising entities' or NPEs. Another less polite term that is commonly applied to some NPEs is 'patent troll'. Although this expression lacks a precise definition, it is often understood that a patent troll is an NPE that seeks to obtain a financial return that is disproportionately higher than the technical or commercial value of the IP – for example, a 'troll' might threaten to obtain an injunction against a company, forcing an entire product to be withdrawn from sale, when only a small component or aspect of the product is protected by the IP in question. Many of these businesses seek to 'aggregate' or accumulate portfolios to build a so-called 'patent thicket' which production businesses may find it easier to pay for than to navigate.

This in turn has led to the development of intermediaries such as IP auction houses which offer portfolios for sale on behalf of owners in the hope of attracting competitive bids from a wider community than competitors or those in the vertical supply chain, the more traditional buyers of third-party IP rights.

Monetization-based business models such as those adopted by NPEs will typically be highly specialized and require significant expertise, manpower and financial resources. However, this does not mean that monetization is beyond the means of other businesses. In particular, a conventionally assembled IP portfolio can often be used to generate revenue as a supplement to the defensive duties of the IP.

Apart from a general desire to maximize revenue, there will sometimes be particular reasons for a company to consider IP monetization. Examples of this include: the existence of IP that is no longer relevant to the core business (eg due to a change in commercial strategy or corporate structure); overprotection of the core business; and corporate distress.

Often, the most likely purchaser of any IP will be a commercial competitor, which can make a conventional sale undesirable. In view of this, licensing or enforcement would traditionally have been the main alternatives. While some owners have had the ability and the inclination to undertake these activities using in-house resources or external professional representation, this has not always been the case – particularly where resources were limited. With the recent growth in the monetization market, NPEs now offer an alternative route to revenue, because their business models attract them to the purchase of IP that has a credible assertion value.

While selling IP to an NPE has obvious attractions, there are risks involved, because the NPE could sell it on to a competitor of the vendor, who could then enforce it against the vendor. Precautionary measures are therefore essential and these will typically include retaining a perpetual licence to exploit the IP or agreeing an option to buy the IP back.

Sometimes monetization can be used in less strategic, but nonetheless valuable ways. An example of this is when a company enters administration or bankruptcy. In such a case, the IP can be sold off for substantial sums, thereby enabling the company to address its debts or simply buy sufficient time to restructure its business.

Corporate growth

IP can be used to underpin the growth of a business in various ways and at various stages of the company life cycle. The most obvious and traditional way is by protecting any revenue-generating products, processes and services from commercial competition, thereby optimizing market share. In a similar vein, an obviously strong IP portfolio can offer peace of mind to potential investors, as they will feel more confident that the business will remain competitive and that profits and/or share value will increase.

It is also possible, however, to use IP in less direct ways to develop a business. These generally tend to recognize the capital value of the IP, thereby enabling it to secure a financial benefit of some kind.

Securitization

One established and theoretically simple approach is to use IP as loan security. Providing the value of the IP can be satisfactorily established, this can unlock funds that can be used for a whole variety of purposes. The benefit of using IP in this way is that the value it offers can significantly outweigh the investment in creating it, thereby enabling accelerated growth for a relatively low outlay. Of course, the most valuable IP may well protect core aspects of the business, which means low outlay does not necessarily equate with low risk: losing the competitive advantage afforded by the IP in the event of a default could have serious consequences.

More established businesses may seek to use their IP to overcome more complex barriers to growth. One example of this is where a pension fund deficit exists. As is well known, funding such a deficit can not only cause a severe drain on profits, but regulatory provisions can limit the options that are available to trustees for investment. The consequences to the business as a whole can be so extreme as to be terminal.

By selling IP assets to its pension fund trustees, a company can free up significant sums that not only release the burden of the deficit, but also provide tax benefits and facilitate growth to the extent that the IP can eventually be released back to the company, while leaving the asset in the hands of a non-competitor with an interest in the continued survival of the business. This approach works because the trustees can generate income from the IP through monetization models, such as licensing back to the company, again in a tax-efficient manner. Structures such as these can be complicated and therefore expensive to put in place and they also rely critically upon determining the monetary value of the IP. They also require a cooperative pension fund trustee. In the right circumstances, however, they can be very powerful.

Taxation

Alongside the R&D credits provided for research, the products of such research, if protected by patents, can be a means of mitigating exposure to the tax levied on sales income. Tax relief schemes are often offered by governments in recognition of the economic contribution made by innovative businesses. The precise details of the different schemes vary between jurisdictions, but they have the common objective of encouraging innovation by offering tax breaks on profits attributable to IP.

At the time of writing, for example, the UK government was due to introduce the Patent Box regime, which allows organizations paying corporation tax in the UK to apply for tax relief on worldwide profits made from patented products or products with patented components.

Owing to the way that these schemes are often structured, creating or identifying profit-critical IP and determining the value of its impact upon the overall profit is essential. To maximize the savings, a strategic assessment of technology to identify its innovative aspects and match these with appropriate IP can pay significant dividends.

IP often forms part of a transfer pricing strategy, designed to enable profits to be extracted from the sale of products or services in the most tax-effective manner by allocating these profits to the exploitation of the IP by one member of a group of related companies licensing the rights to another which makes or sells the products protected by the right.

Asset protection

IP is also often held by a company entirely separate from the manufacturing or trading company using it, to secure the IP from the reach of creditors if the operating or manufacturing company should encounter trading difficulties. In many cases the most valuable assets on the balance sheet of a company will be the intangibles, of which IP will be a leading component.

Patent pools and standards

These pools formalize and facilitate cross-licensing in competitive industries, especially those where it is important to have standardized technical solutions to enable effective competition in the marketplace between providers of alternative products – consumer telecommunications being one example. Such patent pools will enjoy more favourable treatment from competition authorities than other cooperation agreements between competitors. Entry into a standards pool can be made easier by possessing patents which themselves contribute to the pool and can be of value as much for the access they provide as in their own right. The pool can be as effective as a means of exposing the patent to a wider user group and is largely self-policing in terms of royalty generation.

Licences of right, certification marks and collective marks

Rarely used today, and regarded as somewhat esoteric, so-called licences of right can be advertised to try to attract usage of a technology by providing a patent or other right on favourable terms while still offering a barrier to others not prepared to pay the royalties attaching to the product. Similarly, a certification trade mark or in some cases a collective trade mark may be exploited by allowing anyone who makes goods to a certain standard or using a certain patent to be able to use the trade mark associated with that standard, the associated kudos helping to promote the product or service in question.

Key points

- IP is not just about protection – it can have value in its own right and generate revenue.
- IP can be a good way to help build relatively rapid growth without high levels of investment.
- IP can be one of the most valuable assets within a business and consequently have a significant impact upon share value.
- Owing to the significant value of some IP, it can be used to help with crisis management.
- Because IP nevertheless has important defensive responsibilities, putting it to other uses or selling it altogether can introduce significant risk.
- IP can be leveraged in other ways, such as in tax planning and patent pools, and to protect assets and production means from creditors.
- Many asset-related uses of IP rely critically upon its valuation.

Simon Mounteney is Managing Partner of Marks & Clerk Consulting LLP, an IP consultancy firm offering a range of wider consultancy services complementary to the mainstream legal and IP advisory services of Marks & Clerk LLP and Marks & Clerk Solicitors LLP. As part of his role, Simon leads the firm's IP valuation and analysis service, together with its product design service. With 25 years' experience working in intellectual property, he is also a Partner of Marks & Clerk LLP, the UK's largest firm of patent and trade mark attorneys.

Tel: 020 7420 0000; e-mail: smounteney@marks-clerk.com; web: www.marks-clerk.com

PART FOUR
Innovation techniques

Knowledge and technology transfer

Whether you are a major player or an up-and-coming venture, you have multiple options for calling on world-class knowledge and turning it into everyday applications, says Dr Douglas Robertson, chair at PraxisUnico

Universities in the UK are truly world class, with over 50 in the world top 200. There are over 140 universities and specialist higher education establishments, and whatever your needs and areas of specialism there will be a UK institution with expertise which aligns with your needs all tightly packed into a geography of 600 by 300 miles – a concentration which is unrivalled around the globe.

In a publication celebrating the 10th anniversary of Praxis, Campbell Wilson, Executive Business Development Director, Science and Technology Licensing, AstraZeneca, notes that: 'The partnerships we have with higher education institutes are key to being a successful multi-national innovation-driven pharmaceutical company. This is nowhere more evident than in the UK where we benefit from a strong heritage of research excellence and many highly skilled and professionally run technology transfer offices.'

The range of interactions

Universities transfer their knowledge and expertise into application through a whole host of routes:

- teaching and producing graduates;
- direct research collaborations and contracts;
- licensing;
- co-supervised studentships;
- knowledge transfer partnerships;
- continuing professional development;
- spin-out company creation;
- consultancy.

The scale of interactions

Projects can vary in scale from a hundred pounds for a short course through projects which scale from a few thousand pounds over a short time period to hundreds of thousands of pounds for major research projects which may run over several years.

In 2010–11, the latest full-year figures available, UK universities undertook over £1bn of contract research in around 30,000 projects. In consultancy there were over 80,000 interactions with a value of £370m of consultancy. Of these two activities, over 40,000 of these interactions were with small and medium-sized businesses.

There are over 1,000 spin-out companies trading at the present time, with some university shareholding. Since 2003, over 70 university companies have gone to trade sale or been floated on the market. At the time of trade sale or floatation, these had a market cap of more than £15bn!

Do intellectual property rights get in the way?

If you don't think about intellectual property rights (IPR) carefully they can indeed get in the way. It really depends on what you want to do. For simple pieces of consultancy the client will usually get ownership of the report and the university is unlikely to want to publish the results; these projects tend to be undertaken on full commercial terms. IPR can get a little more complicated when it comes to research activities. It may assist if I explain what some of these issues are. I have over 30 years' experience in working with industry and the biggest block to effective IPR is when neither party wants to talk about them. With willingness and common sense from all, much is achievable.

Rarely does a research project stand alone

Universities live on ideas and build on ideas. As Ric Parker, Director of Research at Rolls-Royce, points out: 'It's the job of universities to top up the hopper of ideas.' Businesses come to universities because of our pre-existing expertise and our hopper of ideas. If we locked away all developments in collaboration with each client, clients would not gain any real benefit from working with universities. By simply discussing and considering the type of results to be generated, a clear strategy will emerge. For example, when working with a pharmaceutical company, the company needs to ensure that it owns developments to its drug compounds but will often allow universities to retain ownership of enabling technologies. The pharma industry recognizes the benefit in allowing the university to build its pool of enabling technologies with different partners. Every project can generate intellectual property (IP) of different types:

- relating to techniques and methodologies developed by the university over many years;

- directly relating to an existing product, technique or service of the company;
- new ideas which could generate new products or services, some of these in the area of the business partner and others in entirely different fields;
- patentable and non-patentable IPR.

By a simple discussion under cover of a confidentiality agreement, the different outcomes from a research project can be considered and a route through what at first appeared complex can become easier.

But surely if the university publishes the results then my business advantage is gone?

The good news is that universities rarely wish to publish articles about products. They seek to publish in their discipline. They want to advance knowledge. As a consequence, there is rarely a conflict between what a university wants to publish and what a company needs to protect. The patent system itself is a form of publication and universities will agree to a delay in publication to allow a patent to be filed. In over £1bn of research activity with third parties over the past 30 years, I have encountered only three major disputes about publication and even these were resolved by discussion.

Intellectual property and valuation

Research projects are often undertaken on an 'at cost basis', and in many cases are subsidized by public funds (eg research council support). In some senses the university's publication and potential interest in IP are the equivalent of profit for a business. Universities are often accused of over-valuing their IP. In my opinion, the main reason for this perception is that in research the results cannot be predicted and therefore seeking to value IP at the start is pure guesswork which tends to lead to cautious estimates on behalf of the company and over-inflated values from the university; both parties are likely to be wrong. Corporate lawyers like clarity, but many universities recognizing uncertainty are happy to 'agree to agree'. The parties then negotiate in good faith when they know they have something worth talking about. If necessary, an intermediary can be appointed to provide an expert opinion. Universities value their reputations and they will not seek to be unreasonable.

Intellectual property an enabler and not a barrier – Easy Access IP

Easy Access IP exemplifies the way in which universities and research institutes are changing the UK narrative with business and industry, with the clear focus on valuing partnerships with business with a sophisticated treatment of IP within those relationships. Universities taking part in Easy Access IP identify IP that they feel they do not have the capacity to develop or which is so far from market it is difficult to value.

It all started with a simple good idea. Why not offer certain IP from universities for free, using quick and simple licence agreements, and actually get the knowledge out there for public use?

This radical new Easy Access IP approach to licensing was launched by the University of Glasgow in late 2010 and soon gained international interest and support from both the academic community and industry. Easy Access IP has now been adopted by many UK and international universities which are spearheading the concept in North America, Australasia and Europe. The scheme reflects these universities' commitment to make it easier for industry to engage with us and build mutually rewarding and long-lasting partnerships with the business community.

What next?

Why not call your local university and have a chat? It will have a knowledge exchange, enterprise or technology transfer office. It may not have the expertise you are looking for but by working with its colleagues around the country in PraxisUnico it will probably be able to help.

PraxisUnico is the professional association for those who work for the academic community in finding applications for innovation and in commercializing research. It has now trained around 3,000 technology transfer and research office staff in how to develop effective partnerships with industry.

Further details: www.praxisunico.org.uk

Outsourcing innovation

Why might you outsource innovation? And what are the pitfalls?

asks Mike Faers at Food Innovation Solutions

How do I get the innovation I need to differentiate my business and deliver the profitable growth, when I have reduced the capability within the organization to manage overheads?

Most businesses tend to scale back on innovation as hard times hit. Flexing spend and momentum can normally be sustained from the innovation pipeline for a couple of years... but what then?

I am going to share an innovation business model that is already established in the United States and growing in Europe, particularly in the IT field, and is to many leaders counterintuitive.

Warwick Business School recently published a study of 253 business leaders from the largest firms in Europe. The study found that 64 per cent of responding firms believed their ability to sustain innovation contributed to the financial success of the organization, with 70 per cent reporting they had achieved their innovation through outsourcing to specialist organizations.

This has historically been the way large international organizations and governments behave; however, now there is a definite shift for smaller businesses to follow the same business model.

Outsourcing innovation

'Using external organizations to enable our innovation expectations.'

Five questions to ask yourself

1 'Trust' – finding the right external partner that you can trust with your sensitive information; look for an organization that has testimonials that can be verified.

2 'Intellectual property' – ensure that you understand the IP rights and have a clear agreement in place before you commence, as this can lead to difficulties later on – think of it as pre-nup for IP!

3 'Clear objectives' – do you know what you need from a provider? Is it to create the strategy or to accelerate parts of a complex project that need expertise, is it to culture-change your organization, or a mixture?

4 'Cultural fit' – it can be a disruptive or even threatening experience for incumbent teams to have external providers coming into the organization – do they have the emotional intelligence to navigate the political fallout?

5 'Cost' – you will have heard me talk in previous articles about 'bang for your innovation buck'. Outsourcing should not be viewed as a way to save cost – innovation is not a quantifiable discipline to the same degree as a call centre or an office catering contract where the variables are all known and therefore a robust cost can be applied.

Five benefits of outsourcing

1 'Speed to market' – every business faces at some point peaks in innovation activity that cannot be met by internal resource. How you manage those peaks is crucial; it is better to delay than to rush and fail – but if you can find a partner whom you trust to flex with your business needs, then why wouldn't you?

2 'Skills and capability' – certain projects require skills and capabilities to which you may not have access. This can remove information blockages in projects and at the same time up-skill your internal resource.

3 'Cost' – the upside of the cost question is that you do not need a permanent resource but will need a partner to dip in and out whom you can manage cost-effectively vs a permanent resource, where any partner worth working with will invest upfront to understand your culture and business needs, but this only needs to happen once so the next time the partner can hit the ground running.

4 'Unfettered thinking' – do not underestimate the power of external challenge, particularly in cultures heavily dominated by one discipline such as operations. Finding solutions that are internally considered 'off limits' can be raised without risk and a broad range of experience in different industries can be applied, bringing a fresh perspective.

5 'Expertise' – if you have read my previous articles, you will know that I believe that effective commercial innovation is a specialist business skill. Why would you not use specialists to develop your business projects? What makes an orchestra great is the conductor bringing together specialist musicians at the right time to deliver a command performance.

It is not a clear-cut answer, but where speed to market is a key profit driver for innovation, considered outsourcing can make a significant and positive impact, but never abdicate your responsibility as a leader for what is the most important element of any business's future strategy.

Which got me thinking: what is the key benefit of having an iPhone? It's the *apps* which Apple have effectively outsourced – all the innovation comes from a community of developers yet they still control the content of the App Store and the reputational benefit it brings to its brand and core product. Is this a potential model that could dramatically change the retail landscape in the future?

Within the food world we have a lack of good innovators and specialist business and product developers, and I can envisage a continued migration towards external providers as cost management within the industry continues to dominate the board-room agenda – could this be a way to 'develop your cake and eat it?'

Mike Faers is the CEO of Food Innovation Solutions, the international food innovation consultancy. FIS works with some of the largest international food retailers and manufacturers, building innovation capability and brands through strategy and delivery: setting direction, realigning the team, mobilizing resources through training and development, and managing programmes of innovation and new product development (NPD) change.

Tel: 01284 705787; e-mail: mike@foodinnovationsolutions.com

Challenge-led innovation

4.3

Innovation is happening in new ways to meet the kinds of complex, multidimensional challenges now faced in public health, reports David Rhodes at Public Health England

The past 10 years have seen a renewed interest worldwide in the sometimes-neglected field of public health, leading to an explosion of innovative approaches and technologies, with many others yet to be fully explored and developed. In England, this has been a driving force behind the formation of Public Health England, a new executive agency dedicated to promoting national health and well-being. However, the sheer breadth of the challenges and potential solutions in public health can place a significant strain on the limited resources available for technology transfer and will demand a strong focus on those innovations that offer the most attractive health economic benefits.

The challenges facing public health are evident in a visit to almost any city, town or village in the UK, and are replicated across the world. The advances achieved through public health, improved nutrition, and medical advances over the past 150 years have been nothing short of phenomenal, particularly the reduction in premature deaths from infectious disease achieved through clean water and paediatric immunization programmes. As a result, the focus of innovation has tended to shift towards extension of later life at the individual rather than the population level, for example through medical interventions in oncology and cardiovascular disease. In general, with the exception of the very poorest countries, people are better fed, more prosperous and living longer than was the case in previous generations. An unintended consequence, however, is that we are witnessing a renewed need for innovation at the public health level as the scale of public health challenges in our richer, more elderly and better-fed populations becomes apparent.

Challenges and priorities

In the UK we see a number of key public health priorities and challenges that are, to a greater or lesser extent, replicated in all countries that have benefited from the medical and economic advances described above. The first of these is the reduction in preventable deaths arising, for the most part, from non-communicable diseases and exacerbated by smoking, obesity, excessive alcohol consumption and insufficient exercise, issues which are characteristic of most urban populations that have access to at least some disposable income. Disease and disability, particularly from conditions with high impact such as dementia, anxiety, depression and drug dependency, place a significant cost on primary and secondary care sectors and a substantial, though less quantifiable burden on society as a whole. In some cases such as dementia and cancers affecting older people, disease trends are reflective of an ageing population that has resulted from earlier medical advances. Regrettably, improvements in population health have not benefited all sectors in society equally, leading to health inequalities; marked discrepancies in life expectancy still occur across relatively small geographic distances. Despite the shift in the focus of public health towards diseases of ageing and lifestyle, protection of the population from infectious diseases and environmental hazards remains a priority, particularly as new hazards emerge such as new viral strains and antimicrobial resistance. The benefits of health intervention at key 'touch points' is increasingly recognized, in particular during childhood in order to ensure the best start in life for young people, and as employees move in and out of the workplace.

Biomedical innovations

A number of exciting developments are currently creating new opportunities for improving health at the population level, particularly in the fields of vaccines, diagnostics and genetics. Vaccines continue to offer excellent pharmacoeconomics and promising opportunities for growth and innovation, with new recombinant vaccines in particular offering potential solutions to reducing the burden of vaccine-preventable disease. Polio eradication is now a realistic prospect, while a universal influenza vaccine, immunological approaches to malaria and a modern tuberculosis vaccine are key public health goals. Advances in diagnostics are key to personalized medicine, as outlined below, but microbial diagnostics are also an important component of public health strategy, for example in tracking the development of antimicrobial resistance and underpinning emergency preparedness wherever the emergence of new pathogens or variants is suspected. Likewise, developments in genomics, particularly next-generation sequencing, support rapid characterization of emerging pathogens such as novel coronaviruses. The very real threat of antimicrobial resistance is prompting the adoption of new approaches towards antimicrobial discovery, while the experience of managing healthcare-associated infections and the cost of decontamination in anthrax exposure incidents, for example, has stimulated renewed interest in microbial dispersal and decontamination. The advent of nanotechnology has opened new opportunities for medical interventions but also a requirement for a new discipline of nanotoxicology in order to ensure that nanomaterials are used safely. As drugs have come off patent and been approved for over-the-counter (OTC) use, new opportunities have arisen in consumer healthcare.

Information and communications technology

Some of the most exciting innovations in the field of public health are driven by advances in information and communications technology (ICT). Information, particularly when supported by mobile communications, has the potential to empower individuals to make better choices about their own health, supplementing the support provided by existing community networks such as health workers and pharmacists. Telemedicine offers the prospect of remote tracking of biomarkers and consultation with medical professionals, and remote access to medical records. The advent of the analytical potential of 'big data' enables epidemiological trends to be observed that might otherwise be invisible to individual public health consultants at the community level. Simulation modelling enables scenarios such as emergencies to be modelled and potential interventions tested in advance of real-world developments. Perhaps less obviously, ICT has been of great value in enabling the implementation of initiatives such as emergency response, microbial containment and infection control training across wide and diverse audiences in the UK and overseas. Social media has enabled new opportunities in 'crowdsourcing' of healthcare solutions and provision of real-time access to health information.

Health marketing innovations

Innovative tools developed for commercial marketing purposes are increasingly being used to promote health and well-being at the population level. Successful examples include the National Travel Health Network, Change4Life and Smokefree campaigns which aim to promote better health through access to dynamic websites and apps that support smoking cessation, positive dietary choices and travel health, in some case underpinned by customer relationship management (CRM) systems that allow individuals to track their own progress. Advances in technology have encouraged a shift from campaign-based approaches to delivery such as television and poster campaigns to 'always on' services which can be accessed at any time. Cost-effective training of over 50,000 locally based health trainers and partners in the UK has also been achieved in large part through use of online resources. Advances in psychosocial marketing allow important behavioural 'nudges' that are based on sound behavioural science to be delivered in an effective and targeted way. The growth of the consumer healthcare sector is likely to create further opportunities for effective collaborations in health marketing, as is the growing availability of consumer diagnostics.

Promoting and nurturing innovation

Given the diversity of sectors, disciplines and technologies outlined above, the innovation landscape in public health is complex. Access to a broad range of intellectual property (IP) is required, including patents, trade marks, proprietary know-how, database rights and copyright in both written materials and software, and technology transfer professionals must be proficient in protecting such IP and managing the associated transactions. Further adding to the complexity, many aspects of public health require an open innovation approach, in which solutions are built using multiple sources, and from which spin-off opportunities can be applied to a broad range of sectors. In our experience, sustained effort, multiple calls for proposals, and access to diverse funding sources is required in order to support a healthy pipeline of innovations. In addition to investment in the underpinning science, this entails access to proof-of-concept, challenge-led and commercialization funds. An effective open innovation environment also requires access to networking opportunities that cut across multiple sectors and operate at an international level, while ensuring that appropriate governance processes are applied in order to avoid subsequent disagreements over development and commercialization. Despite the complexities and inevitable resource limitations, the opportunities of challenge-led innovation in public health are immense, offering the potential for cost-effective interventions at the population level that can make a real difference to economic growth, health and well-being.

David Rhodes is Head of Business Development of Public Health England (PHE), an executive agency of the Department of Health charged with improving and protecting the nation's health and reducing health inequalities. The Business Development Department is responsible for the external contracts that underpin much of PHE's activity in the fields of microbiology, environmental hazards, public health intelligence and health and well-being, as well as managing a substantial portfolio of intellectual property.

Contact Public Health England: tel: +44 (0) 1980 612100;
e-mail: business@phe.gov.uk; web: www.gov.uk/phe

Design thinking

Be radical, be profitable, says Graham Grant, a lecturer in entrepreneurship at Robert Gordon University

Companies that opt for small, incremental changes to their products and services complain that they are being squeezed out of the market – there is always someone who can do things faster and cheaper. What are required are game-changing innovations that can radically change the nature of the business and their market. But how can SMEs, with their often limited time and financial resources, innovate consistently and profitably?

The answer could be design. Inspired by the process that designers have honed over many years of harnessing creativity to generate innovations, design has burst out of the studio and into the boardroom. Heralded by companies such as Nokia, Coca-Cola and Procter & Gamble (P&G), design thinking can be applied by companies ranging from the FTSE 100 to the smallest one-man bands.

What makes designers special? The answer is in their thinking. Designers have the ability to think, not 'what is?', but 'what could be?'. They are able to envisage multiple solutions to problems, visualize them, create stories about them and prototype them. Designers have learnt to identify problems and contradictions, to create insights from human behaviours and to design elegant solutions to unmet needs.

Design thinking is transformative: no longer just about the aesthetics of toasters and posters, it is equally at home grappling with wicked problems – those problems seemingly so intractable, impossible and messy that they have been left well alone by managers schooled in traditional management techniques.

One of the greatest myths of innovation is that they arrive, fully formed, in the mind of the lone genius. Almost every game-changing innovation – electricity, computers, the internet and lasers – has been the result of creative interdisciplinary teamwork. Edison didn't invent the light bulb: his team of talented, engaged scientists did. Interdisciplinary project teams are vital to the success of innovation projects: they help companies bridge silos of knowledge, increase internal buy-in and create a unified approach to innovation.

So how does a project work? The process starts by looking beyond the brief and identifying the real problem that a company is facing. Designers have developed a range of ethnographic tools to help. In its most basic form, ethnography is the practice of observing people as they go about their day-to-day lives or undertake a particular activity. Designers are immensely curious, and can help garner insights from this process – seeing how people adapt objects to their own use, the little things that irritate them every time they use them, like a door that intuition says should be pulled open, but instead needs to be pushed. These insights can be recorded in many forms, from written notes to video diaries, photographs and stories.

These insights can help reframe the problem and lead into the next, and most exhilarating phase of a design thinking project: the idea generation stage. The success of this phase relies on the ability to think divergently, to imagine multiple solutions to the problem identified and to keep all ideas valid. Again, designers have devised various techniques to oil the wheels of the idea generation process – brainstorming techniques, intuitive idea generation techniques such as image association, and systematic techniques such as TRIZ and the exotic-sounding morphological matrix. Whatever the technique, the philosophy remains the same – defer judgement, encourage even the wildest ideas and build on the ideas of others. Traditionally, businesses have relied on the MD to come up with an idea, and for the rest of the company to make it work. By involving the whole of the company in creating ideas, there is not only a much higher level of engagement, there is a much greater number of ideas to choose from.

Once ideas have been generated, there follows a convergent process: a way of filtering down ideas and selecting the most promising ones to develop. Again, there are various techniques to do this, but the end result is the same: to select a number of ideas to develop and prototype. For design thinkers, early-stage prototyping doesn't mean complex, glossy prototypes – it is about making models out of whatever comes to hand, whether that is cardboard and sticky tape, Plasticine or blocks of Lego. The importance of these prototypes is to give ideas concrete form, however rough, so as to gauge reaction from the people who will actually use them. Other forms of prototyping could be creating storyboards or role-playing, which can be very useful in prototyping a service.

Concepts are then developed in further, iterative, stages before launch. If run as a truly interdisciplinary project, directors, accountants, quality management and marketing will have been involved throughout the project life cycle. Their involvement will make the project less likely to be killed off at this stage as there is a greater buy-in and sense of collective ownership of the idea. By bringing together all these groups, a design thinking project should deliver a concept that is desirable for the user, viable for the business and technologically feasible.

Design thinking has a wider value. It can help create a culture of innovation. Discrete project teams are one step in a process that can completely reconfigure a company to become one which has innovation embedded in its brand DNA. One-off innovations are all very well, but for a business to become sustainable, innovation must become part of what it does.

Cultures of innovation don't come from having a pool table in the office and a fridge full of soft drinks in the corner – they come from a commitment to giving staff the freedom to utilize their natural creativity. Staff need the space to experiment and a management that encourages success but doesn't penalize failure. Projects don't always work first time, but an innovative company will take that failure and learn from it. After all, the Post-it note, that ubiquitous item of office stationery, was created when a scientist at 3M made a glue that didn't stick properly. Had William McKnight, the company's chairman, not embraced constructive failure and allowed employees to exercise their initiative, the invention would have been written off as a disaster. However, by encouraging staff to discuss their failures, collaborate and use their initiative, he established a culture and an environment which allowed innovations to flourish.

Graham Grant is lecturer in entrepreneurship at the Robert Gordon University, Aberdeen. He has a particular interest in innovation and creativity in the entrepreneurial start-up process. Previously, he was Principal Designer at c4di, the centre for design and innovation at the Robert Gordon University. C4di was Scotland's first centre that employed design thinking techniques to help SMEs innovate across their products, services, processes and business cultures.

E-mail: g.grant3@rgu.ac.uk

Crowdsourcing

Open innovation (OI) and crowdsourcing can transform and accelerate the search for new products. Paul Sloane at Destination Innovation reviews the uses to which they are being put

Not long ago, companies primarily used closed models for all their new product development. They focused on their own resources in research, development and marketing to bring new products to market. This model gave them control and seemed to work well.

Nowadays, most CEOs see collaboration as key to their success with innovation. They know that they cannot achieve their innovation targets using internal resources alone. So they look outside for other organizations to partner with. A good example is Mercedes and Swatch which collaborated to produce the Smart car. When Mercedes wanted to produce an innovative town car it did not choose another automobile manufacturer – it partnered with a fashion watch maker. Each brought dissimilar skills and experiences to the team.

The next step beyond collaboration is OI: a concept developed by Henry Chesbrough to describe the process of harnessing external resources to work alongside your team to develop new products and services. This is something that many leading companies, including Procter & Gamble (P&G), IBM, Unilever, Reckitt Benckiser, BMW, Nokia and Kimberly-Clark, have focused on as a way of driving innovation. OI replaces the vertical integration of processes within one company with a network of collaborators working on innovation projects. Using outsiders can speed up processes, reduce costs, introduce more innovative ideas and reduce time to market.

Kimberly-Clark reduced the time it takes to bring out new products by 30 per cent through OI. It launched Sunsignals in just six months by collaborating with a smaller company, SunHealth Solutions. Sunsignals is a self-adhesive sensor that changes colour when the wearer is in danger of burning in the sun. P&G aims to source 50 per cent of its innovations from outside using OI. Early results include new products such as Mr Clean Magic Eraser and Pringles Prints.

Crowdsourcing is an extrapolation of OI in which you throw out a challenge to a group of people that you may or may not know and solicit their ideas and solutions for your issue. Many web-based companies specialize in different crowdsourcing fields. So if you want a name for a new brand of product, you can get many suggestions by using the crowdsourcing site Naming Force. If you have a tough programming problem you could use Topcoder.com which will set the challenge for ace freelance programmers from around the world. Similarly, if you have a difficult technical or scientific challenge you might use Innocentive or Nine Sigma.

In the book *A Guide to Open Innovation and Crowdsourcing*, Jeffreys Phillips of OVO Innovation categorizes four different types of crowdsourcing model. They are as follows:

1 *Suggestive/Participative*. Here a company will encourage anyone to submit an idea and to review and rank ideas from others. A good example of this Dell's Ideastorm. This is a website that invites suggestions for Dell's products or services. It has received over 15,000 suggestions and Dell says that 400 have been implemented. Note that anyone can submit an idea on any topic. This model will potentially generate a large number of ideas in all sorts of areas which makes evaluation and selection difficult.

2 *Suggestive/Invitational*. In this model the sponsor company invites specific individuals, teams or companies to contribute ideas on very broad topic areas. This is what IBM does with its Idea Jams. These are often campaign or event driven and the invitation is limited to a restricted time. IBM receives many thousands of ideas from these campaigns.

3 *Directed/Invitational*. The company invites specific individuals or partners to respond to specific challenges or requests. This is the most popular model and it is the one used by P&G in its Connect and Develop programme and by Innocentive which invites solutions for tough scientific problems. With this model you get far fewer suggestions but they tend to be of much higher value and focus.

4 *Directed/Participative*. Anyone can submit suggestions for very specific challenges. When the 2010 Deep Water Horizon oil disaster occurred in the Gulf of Mexico, BP and the US government used a website to invite anyone to suggest ways to cap the leak or recover the oil spills. This method can generate a large number of ideas for a particular campaign or issue.

In choosing which approach to adopt it is important to first define your strategy and identify what you want to get out of OI. What is your vision and what is the business strategy to achieve it? How can OI contribute to these objectives?

Here are 10 leadership tips to help you grasp the benefits of OI for your company:

1 Define what you want to achieve. Assess in what areas you need more innovation. Ask how effective your capabilities are at developing new products or services. Identify the areas where you need to be more effective.

2 Set goals. Set some measurable and timely goals for what you want to achieve. CEO Laffley at P&G set a target of reaching 50 per cent of new product innovations from outside the company – the goal was met.

3 Assess your level of openness. Most companies are remarkably difficult to approach with new ideas. They are internally focused and there are cultural barriers to accepting initiatives and suggestions from outside. Carry out an audit of how easy or difficult it is for outsiders to contact the right person and then work with your company. You might be surprised. Take actions to fix the problems.

4 Define your challenge. You can just ask for suggestions on any topic that people want to make, but there is a danger that you will be flooded with low-value ideas. It is generally better to be very specific about what you are looking for – eg 'We want new materials that will perform well in corrosive or extreme temperature conditions'. The more specific you are, the easier it is for specialist outsiders to know if they have a fit.

5 Choose your method. There are several different approaches that you can use. For example, you can throw a specific challenge to anyone who wants to submit an idea or you can pre-select a community of potential partners who meet your criteria. It is good to read up what other companies do and see the pros and cons of various approaches before choosing the one that best suits you.

6 Design your portal. Most people approach your company first through your website so you need a portal specifically for potential OI partners. Here you will explain your approach, define the current challenges, explain how partners can submit, give a list of examples, benefits, contacts etc.

7 Think win/win. This is potentially the biggest barrier that has to be overcome for success with OI. Some of your people may see suppliers as adversaries to be ground down. Others might be hostile to the idea of sharing intellectual property (IP). You have to change the culture to one where people think in terms of a win/win outcome. Suspicion has to be replaced with trust and that involves an element of risk.

8 Put the right people on the case. Do not put a junior R&D executive in charge of your OI initiatives. It should be someone reporting to the CEO. He or she must have the clout to change things and overcome the many internal barriers that will be put up.

9 Get a good legal agreement. You are going to share IP, risks and rewards with an outside individual or company. You need an agreement which is fair to both parties. Your legal department is used to making your interests paramount, but here you have to be fair and flexible. See if you can get hold of sample agreements from other companies.

10 Maintain high-level involvement. Do not initiate OI with a great fanfare and then delegate and forget it. There will be many difficulties and issues along the way so it requires continual monitoring and support. It is risky and fraught with possibilities for error but the potential rewards are huge, so it needs the leader's time and commitment.

OI and crowdsourcing hold out the prospect of transforming and accelerating new product development. These concepts have been proven to work by major players. However, they require a change in the corporate mindset, culture and processes. They require top-level commitment. Fortunately the pioneers have shown us the way. There are many examples to help the newcomer to develop a successful approach.

Paul Sloane is the editor of *A Guide to Open Innovation and Crowdsourcing* and the author of *The Innovative Leader*, both published by Kogan Page. He writes, speaks and leads workshops on lateral thinking and innovation.

Further details: www.destination-innovation.com

Emergent technologies

Ilya Kazi at Mathys & Squire discusses the challenges in bringing emergent technologies to market

By embarking on any new business venture you are likely to be met with a host of different challenges, but when the new business is based on an innovation in an emergent or previously unknown technical field, the issues it is possible to encounter are variable, far-reaching and often unique.

The upside

In many ways, an entrepreneur starting a business based on an emergent technology is in an enviable position. As a pioneer in a new technical field, it is often possible to pursue broad patent protection that can not only provide long-term protection for different aspects and applications of the technology but, as a result, can also present significant barriers to competitors entering the field.

Having broad patent protection provides opportunities and space for the business to grow and diversify once the technical concept has been proven or once the first version of a product is established. It can also enable licensing of intellectual property and other know-how to become an integral part of the business model and generate additional revenue.

There is a significant advantage to a business in being the first to identify or even create a new market. If a company moves quickly, a large market share can be captured before other players start to operate in this area and the company can become the leading name in the new technical field.

With a significant new discovery or a leap forward in technology comes the potential of media interest which can be translated into profile-raising column inches, an invaluable publicity vehicle for a new business venture. One example is in technologies relating to graphene, which generated much publicity and media attention following the award of the Nobel Prize to researchers working in this area at the University of Manchester in 2010. Companies that moved quickly to develop practical applications for and commercialize the technology found a willing audience of both scientific and mass media keen to learn more about their activities.

The challenges

Although there are many advantages to working with emergent technologies, such as a lack of competitors, the downside is that there is no established market or demand, which presents a number of challenges to overcome.

Potential customers, partners and suppliers may first need to be educated as to what the technology is, how it works and improves upon existing technology, and what the benefits are to them. This can be an expensive process which is laden with risk, as there is no precedent for how receptive they will be to change.

New technologies can also sometimes require new ways of doing business, with bespoke contracts and supply agreements needing to be developed to commercialize the technology. In some cases, entrepreneurs with an emergent technology essentially have to build the market before they can start to sell their product.

Inertia can often be another significant barrier to success. Rather than taking a risk with a new technology, many customers prefer tried and tested products that are known to them. The adoption of new products or a new way of working may require staff retraining, investment in new equipment and short-term upheaval, even if it brings significant benefits in the medium or long term.

Getting your intellectual property strategy right can also be difficult in a new technical field. Building a vision of the future direction of the technology and how it might be commercialized in many different ways is essential in obtaining broad, but commercially useful, protection for the technology. In some cases, it can be useful to pursue both broad protection for the general technological developments and more specific protection for products and particular applications of the technology. However, in an emergent field, such as that of graphene or synthetic biology, the array of possible commercial applications for a technology can be overwhelming.

Another issue is that the technology will take time to commercialize and early broad patents may have limited life when the technology becomes mature. With recent changes in US law, it is even more critical to think strategically about what to file and disclose and when.

It is therefore crucial to think laterally at an early stage about how the technology might be used by the business and its competitors, and how and when it might be applied in different industries. While only some of these opportunities will be commercially viable, and it is unlikely that a single business will pursue all applications, having appropriately targeted intellectual property protection in place can keep options open as both the technology and the business develops. Such protection may also provide a source of secondary revenue, for example through licensing.

Reducing the risk

With the opportunities and challenges presented by development of businesses in emergent technologies, it is perhaps surprising and frustrating that so many still fail and that the factors leading to that failure are often the same as those experienced by start-ups in more established markets.

In particular, business leaders need to ensure that funding cycles for the business correspond to its funding requirements. This ensures that there is enough cash in the business to cover spikes in funding requirements that may be caused by, for example, investments in stock or materials, patent costs, investment in marketing or building a prototype.

Another common problem is that businesses fail to deliver what they are contracted to provide, in terms of both the timing and quantities of the product but also, particularly in an emerging technical field, in terms of the market-readiness of the technology itself.

To secure strong intellectual property protection for a new technology, it is essential to find an IP adviser who understands the strategic issues as well as the technology at an early stage in business planning, and well before any disclosure of even the broadest concepts relating to the technology. It is usually not possible to obtain patent protection for inventions that have already been publicly disclosed. A patent attorney can also help to further protect or commercialize the technology, for example by putting into place non-disclosure agreements and developing licensing agreements for the technology.

It is also useful to consider trade mark and branding issues at an early stage of business planning. Expert trade mark searching and advice can prevent a business investing significant resources in branding and marketing under a particular trade mark only to find that there is a conflict with a competitor's existing trade mark.

The key to success

So, what does the entrepreneur in an emergent technical field need to do to get it right? A key factor in success can be to get the right people into the business and know when to step back.

Many inventors start small businesses to commercialize their inventions but, often, the ones who succeed are those who know when to detach themselves from the business and let others take it forward. While inventors have many skills, most are not experienced in the particular challenges associated with running start-up businesses. Similarly, the skills required to grow a new business and to manage an established business are not the same, so a change of personnel is often required.

As well as building a skilled management team, it is important to develop a team of specialized legal and financial advisers that you are comfortable with. In an emergent technical field particularly, it is important to develop a network of contacts in the field. In some cases, this may be an entirely new network in a previously undeveloped field, but bringing these people together, with your business at the centre, can yield great rewards.

The development of businesses in the field of synthetic biology is a good example of this. While technological developments in this field first arose from biological research, the wide application of the technology saw people brought together from fields as diverse as information processing, materials science, food production and healthcare. As a rule, most successful businesses spread their net as widely as possible to establish where their most important contacts lie and can foster relationships accordingly.

The advantages associated with being the first into a new market have already been discussed above, but seizing these advantages is often reliant on a new business moving fast. Time to market can be a critical factor in gaining first-mover advantage and building up significant market share before competitors enter the field.

Finally, don't stop innovating. A balance needs to be struck between commercializing and consolidating version one of a product, and looking ahead to the second version and future developments. The second and subsequent versions of a product may form the basis of the future growth of the company and enable it to stay ahead of its competitors.

In summary, while there are significant challenges specific to starting a business in an emergent field, the opportunities that such ventures present cannot be ignored. With much foresight and careful planning, pioneering businesses can be built, bringing great rewards to the entrepreneurs involved and pushing forward the technological and commercial landscape.

Ilya Kazi is a Partner in the major UK-based IP firm Mathys & Squire which has offices in London, Manchester, Cambridge, Reading and York. Ilya has represented clients in over 2,000 cases before the European Patent Office, has received personal commendations in leading directories such as the Legal 500 and has been named by *Intellectual Asset Management* as one of the world's top IP strategists. He acts for clients ranging from start-ups and UK SMEs to major multinationals, specializing in complex software and IT, clean tech and medical device technology and providing strategic advice on IP to growing businesses.

Tel: +44 207 830 0000; e-mail: ikazi@mathys-squire.com; web: www.mathys-squire.com

PART FIVE
Research models

How to engage with the research base

Massive transformations are happening in how industries at the leading edge, such as digital media and life sciences, are engaging with the research base, says Dr David Doherty at the National Centre for Universities and Business

It is somewhat of a simplification to say that the unique role of universities is to be inventive whereas the purpose of businesses is to create innovative products and services. But this thought does point to something fundamentally important to a market-based innovation system. University researchers are mainly driven by an attempt to discover fresh insights about the world around them, and are mostly rewarded for the quality of publications based on those insights. Companies, by contrast, are and should be driven by innovations that increase their revenues and profitability.

The state chiefly invests in the former for the public good, and the private sector largely in the latter for shareholder benefit. Therefore, a major issue is how best to understand and manage the connections between the two to get the best out of public–private collaboration and maximize this investment.

The quality of intellectual inventiveness in the UK is self-evident. Four of the world's top 10 universities are within 50 miles of one another in south-east England, 31 UK universities are in the top 200, and the UK is second only to the United States in academic article citations. Over the past 10 years universities and businesses have been working successfully to improve their relationship. And a new National Centre for Universities and Business (NCUB) has been established as a venture supported by all four UK governments, the TSB, major companies and universities to further facilitate the means of world-class collaboration.[1]

The UK is not alone in pursuing this drive. Indeed, despite increased investment into universities, there is an R&D funding gap between the UK and comparable competitor nations: Great Britain is eighth in the list of countries investing in R&D relative to their gross domestic product. Furthermore, this investment is concentrated in relatively few firms – almost 60 per cent is made by the top 50 companies, and less than 4 per cent comes from small independent firms. Over 40 per cent of business spend in R&D is carried out by subsidiaries of foreign companies, which makes it the most international (and most vulnerable) among the big industrial nations.

To compete in this intense global environment firms must be supported by policy and practice to support their innovation. And this means understanding different sectors and creating the right mix of relationships to ensure high-quality collaboration.

At a generic level, there are five Cs to achieve success:

- company recognition of a business opportunity or problem that can be solved by working with a university;
- co-recognition by the university that this is an interesting research challenge to work on;
- co-formulation and specification of an open innovation project to be developed together and which satisfies the needs of both parties;
- co-creation of the new ideas, processes, technology or solution;
- commercialization by the company.

These five Cs work best for small companies, but they are relevant to divisions within major business as well. But the generic needs also to be specific to sectors. For example, the Creative and Digital and Information Technology (CDIT) and Pharmaceuticals and Biotech are radically different in many ways.

CDIT is emerging like a thousand archipelagos. Its birth has been so rapid, and the growing pains so racked by booms and busts, that universities and governments have struggled to keep up with its innovation needs. It is marked by some large companies investing heavily in chips, servers, and distribution technologies and algorithms, and tens of thousands of small firms and hundreds of thousands of freelancers developing content, software and services. The 'clock-speed' of innovation is often extremely rapid, with quick pay-offs or exits, and intellectual property (IP) is not often at the heart of a firm's differentiation.

Although most such companies are time-pressed, there is a trend towards collaborating with universities. The internet is such a complex phenomenon that CDIT firms need to engage with the long-run thinking in the public knowledge base to develop short-run solutions to business challenges. And the characteristic approach of this sector to fluid open innovation means that firms are thirsty for fresh ideas and thinking.

The NCUB is working with around 5,000 small CDIT companies on two projects in London and Brighton to explore in detail how innovation partnerships would best work in this area. This includes advice on developing IP and investable intellectual assets, the kinds of graduate and post-graduate talent that companies need to innovate, and the business models that will help firms develop from micro and small to mid-sized and beyond. Hard-core technology transfer models of innovation are not the most appropriate way of thinking about how to build productive, collaborative relationships in CDIT.

It would be easy to assume that the innovation system of the pharmaceuticals and biotech sector is mapped and clear and that the relations are strategic, long term and understood. In fact, we are in the middle of a massive transformation in this industry. The fully integrated R&D model is out of date and has to be reinvented to turn fledgling ideas into life-changing medicines.

Pharma companies are increasingly embracing open innovation, outsourcing their R&D, acquiring and partnering with young biotech companies, and gathering themselves into basic research clusters with universities to get better access to academics, talent and the ability to tap into small innovative firms. As GSK notes in a recent NCUB report, they want to create 'a powerhouse of problem solving'.[2] And to achieve that, the boundaries between academia, the NHS, research institutes and their supply and value chain have to become more porous.

If the UK bio-pharma clusters are to rival those of the Boston or Bay Area, government policy must recognize and ensure that the right regulatory and infrastructure developments are in place to underpin world-class collaboration between our top companies and universities.

The different approaches to innovation, and the 5 Cs of successful collaboration, are two keys to ensuring that firms in the UK have access to, and can work with, our universities to increase both their profitability and the UK's current and future prosperity.

Notes

1 www.ncub.co.uk

2 Growing Value: Business University Collaboration for the 21st Century, http://ukirc.ac.uk/knowledgeexchange/reports/article/?objid=8094

David Doherty is Chief Executive of the National Centre for Universities and Business (NCUB), and Chairman of the Digital Television Group, the industry body for digital television in the UK. He was the first BBC Director of New Media and Deputy Managing Director of BBC Television. After leaving the BBC he led cable company Telewest's (now Virgin's) drive into broadband content and services as MD Broadband, and has been chief executive of two television and interactive media companies. In the public sector, he was Chair of Governors of the University of Bedfordshire, and a member of various government advisory panels on new media, technology and higher education.

Further details: www.ncub.co.uk

Knowledge Transfer Partnerships

Solve one of your business challenges by bringing in a recent graduate and applying some academic expertise? Dr Alison Reith at the West of Scotland KTP Centre discusses how one flagship national scheme works

The Knowledge Transfer Partnership (KTP) is an effective way for companies to work in a structured way with an academic partner on a designated project which will enable the company to gain new skills, expertise and knowledge and allow them to drive their business strategically forward. The transfer and embedding of this knowledge capability acts as the foundation for the company to build new expertise, innovative processes or develop new methodologies, technologies or products which enable the company to expand their market presence, generate wealth and create new employment opportunities.

A KTP project is driven by the strategic need for a company to develop a new skill or capability through the acquisition of new specialized knowledge. The academic team possessing the required skills will scope out the finer details of the project and the milestone targeted deliverables required to deliver the outcome that the company has identified. The nature and complexity of the project will determine the project length, which can range between 6 and 36 months.

While the KTP is defined and driven by the strategic need of the company, it is a partnership in which all parties will benefit from the interaction. The academic team have the opportunity to apply their specialized area of expertise and research interest in an industrial application. The experience of working with an industrial partner can be far-reaching and extend well beyond the period of the KTP project through developing a relationship between the company and the academic partner. This can lead to further student research projects, consultancy work or further KTP projects addressing other areas where new skills are needed within the company. The outcomes of the KTP project can lead to peer-reviewed publications, which can also enhance the company's credibility when moving into new areas of development or new markets. The KTP project can impact on the academic team's own research interests, bringing a new focus on the needs and challenges of industry. Frequently the project outcomes align with areas of student teaching and can provide an industrial relevance to the course material being taught within undergraduate courses.

The key individual within the partnership is the KTP Associate; a recent graduate recruited to work full time on the KTP project. They are employed by the Knowledge Base Partner but work full time within the company, focused on delivering the planned outcomes of the project. The KTP Associate is given the opportunity to work with and learn from individuals across all areas of the business and receives, in addition to the training and support from the academic team, basic management training in skills required to deliver a successful project. KTP Associates also have a designated development budget of £2,000 p.a. which can be used to develop any skills complementary to enhancing the delivery of the project outcomes. Combined with the opportunity to undertake a higher degree with the academic institution involved in the project, and frequently certification with relevant professional bodies, this makes the KTP Associate highly employable, and around 75 per cent of Associates opt to take up employment with the company at the end of the project.

A KTP project costs in the region of £65,000 p.a, which is determined by a fixed salary budget of £27,000 for a KTP Associate with an honours degree, a travel budget of £2,250 p.a., a consumables budget of £1,500 p.a. and a £2,000 development budget; the remaining cost is made up of the academic salary costs for 0.5 days a week. The academic supervising the project will commit to spending this time at the company for its duration to ensure that the project deliverables are met and that the knowledge is successfully transferred and embedded into the company through targeted milestones. For projects which require specialized skills, it may be appropriate to recruit a KTP Associate who has been trained to masters or doctorate level; in this situation salary budgets of £31,000 (for masters) and £35,000 (for doctorate) can be specifically applied to secure a suitable candidate.

KTP is open to both SMEs and large multinational companies from all industrial sectors, but clear transfer of new knowledge into the company has to be demonstrated in all projects. Large organizations are also required to show how the project will impact on SMEs who are involved in their supply chain.

SMEs are eligible for a grant rate of 67 per cent of the project cost for the first three KTP projects they undertake; the grant rate drops to 50 per cent for their fourth project. Large organizations are eligible for a grant rate of 50 per cent of the project cost for the first project and 30 per cent thereafter for their second, third and fourth projects.

In real terms this means that a company can have the advantages of employing a recent graduate, supported by the academic transferring their knowledge into the company, giving credibility to the results of the project through their professional academic reputation and research and publication track record at a cost that is affordable to the company, bearing in mind that the business case provided by the company for undertaking a KTP project will demonstrate that the project will result in revenue generation and profits that far exceed any financial outlay by the company in this partnership.

Companies may embark on a KTP as a follow-on from an existing relationship or collaboration with an academic partner, or they may identify a challenge and require support from a KTP centre, KTP Adviser or academic institution in identifying an appropriate academic with the skill and expertise required for their project. In Scotland SMEs can make use of the Scottish Funding Council Innovation voucher scheme to work with a University partner, gaining access to a few days of academic time. This can be a particularly useful vehicle for developing relationships between the company and the University and scoping out – via a feasibility study – a potential KTP project.

The long-term value of the KTP is the building of strong relationships between industry and academia, leading to ongoing collaboration and exchange of knowledge, from cutting-edge research into industry and conversely an understanding of the challenges being faced by industry, feeding into academic research and teaching aligning with priority areas for future research, development and collaboration.

Dr Alison Reith is a Business Development Officer at the West of Scotland KTP Centre. The Centre raises awareness of KTP through providing information and support to companies and academics who are interested in Knowledge Transfer Partnerships. The West of Scotland KTP Centre assists with scoping out a KTP project, developing the application to secure funding, and assisting with associate recruitment and project management following the award of the KTP grant.

Telephone: 0141 5483733, e-mail: alison.reith@ktpws.org.uk, web: www.ktpws.org.uk

The Pirbright Institute is a world leading centre of excellence in research and surveillance of virus diseases of farm animals and viruses that spread from animals to humans. The Institute contributes to global health and wellbeing and economic, food and health security by improving understanding and control of virus diseases.

THE
Pirbright
INSTITUTE

Redevelopment:

- Recently received major financial investment of £255 million from the Department for Business, Innovation and Skills via the Biotechnology and Biological Science Research Council.
- Current redevelopment will establish The Pirbright Institute as the world's foremost state-of-the-art institute in its field.

Impact:

- Played a major role in the global eradication of rinderpest which is estimated to have saved the economies of Africa around £1bn per annum.
- Is the World Reference Laboratory for a number of exotic viral diseases including foot-and-mouth and bluetongue.
- Provides expertise to deal with major economic and health threats; played a pivotal role in the control and surveillance of the 2001 foot-and-mouth epidemic and in the eradication of bluetongue virus from the UK in 2007, saving the UK millions of pounds and safeguarding thousands of jobs.
- Develops vaccines to protect against emerging virus disease threats such as African horse sickness and the highly pathogenic avian influenza virus.

- virus diseases
- research
- diagnostics
- innovation

- vaccines
- bioscience
- animal health
- surveillance

- food security
- national capability
- zoonoses

The Pirbright Institute
Ash Road
Pirbright
Woking
GU24 0NF
United Kingdom

Tel: +44 (0)1483 232441

Email: enquiries@pirbright.ac.uk

Website: www.pirbright.ac.uk

The Pirbright Institute receives strategic funding from the Biotechnology and Biological Sciences Research Council (BBSRC).

BBSRC
bioscience for the future

Working with research institutes

Dr Emma Fadlon at The Pirbright Institute discusses how to access national capability resources

Research council institutes undertake fundamental and applied research that addresses the 'big problems' facing today's society. This is delivered through defined programmes that are aligned to national and international societal needs and issues. Funding for these programmes is long term and is supported by both strategic and competitively funded research.

Addressing these big problems requires a commitment to the 'long haul' and high investment has been made in recent years into the associated infrastructure, resources and allied facilities required to achieve this. In many cases this investment has contributed towards the UK's national capability (NC). NC is defined as the capability, including personnel, infrastructure, facilities, biological collections and databases, which is essential for UK national strategic purposes and/or an essential, strategic component of the international research base. The Biotechnology and Biological Sciences Research Council (BBSRC) funds a number of NCs that are hosted and maintained at institutes.

By definition these NCs are externally facing – engaging with their user community both in the UK and overseas. The facilities are accessible to national and international academics, public sector research establishments and to the commercial sector as well as the general public.

Innovation and national capabilities

The organizations housing NCs share an important culture with the private sector as they are both challenge led. Funding for their research is aligned to and encompasses the current market needs and issues and is therefore looking to address the future markets and end-user demands. On a national level, these facilities are there to help government predict, prepare and respond to challenges, but in order to do so a multifaceted and multi-partner approach to innovation has been created. In the public–private sector interface there has been a shift towards a more collaborative, knowledge exchange culture. This approach opens up access to these unique facilities and resources, the scientists' ability to interface and collaborate is enhanced, and innovation is underpinned through various funding schemes that support academic collaborations, joint public–private collaborations and translational research. These collaborative schemes can support early engagement by lowering costs, reducing risk and by giving the private sector improved access to unique know-how, innovative solutions and technology.

Adding value

Using institutes to conduct research may not necessarily be the expensive option as the cost to construct, maintain and source the resources offered by the NCs is in itself inherently expensive. The institutes also add considerable value as they have a wide network of established international collaborators and are often key influencers in the market through links with major stakeholders on directing and advising policy.

The Pirbright Institute (formerly known as The Institute for Animal Health) is a BBSRC-funded institute that undertakes research focused on virus diseases of farm animals. It comprises of a range of NC resources that are key to underpinning the BBSRC strategic objectives relating to food security and safety. In addition to the highly trained personnel, it houses specialized high-containment facilities and international reference laboratories that provide surveillance and diagnostics services for the UK, EU, FAO and OiE. It also maintains a number of nationally unique repositories, including: well-characterized animals, viruses, insects, ticks and cell lines. These resources are central in providing the national and international research community with the necessary resources to develop novel vaccines and next-generation diagnostics and undertake pivotal research and development in preparation for emerging risks. It is a research-rich environment that shares the enterprise- and impact-driven culture of higher education institutes but is more closely aligned to national and international governmental policies and strategy.

Innovation in the animal health landscape

The greatest societal challenges for animal health are in food security, food safety and trans-boundary disease control. These challenges have been driven by globalization, climate change and economics. Increasingly, the interface between human and animals is becoming a major health challenge and the 'One Health' approach to dealing with known and emerging zoonotics is a new challenge-led innovation landscape.

The animal healthcare market is growing but the greatest commercial growth is seen in companion animals. Unlike human health, there is not the same level of funding from the biotechnology sector. It is not well capitalized and few venture capitalists (VCs) are investing in this area. The costs to enter the animal health market are high, as the resources and facilities needed to develop and validate a therapeutic or diagnostic, establish a market and/or displace established technologies are as high as for human health. The costs, effort and margins are significant barriers to entry for both SMEs and pharmaceutical companies with established markets.

When it comes to sourcing new innovations, businesses look at their costs but with that comes an inherent risk: it is too easy to look at the short-term view and miss the opportunity for long-term gain. By engaging early and working with an institute there is an opportunity to leverage funding for early-stage high-risk projects, while building collaborative relationships and benefitting from the wider know-how and influence that individuals and organizations can offer.

In production animal health the smaller organizations tend to be in the diagnostics sector. Here there is a greater opportunity to be commercially viable within a window that is associated with traditional VC capitalization.

Collaborating with institutes

Institutes are an excellent environment in which to do your research, prove principles and develop your intellectual property (IP). At The Pirbright Institute vaccines and diagnostics can be taken from concept to validation and clinical evaluation by utilizing its facilities, resources and collaborator networks. It can be a cost-effective option once the real costs associated with maintaining complex facilities, managing projects and wider collaborator networks are taken into consideration. Like universities, institutes are focused on commercial exploitation, with effective mechanisms to capture, protect and manage the arising IP; but they also operate under the funders mandate to deliver maximum impact.

Contract research and consultancies must be calculated under a full economic cost (FEC) model due to legislative frameworks. However, costs can be reduced through revenue-sharing agreements, where the project is undertaken as a joint risk, with rewards reflecting the costs and risks of the initial project. This is especially attractive where initial costs are an issue. There are also many public sector funding mechanisms and awards where industry contributes a percentage of the costs and the rest is matched by the funding body.

Furthermore, with early engagement comes the opportunity to either license or shape the arising IP and the patent protection strategy. Licensing and assignment of IP can also incorporate elements of the revenue sharing, thus reducing costs at an early stage and encouraging a collaborative approach to the development of the technology which benefits both parties.

Conclusion

Institutes provide intellectual assets coupled with unique facilities and resources. The work undertaken within them is a balance between challenge-led and technology-inspired innovation. They can therefore offer a cost-effective mechanism for sourcing new innovations and increasing the value of existing intellectual assets. They can minimize the financial risk through leveraging external funding or through collaboration agreements, offsetting costs until there are tangible monetized assets.

Examples and outcomes

- The Pirbright Institute played a pivotal role in the eradication of rinderpest, only the second viral disease to be eradicated globally. This was achieved through the development and supply of diagnostics while informing organizations such as the FAO and OiE on best practice for disease control and eradication.

- Internal expertise and engagement with international stakeholders identified the key technical and commercial challenges which needed to be addressed in order to deliver the next generation of foot-and-mouth disease vaccines. This led to a programme of research to engineer a novel vaccine with increased stability and that is safe to manufacture. The science has far-reaching implications as the process could be used to develop vaccines for similar viruses such as polio.

- Through expertise in disease surveillance, the ability to develop novel diagnostics combined with the utilization of our facilities, the Institute was able to influence end users in vaccine uptake and disease monitoring to combat an incursion of bluetongue virus in England in 2007. By collaborating and interfacing with an extensive network of stakeholders, including trade associations and farmers, a rapid response was achieved which led to the quick eradication of the virus, saving the UK millions of pounds and safeguarding thousands of jobs.

- The Institute has developed reverse genetics platforms that are powerful tools for understanding disease and developing novel vaccine candidates. This platform technology is being utilized by a number of commercial and public sector collaborators to develop vaccines for new virus strains.

- The Institute's insectary produces and maintains colonies of arthropods that spread viruses, including midges, mosquitoes and ticks. This unique resource of vector colonies is available as an NC for fundamental research as well as commercial studies into understanding transmission and control of disease, including efficacy of insecticides. This work is supported by the commercial disinfectant testing services.

- Contract research is undertaken to evaluate the safety and efficacy of a wide range of vaccine candidates. The studies are undertaken in-house and are supported by the reference laboratories' diagnostic and mathematical modelling services. These products are licensed and marketed internationally.

- The Institute has development and validation capabilities for diagnostics, including testing in the field with international collaborators.

Emma Fadlon is Head of Business Development and leads on the Knowledge Exchange and Commercialization activities at The Pirbright Institute. The Institute, which receives strategic funding from BBSRC, is a world-leading centre of excellence in research and surveillance of virus diseases of farm animals and viruses that spread from animals to humans.

Tel: 01483 232441; e-mail: emma.fadlon@pirbright.ac.uk; web: www.pirbright.ac.uk

Financial support for research

William Garvey at Leyton reviews the international grants and incentives on offer for research from the blue sky to the close to market

Governments around the world have realized that providing financial incentives for companies performing research & development (R&D) activities can have considerable positive effects on the economy. Despite the global economic downturn, many countries continue to introduce new benefits and enhance existing schemes to ensure that they remain the location of choice for R&D investment.

For a company, the benefits of investing in innovative products, processes and technologies go to the heart of competitive advantages. For a country, there are also demonstrable benefits to encouraging companies to invest in innovation, such as attracting new investment, nurturing entrepreneurship, increasing employment opportunities and, above all, increasing its global competitiveness.

How to obtain the crucial funding for further R&D investment has always been the key. Aside from private funding opportunities, there are numerous measures that governments can take to help local businesses. Such incentives can be sought after at any stage of the innovation process, supporting activities ranging from fundamental, blue-sky research to applied research and experimental development. In many cases, activities that support innovation can also be incentivized.

With extensive experience of helping UK companies secure public funding for innovation, the author highlights some of the key issues related to the claim of grant support and R&D-based tax incentives. General principles illustrated in this chapter should be seen in the light of local environment. Where needed, seeking professional support may help a long way in the process.

Grants

This is the most common form of financial support available to industries. Many countries and the EU administer a variety of grants to promote specific industries key to their economic growth or boost their national status on the world stage. Regardless of the type of grant, it often involves an application process that requires the applicant to put across a clear case as to why such financial support should be given to their future project choice.

The grant-issuing body can be a government agency such as the Technology Strategy Board in the UK or a geographical governing body such as the European Commission. They often have a prescribed process to call for and select applications.

Tips

Given the variety of grants available in each jurisdiction, it is important to carefully identify at the initial stage the most appropriate grant fitting the company's goals, the size of the R&D project and the company's resources. Performing a thorough cost–benefit analysis will not only help gauge the suitability of a grant but also assess the potential success rate and the amount of grant required. Typically, a company needs to consider the total grant budget available, number of competing applicants, maximum funds available per project and the cost percentage covered by the grant. Some of the larger grants may also require technological partnerships to be formed.

When applying for a grant, a company needs not only to present a project to demonstrate how it will meet the issuing authority's requirements but more importantly to make commercial sense for the business. Typical factors to consider include how the claimant may maintain/increase employment through sustainable and substantially increased sales and extend the level of technological expertise in a specific sector.

It is also wise to seek advice/support from the grant-issuing authority. Some of these organizations have their own advisers that can pre-assess the project and provide useful feedback on the application. The grant provider should, however, also be regarded as a private investor seeking potential positive social and economic impacts on the local community.

Tax incentives

In addition to direct funding through grants, countries also provide financial support through fiscal means to attract investments into specific industries. These may include tax holidays, lower tax rates or schemes specifically designed to reward R&D innovation. The types and amounts of such benefits available vary from country to country, but most schemes employ either an expenditure-based or income-based mechanism.

Expenditure-based tax incentive schemes

Such schemes offer tax incentives largely based on volume of actual R&D expenditure or the amount over and above a set baseline spend. Often, they can be claimed retrospectively and have long been available in many countries. Canada started its first scheme just after the Second World War. The UK introduced its own scheme to help small and medium-sized enterprises (SMEs) in 2000, followed by the introduction of a second scheme designed for large corporates and groups two years later.

The actual relief is given through either of two means. One is by increasing the company's tax deductible expenditure, which in turn reduces the company's tax liability. This is often termed a 'super-deduction'. Alternatively, a direct tax credit as a percentage of the qualifying expenditure can be given to offset the company's tax liability. A comparison is hardly meaningful between these two delivery mechanisms in terms of net incentive intensity unless details have been examined to ensure a like-to-like comparison.

Global comparison

The UK R&D tax relief scheme provides examples of both super-deductions and tax credits. For any company, super-deductions based on qualifying R&D expenditure (130 per cent for large companies, 225 per cent for SMEs) can be used to reduce the company's taxable profit. For SMEs, the scheme can potentially represent a 25 per cent return on investment. Furthermore, from 1 April 2013, large companies are eligible to convert 10 per cent of their qualifying R&D expenditure into a taxable credit, regardless of their profit/loss position.

Other established R&D incentives follow a more simplified model. Canada provides tax credits at the rate of 20 per cent of a company's qualifying R&D expenditure (with enhanced rates of 35 per cent available for Canadian-controlled private corporations). Similarly, Ireland provides an incremental tax credit at a flat rate of 25 per cent for all expenditure exceeding a base amount.

Tips

Despite the availability of these schemes in many countries, they are not necessarily well known or well understood. The author's experience suggests that, for example, the UK schemes still contain certain elements of a myth that needs dispelling.

Many companies feel that the schemes are too complicated and require too much resource to develop a successful application, while others may not consider that their innovative activities can qualify for tax relief. While blue-sky research is rightfully rewarded in R&D schemes, the reality is that most companies do most of their innovation with commercialization in mind. It is important to note that even activities that appear to be within the remit of normal commercial development may contain elements of R&D and should be analysed against the qualifying criteria for R&D tax incentives.

On the reverse side, it is also important to note that the existence of a patent or other intellectual property protection for a product or process does not necessarily signal the existence of qualifying R&D; those activities must also be assessed against the relevant local regulations.

Often, a company may choose to shy away from unnecessary dealings with tax authorities in order to avoid conflict. While a system of checks must be in place to discourage fraudulent claims, these schemes have been deployed primarily to reward companies for investing in innovation. As such, companies are encouraged to apply if they feel that their work qualifies under an R&D tax relief scheme.

The benefits of R&D tax relief schemes are not always immediately apparent. For instance, a super-deduction-based scheme may not provide immediate cash benefit for a company that is not tax-paying, but rather will help reduce future taxable profits and tax bills.

Income-based tax incentive schemes

Income-based tax incentives are another form of funding mechanism for innovation, whereby preferential tax treatment is applied to profits derived from sales related to qualifying intellectual property (IP) held by a company. This serves as an effective supplementary support to businesses' R&D investment by encouraging commercialization of innovative ideas.

An example would be the newly introduced Patent Box regime in the UK, where qualifying profits are taxed at a lower rate.

Global comparison

A number of countries around the world have introduced similar tax regimes to induce companies to patent more locally and maintain the relevant IP to help boost local employment. While the aim of the incentive is universally similar in promoting IP creation and ownership in a country, there are some fundamental differences inherent to the design of each local regime that businesses need to be aware of. These are predominantly related to the qualification to the regime and the quantification of the relevant IP profit that is entitled to the preferential tax treatment.

The starting point would often be what IP qualifies. While patents are the main stream of qualifying rights, some countries also allow rights that are similar to patents in nature to be included, such as Supplementary Protection Certificates related to medicinal and plant protection products (UK and France). Some countries will also allow copyrights or trade marks to be included (Luxembourg).

Treatment of acquired IP rights can be different too. The UK allows such rights to be admitted into the Patent Box, as long as continuous development follows the change of IP ownership to the new owner. The Dutch Innovation Box, however, only bestows the preferential tax treatment on indigenous IPs.

The tax benefit can be delivered by either applying a lower than standard tax rate to qualifying profits (France) or a reduction of taxable profits, which in turn lowers a company's tax liability (UK and Belgium).

A majority of the countries offering these incentives are in Europe. China is an Asian country that has been seen recently as proactively promoting IP ownership by offering not only tax holidays but also a reduced tax rate on profits generated by companies in certain industries.

Tips

Patent Box regimes are designed to help local companies to keep innovating, the spillover of which will also benefit a country's competitiveness. As with any tax incentives, it is designed to help the right companies that meet the qualification criteria. For companies receiving significant amounts of patent-related income, it is worthwhile to understand the local rules and to be aware of any potential pitfalls when making such a claim.

Sharing experience among peers who may have made similar claims in the past can potentially be both a benefit and a limitation to a company's own claim potential. Because companies' circumstances differ, detailed examination of all the facts is required before a sensible conclusion can be drawn. This is why tax inspectors and practitioners often ask questions beyond a company's tax affairs.

Most of the countries with a Patent Box regime have introduced it within the past 10 years. The relatively new incentives can often present problems at the initial implementation and produce unwanted results for certain industries or companies. However, it is conceivable that such incentives will evolve and their applicability to a company may change over time. Companies with complex tax affairs are advised to seek professional advice in order to stay abreast of the incentive's development.

Conclusion

Regardless of which kind of financial support a company seeks to secure, there are some common principles that need to be applied to increase the chance of success:

- Understand the application conditions and the resource input needed weighted against the potential benefits and a logical presentation of the case with supporting evidence where needed.

- Understand the issuing authority's mindset and approval process. For example, tax authorities are tasked to provide R&D-related tax incentives. They may have a more sympathetic mentality and adopt a more open-to-discussion approach when reviewing claims. They can, therefore, be a good source of support to companies when making a claim. In the UK, for example, specialist R&D units are set up not only to process claims but also to guide companies making claims.

- Enlist external support where needed. Specialist tax or funding advisers can provide professional support to ensure that a company qualifies for innovation funding, has sufficient supporting documentation to meet a country's specific requirements, and submits a thorough application to secure the incentives. They can also help companies lay the framework for better tracking of innovation activities for the benefit of securing future funding.

William Garvey is Managing Director of Leyton UK and Ireland, a leading international consultancy dedicated to providing tailor-made cost-optimization solutions to its clients. In the UK, Leyton's multidisciplinary scientific, engineering and tax teams specialize in R&D tax relief claims, HMRC R&D enquiry support, R&D grant applications and Patent Box claims.
Tel: 02070 432 300; web: www.leyton.com/uk

Research collaborations

Simon Portman at Marks & Clerk Solicitors navigates through the potential difficulties that intellectual property can cause when research is conducted jointly

In a research collaboration, two or more parties cooperate in carrying out a research project, usually with a view to the technology generated by that project being used commercially. By cooperating with each other in this way, the participants can pool resources and expertise and take advantage of intellectual property and facilities they may not necessarily own themselves.

For example, a company with a drug and a company with a drug delivery device may collaborate in exploring how the drug can be incorporated into the device so that the two can be sold as a single product. Existing intellectual property will be applied to the project and, if either the drug or the device needs adapting in order to ensure compatibility, new intellectual property will come out of the venture. The parties will then need to determine how that intellectual property will be owned and what exploitation rights will apply to it.

Alternatively, one or more industrial partners may commission a university or research body to carry out an agreed project. In return for granting exploitation rights over the results, the university may be given funding, the right to continue to use those results for internal research purposes and publication rights.

This chapter explores the intellectual property and commercial issues thrown up by such collaborations, the problems which can arise and how to avoid them.

Many research collaborations qualify for funding available under UK or European schemes such as the European Seventh Framework Programme (FP7). A non-exhaustive list of such schemes available in the UK and the EU can be found within the box in this chapter.

Most such grants require that the parties enter into a research collaboration agreement containing terms acceptable to the grantor. Even if this is not the case, or if no grant funding is being used, formalizing the collaboration with a written agreement is obviously a good idea. If they have signed such a contract, it should be clear what each party's obligations are and what its rights and remedies are if any of the other parties fails to meet its obligations. There is far less scope for a misunderstanding or a dispute if one can refer to a written document in order to confirm who is required to do what under the project and what happens if any given circumstance arises.

Funding available under UK or European schemes for research collaborations includes:

- EU Framework Programme for Research and Technological Development ('FP7') – **http://cordis.europa.eu/fp7/home_en.html** or **https://www.gov.uk/eu-framework-programme**

- Eurostars Programme – **http://www.eurekanetwork.org/activities/eurostars**

- Technology Strategy Board (the TSB administers many of the competitions, including for example, FP7 and Knowledge Transfer Partnerships) – **http://www.innovateuk.org/deliveringinnovation/collaborativeresearchanddevelopment.ashx**

- Arts & Humanities Research Council – **http://www.ahrc.ac.uk/Funding-Opportunities/Knowledge-exchange-and-partnerships/Pages/Knowledge-exchange-and-partnerships.aspx**

- Biotechnology & Biological Sciences Research Council ('BBSRC') – **http://www.bbsrc.ac.uk/business/collaborative-research/collaborative-research-index.aspx**

- Engineering and Physical Sciences Research Council ('EPSRC') – **http://www.epsrc.ac.uk/funding/guidance/preparing/Pages/multiproposalprojects.aspx**

- Medical Research Council – **http://www.mrc.ac.uk/Fundingopportunities/Grants/MICA/Specification/MRC005438**

- Natural Environment Research Council – **http://www.nerc.ac.uk/funding/available/schemes/2collaborative.asp**

- Royal Society, Innovation and industry schemes – **http://royalsociety.org/grants/schemes/#innovation**

- Science & Technology Facilities Council – **http://www.stfc.ac.uk/1788.aspx**

- Wellcome Trust (several collaborative grants in several research areas) – **http://www.wellcome.ac.uk/Funding/index.htm**

- Knowledge Transfer Partnerships – **http://www.ktponline.org.uk/**

The research collaboration agreement should deal with the following:

- exactly who the contracting parties are, including name, address and legal status;
- the scope of the project and what each party's role will be – if any project phases must be completed by set dates, these should be included;
- a non-disclosure obligation requiring each party to keep confidential any sensitive information disclosed to it by any of the other parties;
- what existing or 'background' intellectual property each party is applying to the project – if a party needs a licence to use another party's background

intellectual property in order to perform its own role under the collaboration, it should be clear that that licence is restricted to use under the project only;

- how intellectual property generated will be owned and used (this is dealt with in more detail in the next section);

- whether any party may use subcontractors – if so, they should also be tied in by confidentiality and restrictions on use of intellectual property in the same way that the main collaborators are;

- what will happen if any party drops out of the project, if a new one is admitted or if the requisite funding is no longer available;

- what will happen if a party sells its business or undergoes a change of control – for example, if a party is acquired by a competitor, it needs to be considered whether it is still desirable to have it as part of the collaboration;

- what contractual breaches merit a party being expelled from the collaboration – these may include failing to perform its role under the project in a timely or competent fashion, disclosing another party's confidential information, becoming insolvent or using another party's intellectual property beyond the scope permitted by the agreement.

Legal advisers need to ensure that the agreement is clearly drafted and legally compliant. It will also have to be consistent with the terms of any grant offer letter and not contravene any applicable competition or anti-trust provisions. For example, collaborations in the European Union must comply with the European Commission's 2010 Block Exemption Regulation covering research and development (R&D) agreements.

Negotiating a research collaboration agreement can be a lengthy process, particularly if it involves numerous parties with differing concerns and agendas who all have to sign off on it.

Ownership and use of foreground intellectual property

The purpose of a research collaboration is to generate intellectual property which can be used in the exploitation of useful and profitable products and processes. Consequently, how this resulting or 'foreground' intellectual property will be used, who will exploit it and how any exploitation revenue will be shared out will be the most crucial issues to agree on. In deciding them, the parties should bear in mind the following:

- Although the most acceptable solution may be for all the collaborators to own the foreground intellectual property jointly, joint ownership of intellectual property can give rise to problems. If the co-owners have equal exploitation rights, they could end up competing with each other. Moreover, they will have to agree on how to share the responsibility of applying for and maintaining patent rights and defending those rights against infringement.

In some jurisdictions a co-owner of intellectual property cannot grant licences to it or take action against infringers without the cooperation of the other co-owner(s).

- An easier solution may be for each party to own the intellectual property it generated under the project or in a defined field. In the example of the drug and drug delivery device companies above, the drug company could own improvements to the drug and the device company could own improvements to the device.

- A company may need access to another party's foreground and background intellectual property in order to exploit its own, meaning that an appropriate royalty would have to be negotiated.

- The parties should carry out freedom-to-operate searches in order to confirm that background intellectual property can be applied to the project envisaged and to any future commercialization. If it can't, the efficacy of the foreground intellectual property could be drastically undermined.

- If the foreground intellectual property has been generated by an academic party and is to be exploited by a commercial one, the academic party may also want the right to publish the project results. In such circumstances the commercial party will want to ensure that no confidential information is included in the publication and that, if necessary, publication is delayed until patent applications have been filed.

What happens with foreground intellectual property need not be agreed right at the beginning of the project but, if it is successful, agreement will definitely have to be reached at a point soon after.

Parties need to be realistic with their expectations of the financial return from the collaboration. Commercialization may be a long way off and, when it comes, the revenue may not be as significant as had been hoped. Even if the technology is successful, if it ends up being just one facet of a bundled product or process, any royalty due may have to be split between a number of licensors and the collaborators' share could be eroded significantly as a result.

Some practical considerations

Any given research collaboration may fail for scientific or technical reasons, the intellectual property generated may be blocked by existing rights or commercialization may ultimately fail due to market considerations.

However, failure can also result from personal or organizational factors. This risk can be limited by bearing in mind the following:

- If setting up the project is fraught with difficulty because another party is obstructive or acts in bad faith, or because there are significant personality clashes, matters are unlikely to improve once the project is under way. In such circumstances serious thought should be given to whether or not to enter into the collaboration.

- To achieve what it wants from the collaboration more easily, each party should secure a champion in each of the other parties, but there need to be contingency plans in place should any such champion leave.

- In negotiating the research collaboration agreement, each party should think of all the possible eventualities and accommodate them. Even then, something may happen that no one will have thought of, in which case whether the problem can be surmounted or not will depend significantly on the quality of the relationship between the collaborators.

- It is advisable to set up a project steering committee to oversee conduct of the project, allocate funding, identify intellectual property generated and regularly report back to the parties. As well as making project management more efficient, this makes it easier to identify and address any problems early on, rather than leaving them to fester until they develop into insurmountable obstacles or full-blown disputes.

Conclusion

The above summary gives general pointers and is not specific to any particular technology, grant funding scheme or commercial arena. However, it illustrates that anyone considering a research collaboration is well advised to conduct extensive due diligence in these areas and in connection with their prospective collaborators.

Simon Portman is a commercial lawyer at Marks & Clerk Solicitors LLP, one of the UK's largest intellectual property law firms, which has a unique association with patent and trade mark attorney firm Marks & Clerk LLP and IP consultancy firm Marks & Clerk Consulting LLP. Simon's main specialism is commercial contract law. He advises on a wide range of contracts, including licences, R&D collaborations, manufacturing agreements and procurement documentation.

Tel: 01223 345539; e-mail: sportman@marks-clerk.com;
web: www.marks-clerk.com

Innovation and research – the role of the research councils

In a system as complex and non-linear as the UK's system for innovation, the research councils can link up many of the components

Research Councils UK (RCUK), and the individual research councils, have a vital role within the UK innovation system. We invest in knowledge creation in universities and research institutes; support knowledge translation to business, policy and wider society; and enable knowledge generation, innovation and impact through our policies and delivery mechanisms. Through investment in research careers and postgraduate training we ensure that the UK has world-class skills for both business and academia. In particular, all research councils seek to ensure that the outputs and outcomes of their funded research have significant short- and/or long-term benefits for the economy and society.

The seven UK research councils are:

- Arts & Humanities Research Council (AHRC)
- Biotechnology & Biological Sciences Research Council (BBSRC)
- Economic & Social Research Council (ESRC)
- Engineering & Physical Sciences Research Council (EPSRC)
- Medical Research Council (MRC)
- Natural Environment Research Council (NERC)
- Science & Technology Facilities Council (STFC).

RCUK recognizes that impact – the measurable positive difference achieved from the outputs and outcomes of research – takes many forms, and therefore is achieved through many different routes. These can involve a wide range of partners, including: businesses; investors, including those overseas; government at all levels; charitable and voluntary organizations; and the public itself. Alongside the opportunities afforded by these partners in their own right, the research councils support a variety of approaches to enabling research outputs and outcomes to achieve impact, including through the skilled people we support. These partnerships and initiatives seek to ensure that the research councils make a wide and valuable contribution to the UK innovation ecosystem.

In particular, we work with business in order to support their engagement with researchers, thereby enhancing their innovation potential. For example, researchers funded by the Arts and Humanities Research Council (AHRC) at the University of the West of England worked with Denby Potteries to develop new methods of creating ceramics using 3D printing technology. 'Printing' ceramics in this way means that highly intricate ceramics can be created much more easily than by traditional methods, opening up commercial potential through quicker manufacturing processes and new design options. Research councils also develop strategic relationships with companies and industry sectors, enabling us to build aligned and complementary R&D programmes and enabling a dialogue that influences all parties, to the benefit of business, the research councils and the UK.

Knowledge, its creation, sharing and translation into application, is a central component of innovation. Individuals and organizations learn new things from existing knowledge, and apply this to achieve innovation and business transformation, be it through new products and services or improved processes and practices.

Research councils, through collaboration and cooperation with our various partners, invest in the creation, translation and application of both the generic knowledge base, relevant across many businesses and industrial sectors, and industry-level knowledge bases that have a focus on knowledge shared by all businesses within an industry or sector.

The UK innovation system is complex and non-linear, and includes a variety of actors and capabilities that have benefited from long-term investment from the public sector. The research councils provide, directly or indirectly, a variety of significant and important components of the system.

Within the RCUK contribution to the UK innovation system, the research and innovation campuses represent both a particular achievement and an opportunity for delivering impact. These are substantial campuses based around major, internationally leading and long-term investments in research capability, developed and sponsored by a research council, such as the STFC Harwell facilities, or the BBSRC-supported Babraham Institute, with significant business and commercial activity on site, in part attracted by the research capabilities at the campus.

Research council commitment in these campuses includes investment to support impact from research, through ensuring that there is:

- excellent access for users to research-led facilities and capabilities;
- appropriate and sufficient infrastructure to support business presence and use of research and other facilities;

- very early stage company incubation;
- amenity provision (catering, business interaction space, landscaping and social facilities etc) that enhance the attractiveness of the location to users.

For example, Norwich Research Park (NRP) is a major UK asset. It has internationally recognized research expertise and facilities which focus on the biosciences to realize opportunities to grow the bio-economy while addressing global challenges such as sustainable food, healthy ageing and renewable energy. The commitment of NRP partners (BBSRC, UEA, Norfolk and Norwich Hospital, John Innes Foundation, John Innes Centre, Institute of Food Research, The Genome Analysis Centre and the Sainsbury Laboratory) is to jointly develop the whole of the current Norwich Campus as a UK Research and Innovation Campus. The plan is to generate 2,800 new, high-value-added jobs on the NRP by 2026 and that these, in turn, will generate a further 2,000 jobs in the wider community.

Through these and other investment in the research and innovation campuses, RCUK seeks to ensure that there is immediate and long-term impact from research. In particular this is achieved through, for example:

- advances in specialist facilities design and the creation of jobs in construction;
- creation and support of high-value jobs;
- spill-over effects in job creation and economic activity.

Research and innovation campuses are just one of the many routes through which RCUK delivers impact and innovation from research for the UK.

In the complex innovation system of the UK, research councils have a vital role individually, together and working with a wide variety of other partners. Building partnerships, investing in the creation, application and sharing of knowledge, and support of significant innovation infrastructure are among the major contribution that the research councils can make. This is made both as individual and distinctive organizations, but also as the collective RCUK.

For more information about Research Councils UK, visit www.rcuk.ac.uk

PART SIX
Innovative capability

Six steps to successful innovation

Professor Richard Brook and Dr Jane Gate at AIRTO discuss the pre-conditions for making an innovation happen

The process of successful innovation is complex and in real life does not always follow a simple linear pathway. Critical pre-conditions for success include: ensuring that there is a market or client for the innovation, developing a financially viable business case or business model to support its uptake, being able to successfully convince others to buy in to the vision, being able to secure appropriate financing arrangements, and putting in place a strong implementation team. However, when it comes to harnessing a technology to successfully drive innovation, it is sometimes useful to approach the process systematically to ensure that the following basic requirements are also addressed.

FIGURE 6.1.1   Steps to harnessing technology to drive successful innovation

1. Networking:
   Do I know the right experts?

2. Identifying technologies:
   Have I found the right technologies?

3. Protecting Intellectual Property:
   Do I have the right to use the technology?

4. Proving the technology works:
   Do I have the evidence to prove the product/process concept?

5. Demonstrating compliance:
   Have I met regulatory requirements?

6. Supporting the technology:
   Do I have the right post-marketing support?

Step 1: Networking

The key to finding helpers is to network (relentlessly) and to talk to a lot of people in the process, both informally and through formally organized events and networks, like the Knowledge Transfer Networks[1] for example. Much has been written in recent years about the value of adopting an 'Open Innovation' approach – for entrepreneurs and start-ups it is vital.[2] It is important therefore to explore these networks and the plentiful sources of online assistance that are available.

Networking can also be vital to stimulate innovation. It is often said that innovation is a contact sport. Sharing ideas with others from a variety of different backgrounds can encourage lateral thinking and lead to the elusive 'Eureka moment'. Another way of stimulating the flow of ideas is to read extensively in relevant literature and journals, keeping an open mind and looking at how others do it in other sectors.

Step 2: Searching for technologies

So where do you look for new technologies and how do you handle them? Universities are potentially good sources of technology, generally for those technologies that have not yet reached the stage of commercial application in the marketplace. There are over 134 universities in the UK but only a subset are research active/intensive, and only a fraction of those will have the specific expertise relating to the particular technology that may be of interest.

Research and technology organizations (RTOs) are another good source of technology, expertise, advice and help. They come in various forms, from the public sector research establishments (PSREs) to research associations (RAs) and private companies. A listing detailing 50 of them may be found on the website of the Association for Independent Research and Technology Organizations (AIRTO).

Efforts are being made to construct portals to facilitate access to databases of expertise that will enable technological know-how to be identified more easily and quickly. Useful starting points include the RCUK's Knowledge Transfer Portal,[3] AIRTO's portal[4] and the Easy Access IP portal.[5]

Finally, there are business support schemes from government (the Growth Accelerator being the main one-stop shop for growth-orientated businesses in England; the devolved administrations have equivalent schemes). There are also routes to help, advice and support available through the Technology Strategy Board (TSB), the Intellectual Property Office and other public sector bodies.

Investing time in rigorous groundwork at the outset will pay dividends later, as there is really no substitute for thoroughly researching what's out there, to find the best and most appropriate technology and the expertise that goes with it.

Having identified an appropriate technology for the intended purpose, there will be many aspects of its use that will require attention. Many of these aspects relate to the practicalities of deployment. Who better to ask than experienced practitioners? Some of the more important considerations and pointers to sources of assistance can be found in the following paragraphs.

Step 3: Protecting the intellectual property

Securing and protecting legal rights to access or use a technology or concept is essential to establish a firm basis for building a business stream driven by technological innovation. This is a specialist and complex area requiring professional guidance. The importance of securing clear rights to access the intellectual property should not be underestimated, either via demonstrable freedom to operate or via ownership of the intellectual property as appropriate. Attention should be given to the resource required to ensure that this is done properly and also to the disclosure of inventive steps prior to obtaining patent protection.

Negotiation of licences for third-party use of intellectual property rights is another specialist area of expertise. This requires legal expertise and knowledge of contracts but also in-depth familiarity with the technical and financial drivers conditioning the business of the intended licensee.

Step 4: Proving that the technology works

There is a world of difference between seeing technology working in a research laboratory and proving to everyone's satisfaction that it will work reliably in the 'real world' of an everyday application. There is now a commonly used system for assessing the state of maturity of technologies, using a set of well-defined technology readiness levels[6] moving from early-stage research and concept development to readiness for commercial or operational deployment. Figure 6.1.2 details the spectrum of the nine readiness levels. The system was originated by NASA and is now used by the research councils, the TSB and many others in the field.

In simple terms:

- University research and research council funded research generally encompasses TRLs 1 to 3.
- Development as undertaken by RTOs and similar bodies, together with TSB support, generally spans TRLs 4 to 6.
- Industrial commercialization covers TRLs 7 to 9.

The extent of proving trials for a technology will depend on the intended application. What will ultimately be required is a demonstration of a working product/process and test results showing that it 'does what it says on the tin'.

Assistance with establishing the necessary evidence can be obtained from a variety of sources, including many members of AIRTO, and from contract research organizations (CROs). Typically such assistance will come from independent test houses and in some cases from universities. The option of testing with an end user shouldn't be overlooked if a friendly and cooperative partner can be found. In many ways this is the best way of assessing the fitness of the offering for real-world application. Financial support for such projects may be available from the schemes that are offered by the TSB.

Testing across a realistic spectrum of working conditions can be a lengthy and complex process and specialist RTOs and testing providers will frequently be able

FIGURE 6.1.2   Technology readiness levels: a white paper

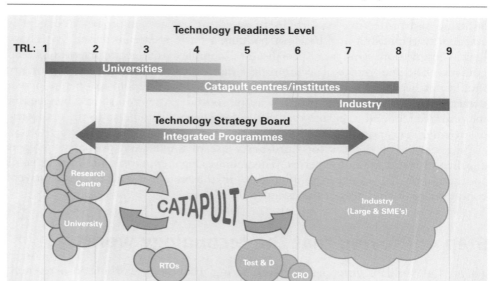

TRLs: **1** Basic principles observed and reported; **2** Technology concept and/or application formulated; **3** Analytical and experimental critical function and/or characteristic proof-of-concept; **4** Technology basic validation in a laboratory environment; **5** Technology basic validation in a relevant environment; **6** Technology model or prototype demonstration in a relevant environment; **7** Technology prototype demonstration in an operational environment; **8** Actual Technology completed and qualified through test and demonstration; **9** Actual Technology qualified through successful mission operations.
SOURCE: Mankins, JC (1995) *Technology Readiness Levels: A White Paper*, NASA, Office of Space Access and Technology, Advanced Concepts Office. Reproduced with kind permission from TSB

to anticipate and head off practical problems of application and in-service use that are likely to arise later on. The cost, disruption and reputational damage of in-service failures that could have been prevented by pre-launch testing should not be underestimated.

Step 5: Demonstrating compliance

The next step is to obtain any necessary approvals required before deployment of the product or process can take place. The precise regulatory framework and authority varies from field to field and from territory to territory.

Some applications will require proven compliance with regulations and standards; for example, if electrical equipment is to be installed in potentially flammable atmospheres, compliance with specific Health and Safety standards will be mandatory; and in the medical and healthcare arena, for example, the necessary compliance processes are onerous, time consuming and expensive, particularly where new medicines and devices are concerned, but clearly these are essential for the purposes of proving efficacy, cost-effectiveness and ultimately patient safety.

In some other respects there is an onus on the supplier to ensure that the new technology and the equipment incorporating it do not expose users to any unexpected hazards, alerting users by means of appropriate labelling and warnings, for example, and protecting them by preventing access to exposed hazardous components, areas and features.

In other instances, and particularly when marketing a product/process, it is up to the supplier to determine what is needed and what steps to take to ensure compliance with Health and Safety good practice. Again there are many sources of advice and various bodies that can help, many of which are to be found online. A good starting point for detailed guidance on such requirements is the Health and Safety Executive.[7] Once again, AIRTO members offer many of these services. The BIS Growth Accelerator[8] can also put developers in touch with the requisite expertise.

Step 6: Supporting the technology

The final step from a technology point of view is to ensure that the skills and know-how needed to support the technology once in use are present, to make sure that the technology and its performance are understood and that the inevitable problems can be sorted out quickly. The availability of skills for this is extremely important and is frequently a non-trivial issue. Close connections to universities can help with recruiting the necessary capabilities.

This after-care process is commercially extremely important; it can provide extensive end-user feedback and the data needed for the design of incremental improvements. In certain fields, for example in pharmaceuticals, this data can also guide future marketing and product development strategies.

The management team and resourcing

While this chapter seeks to summarize the key success factors for harnessing technology to drive innovation, the main prerequisites for success are, as always, the people and resources required for development and deployment. Above all else, it is the quality of the team managing the innovation that matters most.

With a good team in place and having followed the steps outlined above, many of the questions and uncertainties associated with adopting new technology will have been successfully addressed. With the technological risks mitigated and under good management and with the right partnering approach, the challenges of financing the development and deployment of an innovative concept are much more likely to be successfully overcome.

Notes

1   http://www.innovationuk.org/informations/special-area/0004-the-knowledge-transfer-networks.html

2   Chesbrough, HW (2003) *Open Innovation: The new imperative for creating and profiting from technology*, Harvard Business School Press, Boston, ISBN 978-1578518371

3   http://www.rcuk.ac.uk/kei/ktportal/Pages/home.aspx

4   http://www.airto.co.uk/our-members.html

5   http://www.ibridgenetwork.org/community/Easyaccessip

6   Mankins, J C (1995) *Technology Readiness Levels: A White Paper*, NASA, Office of Space Access and Technology, Advanced Concepts Office, http://www.hq.nasa.gov/office/codeq/trl/trl.pdf

7   http://www.hse.gov.uk/guidance/industries.htm

8   http://www.growthaccelerator.com/

Professor Richard Brook is President of AIRTO. His expertise as a technology specialist lies in the field of measurement, instrumentation and control systems, with experience extending from research and development in both public and private sectors to proving new technology and products commercially in the field. He is an experienced angel investor and company director. He co-founded early-stage venture capital company E-Synergy, where he still coaches and mentors companies preparing for financing and investment. Current director-ships include NPL Management Ltd (the National Physical Laboratory), The Institute for Sustainability (Trustee, Director and Deputy Chairman) and the Thames Innovation Centre.

Dr Jane Gate joined the National Physical Laboratory (NPL) in 2011, and serves as the Director of Operations for AIRTO. In addition to overseeing AIRTO, Jane has been part of the formulation and delivery team for the National Measurement System International Programme at NPL. Previously Jane held a range of management and leadership roles at King's College London, within the health schools, and within the university's research com-mercialization and research support division, King's Business Ltd, where she was responsible for leading engagement with business.

AIRTO (The Association for Independent Research and Technology Organ-izations) is the foremost membership body for organizations operating in the UK's intermediate research and technology sector. AIRTO's members deliver vital innovation and knowledge transfer services, which include applied and collaborative R&D, frequently in conjunction with universities, consultancy, technology validation and testing, incubation of commercialization opport-unities and early-stage financing. AIRTO members have a combined turnover of over £2bn from clients both at home and outside the UK, and employ over 20,000 scientists, technologists and engineers. AIRTO members include commercial companies, research and technology organizations, research asso-ciations and selected research and technology exploitation offices from univer-sities, operating at the interface between academia and industry. Most of AIRTO's members operate in the important space between pure research and the pull of the market for commoditization of knowledge into new products and services.

For further information please contact Dr Jane Gate, Director of Operations, AIRTO: tel: +44(0)20 8943 6354; e-mail: jane.gate@airto.co.uk; web: www.airto.co.uk

Innovation that works

What does it take to make innovation work in a business? Mike Faers at Food

Innovation Solutions has 10 tips for success

As a business leader, do not underestimate the emotional intelligence, influence and persistence required to make innovation successful within the organization. A steady flow of creative ideas is essential for long-term growth and innovation should be the lifeblood of any business. To minimize wastage and maximize returns, here are 10 techniques for 'lean' innovation.

1. Where to start – leadership and ambition

Most business leaders I talk to recognize the need for innovation within their businesses. However, they don't know how to get there or how to align the language of the R&D team with that of the boardroom. 'Innovation is a commercial function of which R&D is one element.'

The organizations that succeed in my experience have two things in common: a strong leadership and a clearly articulated ambitious vision which can be achieved through an innovative culture, and innovation-driven company KPIs and a place at the boardroom table.

2. The innovation audit

All businesses have some sort of innovation capability. Using the following metrics enables businesses to audit their competence versus their customer expectations and their competitors:

- innovation strategy;
- creativity and idea management;
- portfolio management;
- NPD implementation success rate;
- people structure performance capability of innovation teams;

- service innovation;
- process innovation;
- technology.

FIGURE 6.2.1 The innovation audit

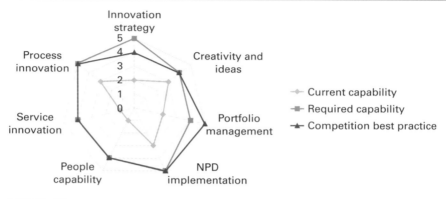

SOURCE: CPI

This gives you a benchmark with which you can measure the year-on-year improvement and is vitally important for cultural and team motivation.

3. A seat at the table – does your structure reflect your ambition?

It may sound obvious, but a lot of businesses do not reflect their ambition with the correct structure to enable success. From my experience and from looking at key innovation studies, we can generalize as to what some of the key criteria might be:

- Give innovation a separate seat at the table.
- Align the senior team behind the structure.
- Make it part of every board meeting agenda.
- Invest in the team through training, mentoring and rewarding success.

4. The burning platform

What is the cost of not innovating?

This is the real question you need to be able to answer. Just like all of us, we put off doing things that we don't really understand or think are seemingly impossible and that we could fail.

A boardroom is no different and needs not only to understand the positive potential, but also the cost of not innovating. I have cited some examples below:

- Nokia to Apple – innovated by making the competition irrelevant;
- Electrolux to Dyson – innovated with patentable invention;
- Robinsons to Innocent – innovated with brand and product, creating new market space.

The above companies have two things in common: they significantly outperform their competition and the market, and they have well-developed innovation management systems and cultures.

So to answer the original question, by not innovating you will eventually be made irrelevant by your competition and your customers.

5. The virtuous circle

The virtuous circle is common sense. However, you need to do all of it well, which is easier said than done!

- Engage your customers continuously and listen carefully.
- Identify the nuggets of insight you can act on now and in the future.
- Can you meet customers' needs better than the rest, or create new ones?
- Develop the products through process innovation and range development.
- Get it right and you will increase frequency, brand trust, relevance and, of course, *profit*.
- Use some of that additional profit to invest in new consumer insight...

6. HOW TO guide for your business?

Process is a fundamental area to get right! Don't underestimate how impactful a good process can be, nor how destructive a dysfunctional one.

If you are implementing innovation into a business, the use of a 'How to' guide can help build belief and behaviour and in turn drive momentum. Whatever your individual innovation process, whether it be a gated NPD, continuous improvement or portfolio management system, it is still important to follow the rules below:

- The voice of the customer must always be at the heart of the process.
- It should be created and integrated cross-functionally.
- It must be flexible to the business's needs and capable of evolving.
- It must be measurable and accountable and included within the key business KPIs.
- It must continually aim to improve the ROI on the innovation budget.
- Staff should be well trained in the process and it should be sponsored within the business.

7. People power

Building capability into the current team/stakeholders with training and development is the quickest way to accelerate change and you can do this by creating: innovation advocates and sponsors; and training and development tools.

Only employees can make lean innovation happen and the tool kit can help them explain how. The quicker you build competence and capability, the quicker you see the results.

8. Balancing the plan

Any plan consists of projects and activities which must be aligned to the business strategy; a common pitfall is that many people think of the innovation plan as blue-sky and that it doesn't have much relevance to the day-to-day business.

It is important that the project portfolio includes short-, medium- and long-term projects, ranked against the key business plan metrics. They need to engage and excite the rest of the business without feeling unachievable... managing the 'tone' is key. This demonstrates to the rest of the business how critical they are and ensures buy-in from all departments.

9. Measure progress and celebrate success

KPIs for innovation can make or break the implementation of any strategy. They need to support the objectives of the broader business plan, including brand trust and quality, and not just be focused on sales.

I would expect to be able to answer the following questions as a minimum:

- What is the total cost of R&D?
- What is the gross and net benefit to the business?
- How many products/services did we launch? What was the success rate at 3/6/12-month windows/intervals?
- Pipeline portfolio NPV (net present value) year-on-year increase.
- Pipeline length – horizon.
- New services – new markets entered and share movement, penetration, frequency and repeat rates.
- Socialize the success of the plan to the stakeholders and reward the success.

10. Challenge – learn – persist

Two great questions to ask of your activity at regular intervals are:

Are we doing the right project?

Are we doing the project right?

Following the LEAN Innovation template will help create a steady stream of big, bold, consumer-relevant innovation that can be rolled out fast, from 'big shifts' to continuous improvement across the portfolio.

Mike Faers is the MD of Food Innovation Solutions, the international food innovation consultancy. FIS works with some of the largest international food retailers and manufacturers, building innovation capability and brands through strategy and delivery: setting direction, realigning the team, mobilizing resources through training and development and managing programmes of innovation and NPD change.

Tel: 01284 705787; e-mail: mike@foodinnovationsolutions.com

Chawton
Innovation Services

Est. July 20[...]

We help clients to appreciate their intellectual capital, assets and property, and to ensure that they then manage these intangibles in an efficient and effective manner.

Chawton Innovation Services has conducted a wide variety of projects;

- IP auditing.
- IP strategy development & implementation.
- IP process development & improvement.
- Benchmarking across a variety of IP topics.
- IP Agent network management.
- Research into NPEs.
- IP outsourcing and off-shoring.
- Helping IP Firms better position their products/services.
- IP data management system selection and development.

- Helping solve IP data management system issues.
- Auditing a company's compliance as part of an M&A deal.
- IP portfolio management.
- IP risk mitigation.
- IP exploitation.
- IP governance.
- Patent product mapping.
- Patent Box exercises.
- IP and IP management education / training.

Chawton Innovation Services Limited.
The Stables, Gosport Road, Chawton, Alton, Hampshire, UK GU34 1SH
T: +44 (0) 7825 081941 E: donal.joseph.oconnell@gmail.com

www.chawtoninnovationservices.co.uk

Inventor reward and recognition

Each business has a potentially broad community of inventors on which to draw. How can you encourage a flow of ideas, asks Donal O'Connell at Chawton Innovation Services

The most important source of patented ideas for any company is the inventor community, and therefore improving the quantity and quality of ideas that are coming from this community should be of the highest priority. Someone needs to invent. Traditionally, inventions come from within research and development (R&D) but the inventor community is much broader than this and, increasingly, it includes people spread throughout the company.

Today, companies cannot survive in isolation. They need to cooperate and collaborate with other companies, universities and external individuals. All these different people must also be recognized as potentially belonging to your inventor community.

The company must know and understand the inventor community, must understand how they see patenting and their views on the subject, as this enables activities to be initiated or amended in order to reach the desired end result of obtaining inventions. If you are aware of factors which work against your patenting goals and targets, there is a need to develop ways of dealing with and controlling these issues.

Benchmark data

Most innovative businesses provide rewards and some form of recognition to inventors and, yes, there are legal requirements in certain jurisdictions to take into consideration. More importantly, however, a good comprehensive reward and recognition programme encourages and motivates innovation and creativity. The elements of such a programme may include such elements as financial awards, but it needs to go beyond this. The recognition element is also important, and serious consideration needs to be given to this part of the programme.

Statutory provisions

More than 80 per cent of inventions are made by employees and it is therefore important that the company knows its own rights with regard to an invention, as well as the rights of its employees. The general rule is that where an employee creates an invention in the course of his or her employment, this invention and any patent will belong to the employer. However, there are statutory provisions in place to ensure that the employee does not go unrewarded. Japan and Germany are two examples of jurisdictions where employee compensation is common, but there are others.

German law

German law regulates matters of employee ownership of inventions and the compensation to which they are entitled by statute. Where inventions are made in the course of the employee's duties, they may be claimed by the employer. The employee must give notice to the employer of the making of an invention and allow it the choice to make either a limited or unlimited claim to the invention. In the case of the latter, the employer is entitled to an assignment but must pay 'reasonable compensation' for this. Similar compensation is due where the employer makes a limited claim, the only difference being that he or she derives his or her rights to the invention from a non-exclusive licence. The German government has published guidelines to be used when calculating compensation. In essence, inventions which produce high turnover will attract high compensation payments.

Japanese law

In Japan, employees are the owners of all inventions they make, including those in the course of their duties. Employment contracts are often used by employers in order to entitle them to ownership over the invention or at the very least an exclusive licence. Where an employee assigns his or her invention or grants an exclusive licence to the employer, Japanese patent law entitles the employee to reasonable remuneration. This is calculated on the basis of the resulting profits made by the employer from the invention and the contribution to the invention made by the employee. Large Japanese companies often have preset scales of remuneration for employee's inventions.

Recent UK court case

The UK Patents Act which came into force in 1978 contained radical provisions on the remuneration of employee inventors who are now, under certain conditions, entitled to a share of the benefits flowing from any outstanding inventions they may make. In 2009, two researchers were awarded £1.5 million under this little-used section of patent law which allows employees extra compensation for inventions which are of 'outstanding benefit' to employers. Companies which hire employees to invent things for them generally retain the patents and other intellectual property for those inventions. By owning those rights the companies in turn control the earnings that result from the inventions. But a clause of the Patents Act allows for extra payments to be made in exceptional circumstances. The High Court made the first public award of such a payment to two scientists from Amersham International, now a subsidiary of GE Healthcare.

From push to pull

Switching from a passive mode to an active mode, or, in other words, actively seeking out new sources of inventions and new patent ideas, also deserves some consideration. How should the company approach this task and how should it be decided whether the efforts needed for this mode of operation will produce adequate results? How frequently should this task be performed? In recent times, there clearly is a trend taking place whereby companies are switching from the passive '*push*' mode, where you wait for inventions to be submitted, to the more active '*pull*' mode, where you seek out inventions in key technology areas and from leading-edge research and technology and product programmes, but at the same time remain ready and willing to handle 'out of the box' ideas from left field. There is also a trend taking place whereby intellectual property experts are working together with the general legal community, as well as the sourcing and purchasing experts within companies, in order to ensure that intellectual property terms and conditions are properly incorporated into contracts with suppliers, vendors and university 'partners'. This includes areas such as idea generation and invention harvesting.

Pull mode activities may include such things as conducting invention workshops on specific areas of interest, actively working with lead technology projects to harvest inventions, working closely with the top inventors and establishing invention targets together with business and technology management.

Reward and recognition

Most innovative businesses provide rewards and some form of recognition to inventors. There are two main reasons for having a reward and recognition programme in place for inventors. The first is that there are legal requirements in certain jurisdictions to take into consideration, and secondly and more importantly, a good comprehensive reward and recognition programme encourages and motivates innovation and creativity.

The components of a programme may include such elements as financial awards, plaques, patent festivals or celebrations and recognition of the inventor by senior management. Other small but simple and effective ways to indicate top inventors are top inventor get-togethers and published league tables of the top inventors within the organization. The value of a simple 'thank you' or 'well done' should also not be overlooked.

Reward programmes

You may grant a financial award for a patent committee approved invention disclosure, and define exactly how much you will award per inventor. You may wish to grant an award when a patent application is filed, but also consider granting an award for a design patent application and a utility patent application. You may decide to grant an award when a patent is issued. You may go further and grant a 'milestone' award which recognizes an inventor who has received a specific number of patents, say 10 or more. You may also grant a 'patent-of-the-year'-type award for an invention which has had a significant or financial impact within the company.

At a number of companies, there are lifetime achievement awards which recognize members of the R&D community whose cumulative technical contributions have had a significant impact on their company's financial growth. The recipient receives some financial awards, sometimes in the form of stock options. These award programmes are basically where good patents are identified and recognized, based on the significance of the invention, and the award is sometimes defined based on the turnover of those products where the invention is implemented.

A few companies grant awards for defensive publications, innovations that are not patented but, instead, are published to ensure the right of the company to use the technical development. A few grant an award for a substantial innovation that is not patented but, instead, is maintained as a trade secret or a confidential process. Some grant awards for the filing and/or issuance of any other type of intellectual property, such as copyrights, service marks and trade marks.

Recognition programmes

Your inventor reward and recognition programme should ideally include other forms of employee recognition and not just financial payments. These recognition programmes may include such things as pins, plaques, luncheons and annual award dinners. A number of companies hold annual inventor award dinners at each of their major R&D locations. One company at least provides special coloured employee security badges for recipients of their top inventor milestone awards. Many companies operate inventor newsletters and patent award wall plaques.

The scope of the reward and recognition programme

One key issue to consider for any multinational company in particular is whether your inventor reward and recognition programme will be global in scope, and implemented consistently across the organization. Alternatively, you may decide that the award amounts will be adjusted by country based on geographical pay differences, or perhaps only implemented in those countries where there is specific inventor award legislation. At first glance it may seem more cost-effective to operate the award programme only in those countries with such legal requirements, but this can increase award administration workload and also cause friction within the inventor community, especially if R&D projects are spread across multiple sites.

Recommended actions

TABLE 6.3.1

Ownership	Assign responsibility so that ownership of any inventor reward and recognition programme is clear within the company
Legislation	Be aware of inventor legislation, and monitor developments so that the company knows what is legally required
Benchmark	Gather benchmark data from time to time, so that the company understands what is considered 'best in class' practice
From 'push' to 'pull'	Move from push to pull mode, so that the ideas generated align with the business needs
Financial and non-financial elements	Consider both financial and non-financial aspects to the inventor reward and recognition programme
Be consistent	Be consistent when deploying any inventor reward and recognition programme
'Thank you'	Don't underestimate the value of a simple 'thank you and well done'

Some final thoughts

Some will argue that financial reward programmes should not be considered at all, as it is the role of R&D engineers to invent. However, benchmark data suggest that a number of companies are rewarding their inventors well. Financial awards as well as annual patent ceremonies and such items as plaques for inventors are good well-established practices in many companies. Increasingly, company-wide recognition of the top inventors, for example based on exceeding some threshold for the number of granted patents, is becoming the norm.

The correct emphasis should be on changing the culture of how businesses view employee inventors away from 'we pay them to invent, that's their job and they are lucky to have job security', while the board often award themselves huge performance-related bonuses. Instead, the business needs to convey that it truly values and appreciates innovation because it is that which drives the company's success and the inventor should rightly share in that. In my view there should be big bonuses for inventors whose ideas generate considerable financial success for the company, so long as there is fair estimation of the value of the invention and its contribution to the business.

Donal O'Connell is the Managing Director of Chawton Innovation Services, which offers consultancy in the areas of innovation and intellectual property management. Put simply, he helps clients to appreciate their intellectual capital, assets and property, then ensures that they manage these intangibles in an efficient and effective manner.

In the past few years, the client base has included some leading universities, some global IP service providers, some major IP firms, a global telecoms company, a global agrochemical company, a maritime technology company, a compliance firm, some global chemical companies, a global food and beverages company, a global heavy engineering company, a major cloud computing company, a regional consumer electronics company, one of the big four financial services companies plus a variety of SMEs.

Donal was formerly a VP of R&D and a Director of IP at Nokia. His first book *Inside the Patent Factory* was published by John Wiley & Sons in 2008 and his second, *Harvesting External Innovation*, by Gower in mid-2011. He is currently researching a third book on the subject of 'buying and selling patents'. He is also an adjunct professor at Imperial College, London, teaching some electives there on 'IP management' and 'open innovation and the role of IP'.

PART SEVEN
Collaborations and partnerships

Eminate Ltd

Realising a world of **innovation** opportunities

Sourcing ideas
We identify and license ideas for new products or services, in the food and engineering sectors, from individuals, universities and companies.

Scoping commercial potential
We reduce risk by developing our products and services in partnership with representative customers.

Realising value
Our IP development process has already turned a novel idea for a salt reduction ingredient into a commercial product that has been licensed to a FTSE100 company.

If you have a great idea, or would like to trial or access market-ready products, please get in touch.

Telephone: +44 (0) 115 74 84130 | Email: enquiries@eminate.co.uk

www.eminate.co.uk

GREAT BRITISH INNOVATION

Open innovation, exits and how to work with a corporate

David Park and Sarah Gaunt at Eminate discuss how to build a partnership

with one of the major players

Most innovators gaze enviously at the multinational corporate world of apparently limitless budgets, global reach and scale. Even if the reality is somewhat different, there are a number of good reasons for an innovative organization, of any size, to treat the effective engagement with multinational corporations as a strategic priority. But how can you even break into a vast, corporate monolith, let alone close a licensing deal with one for your IP?

How can I engage with a multinational corporation?

The idea of engaging with a faceless, global corporation can appear a rather daunting prospect at first. However, it *is* perfectly possible for an organization of any size to proactively engage with, and build a beneficial relationship with, a multinational corporate by following a few simple rules:

1 Do your homework. There will be a wealth of information online about almost every corporation you may wish to target. Understand their core markets, products and strategic aims. See if you can find out about any new sectors or markets they are moving into. Explicitly search for terms such as innovation, collaboration and partnership.

2 Have a clear, concise message about yourself and your organization. What do you do? What are you interested in? What can you potentially do for the corporate?

3 If possible, utilize your existing contacts and connections to facilitate an introduction to a relevant person/level in the target corporate. Who do your board members or consultants know? Do you already have a supplier relationship with the company?

4 Seek out the open innovation team within the corporation; they are explicitly tasked with finding external sources of innovation and will almost certainly be one of the most effective and quickest routes into the corporate and, if all goes well, your main champions on the inside as well.

5 If all else fails, ring the main switchboard at the corporate's head office, or the main office in your country or region, and simply ask whom you should contact if you are looking to speak to someone about providing innovative solutions into the company. You can often get to the PA of a key board member or executive this way (with perseverance!)

What is open innovation?

Open innovation is about reducing risk. It is a concept that describes what many organizations actually do already:

- looking elsewhere for new ideas or solutions to a problem;
- outsourcing or sharing the development of new products;
- jointly launching commercial services.

Many large companies and corporations are increasingly formalizing these activities and forming open innovation teams who are explicitly tasked to:

- identify external organizations, including SMEs and universities, which could potentially support some aspect of the corporate's core function;
- source (nearly) off-the-shelf solutions to existing internal problems or issues;
- discover and secure innovative IP that aligns with the current, strategic, aims for growth.

In recent years, a number of the world's largest corporations have launched online open innovation portals as an explicit, internet-based space to list their current and future areas of interest and to provide a clear mechanism for any external organization to make contact with potential ideas or solutions.

The open innovation team at a large company will endeavour to introduce you to the right people across their apparently inaccessible business: technical, management, marketing, production, financial, IP etc. You don't even necessarily need to target corporate open innovation teams one by one. Trade bodies, governments and supranational organizations such as the EU are increasingly arranging sector-specific open innovation forums or pitching events that provide innovators an opportunity to meet and pitch their ideas to open innovation managers from across the global corporate community. These events are also an excellent opportunity to network with smaller, innovative organizations as well.

How can I license my IP to a multinational corporation?

Many people will ask you about your exit strategy for your latest innovation or business venture, and for many individuals and organizations the default, go-to-Plan-A answer is 'to close a licensing deal with a large company'. So how could you actually go about doing this, and what are the risks and benefits of taking this exit route?

Every large company is obsessed with identifying, and reducing or mitigating, risk. One of the key risk areas for any company relates to the sourcing and development of IP. If you have successfully followed the tips and suggestions detailed above, you should have a constructive relationship with the open innovation manager (or equivalent) in one, or more, multinational corporations related to your sector.

If you can then bring a product or idea to your open innovation contacts that has the following characteristics you will almost certainly have the corporations beating a path to your door, actively seeking a licensing deal:

- protected IP with adequate coverage (patent filed, although probably not granted yet);
- applications data (how to use the product in a relevant, commercial context);
- demonstrable means of viably manufacturing at scale (if relevant);
- initial users who are credible in your sector (repeat business from one or two large clients, who can provide the corporate with credible market feedback, usually provides a far more effective 'voice of customer' than hundreds of small, local, one-off, clients).

It is then a matter of negotiating your terms. This will cost a lot in legal fees and will take longer than you think (multinational corporates don't always move quickly and will have a range of internal processes and hurdles to clear before they can close any deal with you). Some top tips/pointers for this negotiation stage:

- Many corporates will seek a global, exclusive licence. Try to avoid carving up your IP (eg by market sector or geography) too early or you may not be able to close a deal with a corporate later on.
- Ensure that you include explicit terms in your licensing deal that allow you to recover your IP if necessary and to re-license it (eg the corporate may wish to license from you solely in order to 'sit' on your IP to protect their own developments).
- The corporate will probably seek assurances or even indemnities from inventors, the company, maybe even your shareholders, across a range of aspects, including your ability to complete further work/developments in the area of interest and the provision of ongoing technical/market support to the corporate for a period of time. Plan for this.

Rather than waiting until you have a finished article to present to a potential corporate partner, it is also possible to negotiate a licensing deal at an earlier stage of IP development if you have the track record, relationships and luck to do so. One example would be to provide a corporate with an option to license your nascent IP in, say, 12 months, in return for an upfront payment and ongoing support to you (technical, market analysis, production scale-up etc). You may not have filed a patent, you may not have made anything at commercial scales, you may not even have sent samples to clients yet, but it *is* still possible to negotiate a deal which dramatically de-risks the IP development for both your organization and the corporate.

It may take time, and it will take effort, but it *is* possible for an organization of any type and size to build a relationship with a number of relevant corporates. The long-term rewards to your organization could be measurable in terms of both your reputation and your bottom line for decades to come.

At Eminate Ltd, we have consciously identified a small group of multinationals we'd like to partner with and are now working closely with each of them, having made the initial approach through their open innovation team. This strategy is already proving successful. As well as getting a great insight into the commercial opportunities and challenges facing the world's leading companies, we are able to trial and test our new ideas with commercially credible partners and have a clear opportunity to rapidly scale our new products. For example, we have recently celebrated the completion of a major licensing deal with a FTSE 100 company, Tate & Lyle, for our SODA-LO® Salt Microspheres technology. Invented, developed and commercialized by the Eminate team, this product has now been globally launched by Tate & Lyle in over 100 countries. It is already winning international awards for innovation and health and is increasingly being used to reduce sodium levels in popular food products around the world. Further products are in the Eminate pipeline and we continue to engage with global corporations to progress these early stage ideas into de-risked, commercially viable products.

Eminate Ltd specializes in sourcing novel ideas for new products in the food and engineering sectors and turning them into commercial reality. The company already works with a number of multinational companies in Europe, North America and the Far East. Eminate recently worked closely with the open innovation team at a FTSE 100 company to structure a major licensing deal for a salt reduction ingredient.

David Park is Managing Director at Eminate and specializes in successfully running start-ups focused on commercializing early-stage ideas. Sarah Gaunt is Eminate's Research & Commercialization Director and leads many of the external engagement and commercialization activities within the company.

Further details: www.eminate.co.uk

Realizing open innovation

Paul Rodgers and Bill Primrose at Ithaka review the opportunities and challenges in opening up the innovation process in the pharmaceutical industry

Adoption of open innovation models by the pharmaceutical industry and the biomedical research community is a response to growing challenges in bringing new therapies into clinical use and securing an adequate return on investment. Open innovation in drug discovery and development is a term encompassing elements otherwise previously incorporated into licensing, collaboration and research grant funding as the industry seeks to assimilate ideas, intellectual property (IP) and innovation from a wider constituency than previously. Sources of innovation can include internal R&D, other companies (both large and small), academics and clinicians, funded from a range of sources, including the public purse, charities and industry.

These new approaches are rich in potential and are producing a steady stream of innovations that offer the promise of revolutionary developments. However, practitioners of open innovation face a number of significant challenges in bringing the resulting products and services to market. These challenges can be overcome but it requires resilience, adaptability and creativity to do so. Ownership of existing and developed IP is a key issue. Questions arise as to who brings what to the consortium, who benefits from newly created IP and who has the rights to exploit it. This chapter gives a background to the questions inherent within open innovation in the pharmaceutical industry, and provides a number of examples of how it is being addressed.

Why the pharmaceutical industry embraces open innovation

The pharmaceutical industry (Pharma) has undergone a sea change in recent years with regard to its willingness to embrace open innovation. Whereas a decade ago the R&D culture was one of maintaining confidentiality come what may, the industry is now exploring a wide range of open innovation models. This has largely been driven by a 10-fold increase in the cost of developing new drugs over the past three decades, with R&D productivity at a historic low over the same period.

Ithaka
LIFESCIENCES

Pharma is good at many things. It has access to finance, plus a reservoir of tools and resources (including large, diverse screening libraries and clinical databases) and technical expertise that are not available to early-stage companies. It has staff with significant knowledge of the whole drug discovery and development process, whose experience is a valuable asset if shared with others. It has the money and global reach to carry out all phases of clinical trials, and to market and sell the resultant drugs. However, it is increasingly lacking in the innovation necessary to discover new drug candidates.

Pharma can be considered now as being similar to large manufacturing companies, funded through sales and equity markets, but requiring that the new clinical candidates to feed its pipeline be sourced from elsewhere. Traditional licensing deals with smaller biotechnology companies remain important, but Pharma is also now interacting directly with academics, other global pharmaceutical companies, charities and publicly funded health initiatives to source innovation, predominantly in the pre-clinical area. New approaches are being used to identify novel targets and optimize processes, and input is required from this larger number of players. These new approaches are rich in potential and are producing a steady stream of innovations that offer the promise of revolutionary developments.

Models for open innovation

For drug discovery and development, we can consider two different models of open innovation dependent on the type of clinical indication being addressed:

1 those indications with a large market where a sufficient product price is achievable for Pharma to want to develop, market and sell their own products ('mainstream indications'); and

2 indications where the market is small, or where reimbursement is low, but where the pressure for new treatments is driven by public health or societal reasons ('neglected indications'). These latter indications include some infectious diseases in the developed world and many diseases that are prevalent in the developing world. It may be that successes in this category will encourage Pharma to become more involved in open innovation activities for mainstream indications in due course.

Table 7.2.1 summarizes some examples of open innovation initiatives for neglected indications and Table 7.2.2 provides examples of open innovation in the field of mainstream indications.

TABLE 7.2.1   Examples of open innovation in neglected indications

Example	Participants	Notes
Tres Cantos Open Lab Foundation: Malaria Drug Discovery (**www.openlabfoundation.org**)	GlaxoSmithKline (GSK), Novartis, St Jude Children's Research Hospital and others	A combined library of more than 20,000 compounds with some anti-malarial activity was made available for researchers to identify starting points for further lead optimization
NewDrugs4BadBugs: antibiotics discovery and development	Innovative Medicines Initiative (IMI), AstraZeneca (AZ), GSK, Janssen, Sanofi and Basilea Pharmaceutica, and others	Project budget of €223.7 million. Data and knowledge sharing to learn from previous antibiotic development efforts, particularly from failures, which are not normally made public
Tuberculosis (TB) Drug Accelerator (**www.astrazeneca.com/ Research/news/ Article/25062012–seven- pharmaceutical-companies- join-academic-research**)	Abbott, AZ, Bayer, Eli Lilly, GSK, Merck, Sanofi, Infectious Disease Research Institute; National Institute of Allergy & Infectious Diseases, Texas A&M University; and Weill Cornell Medical College	$20m funding from the Bill & Melinda Gates Foundation; Pharma will open up selected sections of their compound libraries and share data with each other and the four research institutions; the companies will work together to develop the best prospects, regardless of where the drug originated
WIPO Re:Search (**www.wipo.int/research/en/**)	Collaboration of private and public sector organizations sponsored by the World Intellectual Property Organization (WIPO) in collaboration with BIO Ventures for Global Health	Development of new and better treatments against neglected tropical diseases such as dengue, rabies and Chagas disease, as well as malaria and TB

TABLE 7.2.2   Examples of open innovation in mainstream indications

Example	Participants	Notes
Critical Path Institute (C-Path, www.c-path.org/consortia.cfm)	C-Path partnerships include more than 1,000 scientists from government regulatory agencies (eg FDA), academia, patient advocacy organizations, and 41 major pharmaceutical companies	C-Path improves efficiency of the development of drugs, diagnostics and medical devices by creating new data standards, measurement standards and methods standards
European Lead Factory (www.imi.europa.eu/content/european-lead-factory)	IMI, 30 academic and industry partners, including Bayer, Janssen, Merck-Serono, AZ, Sanofi, UCB and Lundbeck	€196 million initiative combines a 500,000-compound library and a high-throughput screening (HTS) centre against novel targets proposed by academic groups
Compound library sharing (reported in: *Nature Rev. Drug Disc.*, 2012, 11, 239)	AZ and Bayer	Agreed to make their entire compound libraries (4 million molecules) available to one another for HTS runs
Drug repurposing (www.mrc.ac.uk/Newspublications/News/MRC008918)	UK Medical Research Council (MRC) and AZ	£10 million from MRC to provide UK academics with the means to study 22 compounds, de-prioritized by AZ, for new indications
TransCelerate Biopharma (**www.transceleratebiopharmainc.com**)	Abbott, AZ, Boehringer Ingelheim, Bristol-Myers Squibb, Eli Lilly, GSK, Johnson & Johnson, Pfizer, Genentech and Sanofi	A non-profit organization set up for precompetitive research to address long-standing challenges in new drug development
Stevenage Bioscience Catalyst (SBC, **www.stevenagecatalyst.com**)	Cambridge University and GSK	University researchers will be based at SBC, the UK's first open innovation bioscience campus, co-located with GSK's R&D centre to advance drug discovery and development of new medicines

An open innovation consortium may have R&D contributions from a number of different members, broadly described as ACEs (academic centres of excellence), SMEs (looking to apply internal and acquired innovation to support the needs of larger companies, and with a mix of public and private funding sources), and the Pharma industry.

It is important to distinguish between open innovation and open access. Fundamentally, open access is a one-way, giving process whereby data and information are made freely available to all comers in the hope that this will stimulate innovation. For example, GSK announced in December 2012 its intention to release 'patient-level' raw data from clinical trials of approved drugs and failed investigational compounds. This move, which will begin in 2013, could catalyse a growth in the understanding of disease and help avoid repeating mistakes made in failed trials, particularly if other companies follow GSK's lead.

What are the current commercial and technical limitations on realizing the potential of open innovation?

Potential commercial limitations include the following:

1 *Funding.* Finance is required to bring any innovation to market, but in drug discovery and development, the required investment can be daunting – hundreds of millions of dollars, perhaps up to $2 billion for a new drug, can be spent commercializing an innovation. Timescales are also daunting: it can take 12–14 years to bring a new therapeutic to market. Even a full hit-to-lead optimization project can take up to two years and cost $2.5 million. Attrition rates are enormous: only one out of every 10,000 novel compounds originally screened for a beneficial therapeutic effect eventually makes it to market, and as many as 30 projects need to be initiated to bring one to fruition. The long timescales and high levels of risk combine to make securing adequate funding a particularly onerous challenge.

2 *Benefits.* While the overall goal of delivering new treatments and 'making a difference' is common to all the participants involved in an open innovation consortium, the rewards for each are different and they may lead to tensions within the partnership as each participant seeks to realize its desired rewards. The benefits for each member of an open innovation consortium may be:

   – academic institutions – increasingly look for a commercial return on their research, which has been funded through the public purse;

   – academics – funding, scientific interest, publications, career advancement;

   – clinicians – new treatments, funding;

   – governments – societal benefits, control of healthcare budget;

   – non-profit organizations such as medical research foundations and charities – new treatments for specific disease(s);

- SMEs – funding, service provision, opportunities for licensing and trade sale;
- Pharma – new compounds to fill pipeline, sales, licensing opportunities and, in the case of neglected indications, positive publicity for working on diseases of the developing world.

3 *Business model.* As discussed, the risks and timescales make it virtually impossible for a start-up company to take an innovation all the way to market on its own. Typically, the innovator requires to seek a partner with deep pockets to commercialize the product and provide the innovator with an earlier (though smaller) financial return. However, this brings new challenges with regard to issues such as loss of control, poor communication, different expectations and culture clashes that can cause partnerships to fall apart.

4 *Intellectual property.* IP contributions to the consortium may come from a number of sources, including Pharma, SMEs, research foundations and academia. This background IP may need to be made available to the other participants during the course of the project and appropriate licensing will need to be put in place. IP created during the course of the project (foreground IP) may require access to the appropriate background IP in order for it to be exploitable, and this will also need to be addressed in any initial consortium agreement. The right to exploit the outputs of the consortium will also need to be addressed. In general, this will be carried out by an industry player, and Pharma is likely to have the expertise to do this most straightforwardly.

5 *Management.* There are multiple challenges in managing a consortium of partners with different visions, goals and motivation. These challenges can be magnified by cultural differences between industry, academia, charities and healthcare providers, and further exacerbated by cultural and language issues in international partnerships. Highly skilled and experienced project managers are required, but they can be thin on the ground.

Technical issues include the following:

1 *Sharing of data, know-how, materials and equipment.* For a partnership to be successful, proprietary data, know-how and materials will likely need to be exchanged or shared. The owning party will require comfort that there are mechanisms in place to ensure that there is no 'leakage' to organizations outside the consortium. All parties will want clarity on who owns any improvements and derivatives, and equitable arrangements for sharing of resultant benefits.

2 *Fit for purpose.* Procedures need to be implemented for making project management decisions on issues such as whether a jointly developed product or service is fit for purpose.

3 *Clear pathway to regulatory approval.* There are challenges in meeting regulatory standards with products arising from consortia or from open source developments. How are standardization and traceability of data and reporting, records etc achieved across a partnership when some of the partners may have little or no previous relevant experience of regulatory issues?

The limitations and challenges outlined above require new approaches and this is driving the development and implementation of new innovation models.

Conclusions

Drug discovery and development is a sector with a need for collaborative approaches to innovation yet it faces so many perceived barriers – worries around IP, business models, competitive funding schemes and so on. It is clear that successful open innovation requires careful planning in order to align the partners' goals and expectations, and to develop procedures and guidelines to address the barriers mentioned above. However, the ultimate key to success lies in the participants understanding each other in order to succeed together. This requires the development of mutual trust, which can only be fostered through understanding your collaborator(s), which in turn can only be built through engagement with that collaborator(s).

CASE STUDY

Psynova Neurotech Ltd (**www.psynova.com**) was founded in 2005 by Dr Sabine Bahn and Prof Chris Lowe of Cambridge University with support from Paul Rodgers who then served as Chairman of the Board until its acquisition by Myriad Genetics in 2011. The company is developing novel protein biomarkers for neuropsychiatric disorders and is a participant in the IMI NEWMEDS (Novel Methods leading to New Medications in Depression and Schizophrenia) programme. NEWMEDS (**www.newmeds-europe.com**) is an international consortium of scientists which has launched one of the largest research academic-industry collaboration projects to find new methods for the development of drugs for schizophrenia and depression. Participants include Pharma companies, academia and SMEs.

The participating companies pooled their data into a large collaborative dataset that brings together the data of 23,401 anonymized patients from 67 trials on 11 compounds in over 25 countries. This makes it by far the largest single database of clinical trial data ever amassed in psychiatric research. Access to this database, plus access to clinical samples, was of major benefit to Psynova for validating its novel biomarkers. The consortium facilitated development of relationships with Pharma companies, which resulted in a very real and tangible benefit for Psynova in the form of a significant licensing deal with Roche on a schizophrenia biomarker.

Paul Rodgers is the Founder and Managing Director of Ithaka Life Sciences Ltd, the international strategic advisory firm. Ithaka acts for a wide range of emerging and global life science companies, investors, research organizations and government agencies offering technology commercialization services, including business plans, sourcing of funding, due diligence, market, intellectual property and technology assessments, and management support. He also serves on the board of directors for three emerging technology companies: ProteinLogic Ltd, CYP Design Ltd and Paramata Ltd.

Bill Primrose is a Consultant in Drug Discovery and an Associate of Ithaka. He has broad experience with companies working in drug discovery and associated services. He was a founder of PanTherix, which used structure-guided methods in antibacterial research, and of SioKem, a contract chemistry provider. He has been CEO of both IntelliHep (sugar therapeutics) and Theryte (oncology). He is currently CEO of CYP Design, which provides products and services for metabolism and toxicity testing in early-stage drug discovery.

Contact Paul Rodgers at Ithaka: tel: + 44 1223 703146; e-mail: paul.rodgers@ithaka.co.uk. Contact Bill Primrose at CYP Design: tel: +44 1223 247468; e-mail: bill.primrose@cyp-design.com

How to scan, bring in and de-risk ideas

David Park and Sarah Gaunt at Eminate discuss the process of putting in place a process for trawling and identifying potential winners

Ideas underpin everything...

One of the most stressful activities for entrepreneurs and innovators is the constant hunt for the next big idea. Whether you are embarking on an innovative venture for the first time, or can already celebrate an extensive portfolio of previous success, everything derives from the successful identification, capturing and filtering of new ideas: products, apps, methods of business, markets, brands etc.

So is there an easy-to-understand, low-cost, technique that can magically find you an amazing new commercial idea, at no risk, every time? Of course not. However, there are a number of obvious steps you can take to reduce the risk and cost of finding that Next Big Thing.

Sources of innovative ideas?

Many innovators and entrepreneurs base their first venture on something they've been mulling over for a long time and that first idea is probably already a lot more developed as a result. But what if you want to come up with a second idea? What if your role in your organization is to source innovation in an area you know nothing about? It seems obvious, but if you are in the business of identifying new ideas you should probably have a clear strategy for identifying them! In support of this key activity, what are some of the obvious sources of innovative ideas you could target and what sorts of deals might you do to access those ideas?

Your own organization

The first source of innovative ideas should always be your own organization. Whether you are a two-person start-up or a multinational corporation, your staff and consultants are a rich source of innovation. *Everyone* should be encouraged to propose new ideas (from a whole new product or market to a tweak that optimizes a process or reduces risk). How you reward the members of your team who actively support the generation of new ideas is a matter for you, but the key trick is to ensure that everyone feels happy to engage and isn't put off by fear of ridicule if there is a chance that the idea may not work or sounds silly. On top of facilitated meetings that actively seek new ideas and solutions, our company simply has an 'ideas' e-mail address where people submit their ideas (which has the added benefit of keeping a record of who suggested what and when).

Universities

The world's universities are a historically rich source of very early-stage, innovative ideas. However, it is only in the past few decades that governments around the world have taken steps to actively incentivize both universities and external organizations to try to work together more effectively and generate commercial or national benefit from academic ideas. If you are looking for innovation, you could do worse than start to engage with the higher education sector. Almost every university that undertakes research as well as teaching will have a specific team set up to engage with external organizations (although some are more mature than others). The standard model is for universities to try to license what they have 'as is', which may be at a far earlier stage of development than you require. However, it is possible that your regional or national government has funding schemes in place to help you take ideas out of the academic sector into yours.

Micro companies and SMEs

There will be many start-ups and SMEs in your sector which are really keen to engage with a commercialization partner who can take their ideas and help develop them further. However, it can be tricky to find these companies as they don't usually have the time or budget to engage extensively with external entities. An excellent source of active small companies could be your regional development agency (or similar), local chamber of commerce, regional, sector-specific organizations or government/national organizations whose role it is to encourage innovation and IP exploitation (such as the Technology Strategy Board in the UK). Most small and micro companies are cash poor and may not have completed an extensive due diligence on their big idea yet. Any deals you do will almost certainly have to involve an increased level of investment from your side, with a potentially high degree of risk. Apparently haphazard decision making from small business owners is also sometimes a concern, and it is always best to start any potential relationship with a small, 'taster' project to increase your confidence in both the idea and the other organization.

Large multinationals

Although it may seem counterintuitive, given their apparent scale and reach, multinational corporations are a further potential source of new product ideas and opportunities. Almost every big company will be happy to tell you, either openly or under a suitable non-disclosure agreement, about the challenges they face and the areas where they would like to see solutions. These could be strategic, or relate to a specific product, market sector or geographic region. It is always worth finding out what the big players are working towards and feeding that into your ideas planning and filtering. It is also possible that even the largest multinationals might be interested in outsourcing some of their early-stage innovation to your organization (often because their own internal systems are too restrictive and focused). They might pay for the privilege or be willing to enter into a deal where you take some of the risk in return for a greater share of any future rewards. It's worth asking!

How to filter potential ideas

So, after you've trawled your own organization, universities and other companies for innovative ideas, how do you choose which one(s) to take forward? At Eminate Ltd we follow a few simple steps to help reduce risk and cost, and increase our chances of picking winners:

- Put a small 'ideas' (or IP) review team in place that includes senior staff and is suitably empowered to make decisions. Ensure that it is able to call on expertise inside and outside the organization to support its decision making.
- Select ideas that align with the strategic aims and objectives of your organization.
- Design and implement a stage-gate process for developing and filtering your ideas. The early steps should be quick, low-cost checks to see if there is an obvious reason not to proceed further (patent landscape, competing products, your own skills and resources etc). If no obvious issue emerges, you can move the idea to the next stage. If there is an issue that appears insurmountable, either move the idea into a holding area or treat it as obsolete.
- Try to get a number of ideas into your filtering process; most won't make it through.
- Keep a written (electronic) record of all the ideas you filter. Update this regularly. Ensure that you also record your reasons for not proceeding with an idea.
- On occasion, revisit ideas you have previously parked in a holding area; if they are still no good, bin them.

At Eminate the entire IP identification, review, development and exploitation process is also a core element of our ISO9001:2008 accredited Quality Management System. Since implementing the programme we've had two ideas progress through to licence and a third is in the final stages. We are growing an extensive pipeline of ideas from all of the sources detailed above. It has become very clear that initiating and supporting a formal process that enables our organization to repeatedly identify and de-risk new ideas has been one of the best investments we've made to date.

Eminate Ltd specializes in sourcing novel ideas for new products in the food and engineering sectors and turning them into commercial reality. The company already works with a number of multinational companies in Europe, North America and the Far East. Eminate recently worked closely with the Open Innovation team at a FTSE 100 company to structure a major licensing deal for a salt reduction ingredient.

David Park is Managing Director at Eminate and specializes in successfully running start-ups focused on commercializing early-stage ideas. Sarah Gaunt is Eminate's Research & Commercialization Director and leads many of the external engagement and commercialization activities within the company.

Further details: www.eminate.co.uk

PART EIGHT
Ready for market

Bring Big Ideas Home

Home to the **UK's largest** hydrogen plant; **Europe's largest** integrated processing site; **the world's largest** energy from waste facility.

The **engineering** skill behind **Sydney Harbour Bridge; The Shard, Hong Kong's Convention Centre; 1 World Trade Centre,** New York.

The **manufacturing** resource for the **UK's only** subsea array cables for offshore wind farms; **Europe's largest** producer of bio-ethanol; the **world's largest plastics** processing plant.

The **creativity and initiative** behind **industry leading** gaming; **3D Pain Distraction Units, in-vitro diagnostic products; medicines** targeting cancer, heart disease and strokes.

Incubator Units at leading Centres of Excellence including CPI, Digital City, Teesside University and UK Steel Enterprises. Business Rate Relief on an Enterprise Zone supporting the manufacturing, creative and digital sectors.

Business Support for companies looking to invest, expand or relocate. Join us and make it happen.

teesvalleyunlimited.gov.uk // **01642 524 400**

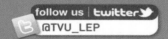

Tees Valley Unlimited is the Local Enterprise Partnership for Darlington, Hartlepool, Middlesbrough, Redcar & Cleveland and Stockton on Tees.

The innovation process

Taking an idea from a basic concept to a working product available in the marketplace is highly rewarding but involves a long and complex process, says Steve Spruce from The Centre for Process Innovation

UK manufacturing industry today faces tough challenges in order to deliver innovative products and services to meet the needs of the technology-savvy consumer. With demand and consumption of goods and services rising, inevitably UK manufacturing innovators are under increasing pressure to drive the industry forward and develop the technology for new and existing products.

However, there are many pitfalls for the innovation industry and the reality is that getting an idea, no matter how great, from the concept to market is fraught with problems, with many businesses failing at the development phase. Therefore, a better understanding of the innovation process can help to overcome the obstacles that you may face and maximize the opportunities for success.

What is innovation?

First, before embarking on a journey to bring your ideas to life, it is important to make the distinction between an invention and innovation. An invention is creating something new that the market has not seen before. An innovation is taking an existing concept or idea and improving it, typically using a step-wise process of developmental stages leading to a commercially viable product.

The innovation challenge and the valley of death

If you are considering taking your idea forward, it is worth taking the time to learn about the challenges that you will inevitably face along the way, as knowledge is most definitely power! We will look at the following challenges and how to tackle them next:

- getting into the correct mindset;
- working with the right people;

- identifying and securing the best financial resources;
- managing your cash flow;
- understanding your marketplace;
- seeing your idea through prototyping;
- setting the cost and value of the products correctly;
- recognizing the opportunities available.

A very well-publicized phenomenon in the innovation industry is known as the 'valley of death', where many new ideas going through the innovation process fail to progress any further and which can take anywhere between 5 to 10 years to work through.

In technology readiness levels (TRL) terms, which are used by NASA and the UK's Technology Strategy Board (TSB) to demonstrate the innovation process, the 'valley of death' or the innovation gap occurs between TRL 4 and 7 (see Figure 8.1.1). It is at this stage that organizations like CPI can support you in assessing the potential feasibility and value of your idea and provide information and advice on the best way forward. It is as important to help businesses make decisions to stop some projects as it is to focus their finances on those projects with the best chance of success.

FIGURE 8.1.1 The innovation chain: converting science into wealth

Technology readiness levels NASA & UK TSB

	ACADEMIA	CPI	INDUSTRY

Knowledge Development	Technology Development	Business Development

TRL 1	TRL 2	TRL 3	TRL 4	TRL 5	TRL 6	TRL 7	TRL 8	TRL 9

Research to prove feasibility   Technology development and prototypes   Market launch and commercialization

Basic technology research   Technology demonstration   Pilot plan and scale up

From innovation to commercialization

cpi ...the future inspired

The valley tends to be at the point where a conceptual idea needs to be turned into a working prototype to demonstrate that it works, to assess production costs and outline the equipment and processes needed for manufacture.

FIGURE 8.1.2   CPI's business model

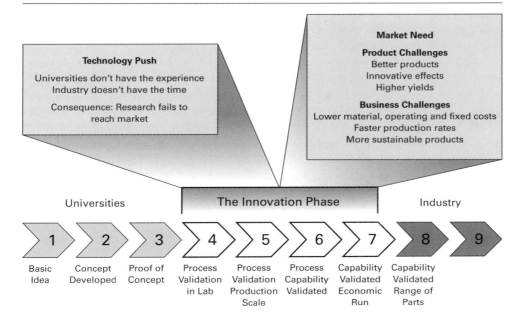

As can be seen in CPI's business model (Figure 8.1.2), which is based on the TRL scale, our approach combines technology push with business pull to drive forward those ideas that universities and businesses are not equipped to develop themselves owing to the high capital costs involved.

Investors will finance ideas to turn them into prototypes but there is a much higher risk involved and therefore a higher percentage of product ownership is usually demanded. A business is in a far stronger investment position to retain value if it has a working prototype with IP protection and production data as the product offer. This is where an independent technology innovation centre such as CPI can help.

CPI and other industry-led Catapult centres offer a wealth of expertise across a wide range of technologies and services, providing equipment to demonstrate the process/product and prove it is feasible before you invest substantial amounts of money in capital equipment and training. This enables you to develop, prove, prototype and scale up your product, which can be demonstrated on paper, in the lab and in the plant before being manufactured at an industrial scale.

The innovation process

Remember – creating new ideas is invention, improving and finding new applications for existing ideas is innovation!

Step 1: Identifying the goals or problems to be solved

The first step in the innovation process is to clarify what your business's innovation goals are and why you want, or need, to engage in this kind of innovation. It is important to involve a good cross-section of the business in developing these goals, utilizing the expertise within the organization and even extending this to the customer and client network to get the market view.

Step 2: Analysis

The second step consists of some real-world discovery of the current situation, customers, their needs, challenges etc. In addition to customers, it is vital to look into what the competition is doing, any trends which will impact on your business, and which innovations companies outside your industry are implementing from which you can learn. You should check inside your own company to determine what assets, resources and core competencies you have within your company that you can apply.

Step 3: Development and design

Based on the information and thoughts gained during analysis, it is advisable to develop an ideas portfolio that includes ways you could innovate to meet these goals and problems. Once you have developed these ideas, an initial evaluation and prioritization will lead to a portfolio of innovations you can test.

Step 4: Conversion

The next requirement is to translate the ideas into practical innovation products that could be targeted towards the identified marketplace. The aim here is not to fully launch the innovative products but to test your ideas within a limited scope to determine whether customers like the innovation, accept it and are willing to pay. This means providing prototypes complete with some basis of costing and a rudimentary process to make or design them, and this is where innovation centres such as CPI become involved.

This is a very important step, as innovations will probably have to be modified and changed in the light of customer or market feedback. Some ideas will work, others won't; it can take some time experimenting to find the best ideas which meet the needs of a commercially viable market. Without a realistic, tangible product offer, this step is very difficult. During this part of the work, the importance of protecting your intellectual property is critical.

Step 5: Commercialization

The final step is where you take tested innovations and develop them to full-scale operations. This will require access to production facilities, routes to market, logistics etc. It is here that collaborative working across the business and in industries outside the business, partnerships and subcontracting management can play an important role.

As you move through this whole process the risk decreases step by step as you build confidence in the products and gain a greater understanding of the technical and commercial issues faced. However, be mindful that the costs increase dramatically as you move from discussion through lab work to prototyping and finally to production.

Innovation requires the careful balancing of risk and reward at all stages and will be influenced by the organization's culture and view on when, and with whom, to share this.

Steve Spruce is Operations Manager for the National Printable Electronics Centre at The Centre for Process Innovation. With a background in chemistry and over 35 years' experience in the process industries in the private and public sectors, Steve has a broad range of expertise in the development, control and implementation of strategic innovation programmes with a track record of successful new product commercialization.

Working in senior positions in the UK and Continental Europe, Steve has developed products for national and global markets. His roles have encompassed training and development, production site operations management, applications development and technical service management.

E-mail: info@uk-cpi.com; tel: 01740 625 700; web: www.uk-cpi.com

Customers before products, before profits

Take your innovation to your customers as soon as possible, says Peter White,

founder of YTKO in Cambridge, and get them to set your price, performance

and profit expectations. And turn invention into innovation

Innovation isn't enough. Without customers, it's just invention: interesting, attractive, newsworthy, but not saleable. Now, this is hardly news – the great business guru Peter Drucker stated that: 'The business enterprise has two – and only two – basic functions: marketing and innovation. Marketing and innovation produce results; all the rest are costs.' He published that in 1953, sixty years ago.

Trouble is, even today, innovators equate marketing with marketing communications – confusing the tactical, such as social media and exhibitions, with the strategic. This confusion means that the innovator's marketing is added post-product, too late to ensure real market fit and a strong value proposition.

Taking the time to do a value proposition, at the earliest possible stage in development, not only shows you what the real worth of your innovation is, but also indicates how – and to whom – the concept should be marketed, and customers' eagerness to buy and implement.

A value proposition attempts to demonstrate quantified benefits to a prospective user: benefits they will receive through the implementation of your offering. You can kick-start the whole, essential, business development process by working with the customer to meet – or better, exceed – their needs and wants. You prove that your offering has value in their situation.

A value proposition isn't simply a sum showing how many times faster, or cheaper, your offering is. It takes into account how much your solution costs to buy, implement and maintain, and then details what the savings, or advantages, are. Value propositions work best when you're selling business-to-business. If you're in the consumer marketplace, you'll need good market research to give you a clear idea of the value your customers will put on intangibles such as status and fashion – even on innovation itself.

Let's be specific: the four steps here should be enough for any company, large or small, to determine whether its newest concept will sell, or sit on the shelf.

Start by describing what the prospect could improve – such as productivity, efficiency, revenues, safety, time to market; what they could reduce – costs, staff turnover; and what they might create – satisfaction, position, new services – by buying from you.

Then project how much this improvement would be worth in terms of cash, or reduced timescales – or provide a percentage/range. You'll need to have done your homework on what the typical costs of people, materials and machinery are. But of course you are talking to the market regularly, and you're not innovating in a vacuum, are you? Now you'll be able to talk to your prospective users about what they'll be able to do differently. Here you can create a scenario of a collaborative, innovative future.

And, at this time, any interested customer may ask you straight out: what will it cost me? Don't tell them. Get them to agree on what the saving really could be, or the extra productivity. Be specific, but keep it experimental and informal. And ask them what proportion of that likely saving they'd be prepared to pay. Sticking to talking value lets you set the agenda, enables you and the customer to jointly agree the value, and makes the customer set the price.

Now, if you can't make it for what they'll pay, this way you'll have saved yourself development headaches, and the pain of trying to sell an unwanted product. It means going back to the drawing board, but now you're well informed and have a clear cost goal.

At the very least, communicating your outline value proposition – and showing how you arrived at the worth of your solution – fashions curiosity in the mind of the client. They will want to know if you have an application for their situation, and they will work with you to help develop the best solution.

Then do it all over again. And again. You can never have too much customer information.

Shouting about innovation still doesn't get you the sales. You must demonstrate the inherent value to the customer that should be integral to your offering. If that value is not obvious, or not specific, or not sufficient to make the customer buy, then you should work together with those customers to find where the value lies. Just because it's innovative doesn't make it saleable.

Like much of marketing – not marketing communications, remember – this stuff is obvious. Yet very few of the many SMEs we see discuss the customer's needs and processes at concept stage. 'We send our business development manager out three times a week to talk to prospective customers', said one founder. 'We're building a terrific database.' Perhaps to those possible purchasers the new product would indeed be suitable, but a 'must-have'? At no time had they talked about value, or about the return on investment the customer would expect in order to justify a purchase.

Companies get overly secretive. 'If we talk to the market now, then our competitors will pick up what we're doing and we'll lose our edge.' Oh yeah? If your competition is so good they can catch up with your R&D in a few weeks, are you really innovating?

Let's agree, then, that every innovative company needs to engage with the customer at the earliest opportunity. A market is not just a single buyer, though. Even within the customer there are different roles, and different value judgements: you must assess and then address.

A buyer determines needs, assesses suppliers, orders and pays for and takes delivery of a product or service. The value proposition to the buyer often focuses on speed of delivery, quality of service, maintenance levels, service level agreements and overall quality delivery.

The user motivation is different. They want to do their job better. These are people who are looking for an outcome. It may be doing a job that they haven't previously been able to do, or simply performing that job better, or removing obstacles in their way. These are the group focused on the performance, and the value proposition for the user needs to reflect these outcomes.

This is marketing. It's creative, strategic and sits neatly alongside your early-stage innovation, and informs those proofs of concept. It ensures that there's no ivory tower of invention, and provides a reality – and profitability – check, so you know you've got a business to back your innovation. And it adds new resources to your innovation team: customers. They're the people who daily struggle with the problems you're looking to solve, and who will tell you exactly the value of what you're working on. They'll do that for free, and then pay you money when you can prove your concept to them. Get engaged. Get marketing.

Peter White is the founder of YTKO, the European economic and enterprise development organization. Peter describes his company's work as 'creating customers for science and technology, and developing companies to meet those needs'.

Peter works closely with scientists and technologists to create sustainable market-driven enterprises. He is a leading practitioner of proof of commercial concept, using innovative processes to develop and accelerate market engagement and revenues at the earliest stages of product and service development.

He sits on several boards as a non-executive, and is an active angel investor. He is also a founder of Outset CIC, a not-for-profit firm that helps under-represented and disadvantaged people start and grow businesses.

Further details: Peter White, YTKO, Brookmount Court, Kings Hedges Road, Cambridge CB4 2QH; web: http://www.ytko.com

PART NINE
Competitive position

The role of information in innovation

Katy Wood at Minesoft reviews the plethora of web-based search tools that can track down technical intelligence

Competitive technical intelligence is a keystone of innovation. Visualizing the landscape in which you are working, identifying gaps in the market and understanding what your competitors are innovating are all crucial components of the innovation process. They will help with long-term strategy and decision making, and ultimately enable a company to drive growth through innovation. Those steps can only be achieved with the collection of relevant information followed by the analysis, evaluation and dissemination of this information throughout the organization – all of which enable it to be converted into useful, actionable intelligence.

Global innovation

A plethora of web-based search tools exist today to locate and manage technical information garnered from sources ranging from patent data to specific scientific journals. While the content may vary, all such web-based search tools share in common the challenges of usability and accessibility. In a global economy, one of the biggest considerations when searching technical information is that of breadth of coverage. Developed markets such as the UK need to ensure that information about new innovation and competitor activity is captured not only from the more established industrial and manufacturing countries, but also from the emerging 'tiger' economies. The volume of patents filed by a country is widely accepted as a key indicator of that country's commitment to innovation, and by this measure the BRIC countries rank increasingly highly on the global innovation scale. Value-added, commercial patent databases such as Minesoft's PatBase will ensure that available patent collections from these countries are included in their products, as well as developing countries such as Thailand and Vietnam. Similarly, competitive intelligence search tools for non-patent literature such as the IET (Institution of Engineering and Technology) Inspec database will collate research published all over the world to offer users a global overview of emerging technologies – from proceedings from a conference in Brazil to a research paper from India.

Global information

Technical information from many different countries, of course, translates to technical information in many different languages. This poses a challenge for the providers and users of technical information resources. The provision of machine translations and the facility to machine-translate text on demand are increasingly important in search tools. In PatBase – the full-text patent database containing over 46 million patent family records – patent documents can be machine-translated as required, while millions of searchable machine translations are provided for patents originating from China or Japan, for example, where no English language text exists. PatBase is developed in partnership with RWS Group – the largest European translation company specializing in patents and technology – whose technical search and translation expertise augments the database. In addition to machine-translation capabilities, we have invested in developing new programming and functionality to cater for searching and reviewing text in both Western characters and non-Latin texts, including Japanese, Chinese, Russian and Thai, in the form of cross-lingual search tools and multilingual interfaces. As our product development is driven not only by major US and European countries but also by a large Japanese user base and growing communities of users in other parts of the world looking to use patent information to gain a competitive advantage, we aim to cater for global users with features such as a Portuguese interface for PatBase Express, the end-user patent search tool. A full Chinese interface is currently in development for PatBase – the Chinese patent office received more patent applications in 2011 than any other country, a clear innovation indicator.

Turning information into intelligence

While patent filings are undoubtedly a barometer of a country's innovative clout and patent information is an essential source of technical information that may not be disclosed elsewhere, it is the analysis and distribution of, and value added to, this information within a company that turns it into actionable intelligence. Many large corporations now invest in customized, internal, web-based competitive technical intelligence solutions in order to keep on top of competitor activity. Such solutions will incorporate not only secondary information sources such as patent data and relevant non-patent literature, including journal articles and business reports, but also primary information specific to the company such as internal classification tags. Minesoft's PatentArchive solution enables companies to generate long-term strategic value in technical information retrieved from patents and other technical literature. Incoming information (generated from regular alerts based on technical search queries of the PatBase database) is enhanced in a structured way by, for example, technical experts, product specialists, and IP and licensing professionals. They can then work collaboratively to establish the commercial value of the information and leverage that knowledge.

Current awareness

Looking beyond patent information, web-based scientific databases such as IET Inspec and IEEE, which index records to global research literature in technology fields, are another key competitive intelligence resource. These information resources (normally subscription based) can be used to uncover historical references as well as discover cutting-edge technologies. We launched Minesoft Inspec in November 2012 to offer an intuitive new online platform for searching the IET Inspec Engineering and Technology database. The IET, based in the UK, is Europe's largest professional body of engineers, with over 150,000 members in 127 countries, and is a source of essential engineering intelligence. The IET Inspec database contains over 13 million indexed records from publications in over 68 countries from both English and non-English sources, with information from 1898 to the present day, and can be used as an effective technological forecasting and competitive intelligence tool. Peer-reviewed engineering and technology literature is abstracted and indexed by experts in the fields. The inclusion of conference proceedings and videos enables users to review information about the very latest innovations that have just been announced (the database is updated on a weekly basis). The benefits of the new platform include integrated visualization and statistical analysis tools that allow users to get a clearer picture of the technology landscape and key players in a certain field. The option to set up current awareness alerts – a feature common to most online databases of technical literature – means that information on a particular technology can be cascaded to all relevant staff, from engineers and scientists to product development managers.

Competitive technical intelligence tools should be an essential in-house resource for every forward-looking, innovating company. A multitude of web-based search tools are available today that offer a single, intuitive platform from which to search aggregated databases of scientific and technical information. Providers add value to the information through translation facilities and analysis tools and by enabling companies to add their internal data and create a workflow to turn information into intelligence that keeps them one step ahead of the competition.

FIGURE 9.1.1   Minesoft Inspec

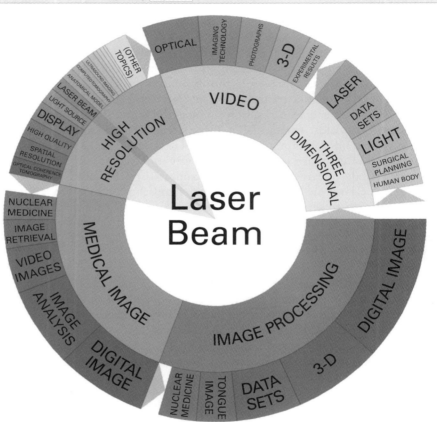

Minesoft is a leading software solutions provider specializing in the legal, scientific and technical information found in patent documents. Building IP intelligence research solutions since 1996, Minesoft's products and services are used by R&D departments in leading corporations, national patent offices and IP law firms around the world.

Combining cutting-edge technology with responsive service, Minesoft has developed a range of products that help research and information professionals to drive innovation forward – from competitive intelligence and patent document delivery services to its prominent searchable patent database, PatBase.

For more information, visit www.minesoft.com or contact info@minesoft.com

THE UK'S FASTEST GROWING SPECIALIST SEARCH COMPANY

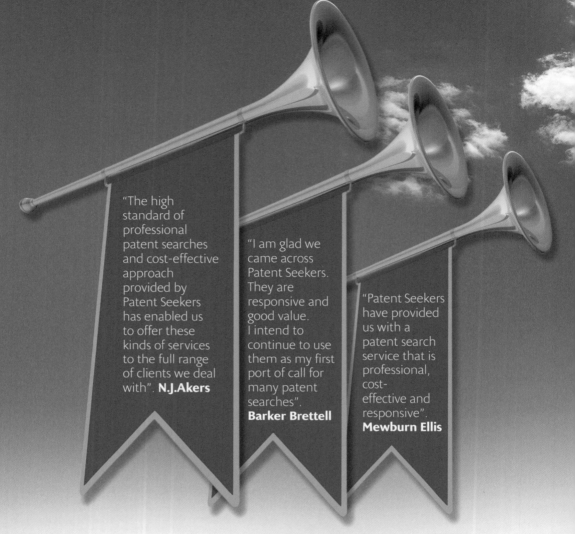

"The high standard of professional patent searches and cost-effective approach provided by Patent Seekers has enabled us to offer these kinds of services to the full range of clients we deal with". **N.J.Akers**

"I am glad we came across Patent Seekers. They are responsive and good value. I intend to continue to use them as my first port of call for many patent searches". **Barker Brettell**

"Patent Seekers have provided us with a patent search service that is professional, cost-effective and responsive". **Mewburn Ellis**

We don't like to blow our own trumpet, so we thought we'd let our clients do it for us.

Patent Seekers is the UK's fastest growing specialist search company. We work on behalf of Patent Attorneys and other organisations and businesses based in Europe and North America. Our staff are all qualified, professionally trained patent analysts (including former UK Patent Office Examiners) providing patent search services for their specific areas of expertise. We work in teams to ensure attention to detail, each follow meticulous processes as well as utilising multiple databases. One of our teams specialises in Pharmaceutical, Biotech and Chemical

searches whilst another provides the same level of expertise for Electrical, Electronic, Software and Mechanical. If you have a requirement for any of our services or want to find out more information about Patent Seekers, please get in touch.

Patent Seekers Ltd., Suite 53 Imperial House, Imperial Park, Celtic Lakes, Newport NP10 8UH.

Tel: +44 (0)1633 816601
Fax:+44 (0)5600 757713
Email: mail@patentseekers.com
www.patentseekers.com

| INVALIDITY | INFRINGEMENT | STATE OF THE ART | NOVELTY | DESIGN |

PATENTSEEKER
The UK's Fastest Growing Patent Search Com[

Patent landscaping

Before you set your research strategy, work out where your market is really heading, says Dean Parry at Patent Seekers

Patenting is arguably a reactive process. Someone has an idea and then takes that idea to an attorney who drafts a patent to protect it.

However, in an increasingly competitive and global marketplace, the role that patents play in a company's strategic planning process is growing. Innovative companies have realized that it is essential they capture the full benefits of their innovation by driving IP considerations into the heart of their future plans rather than treating intellectual property as a legal afterthought.

Instead of leaving the consideration of IP issues until after the plan has been written, the R&D has been completed and the product has been produced and launched, strategic planners and business managers are now identifying and securing the opportunities afforded by their intellectual property much earlier in the innovation cycle. By making this switch they are able to formulate and implement business strategies to handle potential IP problems.

One of the most important tools to emerge in support of this new approach is patent landscaping, which has become pivotal as companies decide where to focus their future. Conducted by patent attorneys or other patent law experts, patent landscaping is a research process that creates an overview of patents pending or in place in a particular area. For example, if you are developing a new drug for fighting prostate cancer, a patent landscape will show you the other drugs in that area under patent or awaiting patent approval.

Unlike traditional marketing reports which blend the author's sector understanding with easy-to-access information from the world wide web, a patent landscape is a deep dive into the 'invisible' web utilizing the more reliable information that can be mined from patent databases.

These databases provide unparalleled insight into a company's 'secrets'. The patent process is unique in forcing the patent owner into disclosing every detail of their product, innovations or technology in return for the patent that will buy them a limited monopoly for that product, innovation or technology. A patent landscaping exercise gathers all of that information and interpolates it, giving you access to a rich vein of unparalleled intelligence on your industry. This insight and intelligence will add enormous value to your business's strategy and help inform the decisions you make on your future activities.

In order to illustrate the power of patent landscaping, we would suggest that patent landscaping offers ten key commercial benefits.

1. You will avoid making potentially expensive mistakes

A patent landscape will indicate how likely you are to get a patent approved. Patent offices will not allow patents that are too similar to each other, so it is vital that you know whether another company is conducting research or planning patents in the same research area. Having a patent landscape will help you understand the likelihood that another company will claim ownership of the same technology before you commit time, resource and investment in pursuing an idea.

However, it is important to recognize that a patent landscape cannot tell you what areas you should conduct research in or if there are any other barriers to research in a particular area, such as where the cost of getting a product to market may be significantly higher than in other areas.

2. You will learn who your competitors are and who your competitors will be

Patent landscapes can be used to visualize patterns of competition on a global scale. As a result, it is a tool being used increasingly by large corporations, as analysis of the vast amounts of data held in patent databases shows users all of the entities filing patents in their area, reinforcing competitor knowledge while also identifying new market entrants. This level of insight gives a business significant competitive advantage and allows you to move quickly in advance of competitor activity rather than reactively.

3. You can determine what each of those competitors is working on

Returning to the idea that all businesses have 'secrets', it is fair to say that it is highly unlikely your competitors will ever be willing to share those secrets. However, all of that information is contained within the world's patent databases. A landscaping exercise will unlock that intelligence and show you clearly what each of your competitors is working on.

4. You can see how rapidly new innovation is taking place in your space

Patents provide an exclusive and valuable source of information on recent developments in highly commercially sensitive areas. Patents can be considered as a direct indicator of not only what is happening but also how quickly it is happening. More importantly, as patent data is made available with – at most – an 18-month delay, it is as close to real-time intelligence as you will realistically get.

This level of overview is essential for the cross-fertilization of R&D efforts at an international level and will help strategic decision making. The information buried within patent databases will create new commercial opportunities for established businesses and help new entrants build up their know-how more quickly.

5. You can identify gaps in your R&D

Patent landscaping is generally performed on behalf of businesses seeking to develop new products in a particular area. The results can make a valuable contribution to developing a business's R&D strategy.

A landscape will highlight the approach your competitors are taking (elements of which could be used to improve your R&D) and identify areas that do not already contain a lot of patents and could therefore be exploited with careful and more focused R&D.

6. You can identify which patents are seminal discoveries and which are incremental improvements

Understanding the speed of development in a certain area will allow you to assess opportunity and viability more accurately. If seminal discoveries are commonplace, the market could be considered to be much more open to exploitation than if incremental improvements on existing ideas are constantly being made.

However, conversely, it could be argued that there is demand for constant incremental change. Meeting that demand that could be more cost-effective (and more realistic) than pursuing something brand new.

7. You can improve your licensing strategy

Once you own a patent covering a particular innovation or piece of technology, anyone who wants to use that idea or technology will have to negotiate a deal with you to use it, a deal which will include them paying you royalties.

According to a 2011 article in the *International Business Times*, you could use patent landscaping to identify where there are opportunities to apply for multiple patents in a particular field. This would allow you to control development of new innovations/technology in those areas and increase the level of royalties your patents realize. Your landscape will also identify those most likely to need a licence to use your patents so that you can approach them and open negotiations.

8. Learn whose innovations could be licensed to your benefit

The development and production of a new idea is an expensive business. The insight that a landscape will deliver will show where the technology you require already exists. From there, you can make a more informed decision as to whether it is more cost-effective to license existing technology or develop your own in order to realize your ideas and take them to market.

9. You can visualize the most densely and sparsely populated patent areas

Understanding where the 'white space' exists in a particular market is essential when you are considering the viability of a new product or market. If it is densely populated, do you risk infringement? Will you be entering a market that is saturated or mature, limiting the likelihood that you will be successful? If it is sparsely populated, is that because there are specific obstacles to progress hidden under the surface? All of this information is crucial if you are to make the right strategic decisions.

10. Help you avoid potentially expensive litigious or defensive action

One key benefit of patent landscaping is that it exposes some of the risks you may face from patent infringement actions, especially useful given the potential size of damage awards. While patent landscaping is historical in its perspective, it offers businesses a wealth of information they can use to inform future strategy and define a successful path forward. Once businesses have a comprehensive awareness of where its competitors are and which way they are heading, their managers will be able to shape both strategic and tactical responses within their product and technology strategies.

In addition, I would argue patent landscaping is essential for any modern corporation because the relatively modest investment involved will not only improve strategy, it will also minimize potential risks and identify significant opportunities.

Dean Parry (BSc, MSc) is the technical director of Patent Seekers. He is a former UK Patent Office Examiner and an expert patent analyst. He has led research projects to provide technical defences for some of the world's largest patent disputes and works with companies in the EU, United States, Australia, Canada, China and Japan.

Further information: http://www.patentseekers.com

Freedom to commercialize

However good your idea, you must make sure you have a clear path to market, say Nicola Baker-Munton and Hannah Kendall at Stratagem IPM

Owning a patent does not grant a company the right to commercialize free from any threat of infringement of third-party rights. Third parties may have patent coverage that dominates your position and the onus is on you to identify these and avoid them, challenge them or take a licence! Failure to do so has a number of possible consequences; the most likely for an early-stage company is that such third-party rights are identified during the due diligence associated with fund raising and the investors refuse to invest or beat you down on value. At a later stage you risk a law suit and the very significant costs of mounting a defence.

Under the law and in summary, a person infringes a patent in a particular territory, if, without the consent of the patent owner, he or she manufactures or sells product or uses a process.

Innocence and/or ignorance of a relevant third-party patent is not a valid defence in infringement proceedings. It is therefore vital that as part of any development plan for a product or process, freedom-to-commercialize analyses should be undertaken, or at least a risk assessment carried out, on each and every aspect of a product, its production methodology, its formulation and its use or the process steps. Carrying out these analyses early in development can help to avoid costly development being wasted on products or processes that are the subject of someone else's patents. It also gives the company an opportunity to devise non-infringing products and processes which are free from third-party coverage or obtaining a licence to proceed.

It is also important to note that no amount of freedom-to-commercialize search and analysis can prevent an aggressive competitor from using the patent system as one of its routes to thwart a company's business, but 'clearing the path to market' and being aware of what a competitor has in its armoury is not only vital for the company but usually a pre-requisite to secure investment.

Identification of third-party patents

Third-party patents should be identified by specific patent searches undertaken by a specialist with expertise in searching the relevant patent databases. Searches may

focus on keywords, classification, structures if the technology is chemistry, sequence searching where sequences of proteins or nucleic acids are involved, or company and scientist names known to be active in the field. The databases used are of great importance as they need to be comprehensive and not merely representative if all potentially relevant documents are to be found.

Consideration should be given to whether the searching should be geographically limited; a search covering UK, EP, US and PCT publications will generally identify all potentially relevant families as these key territories are almost always designated. The searches will require analysis, sometimes by both patent attorneys and scientists, to determine whether any documents warrant further scrutiny for claims that might pose a threat.

As part of the search process, a consideration of costs vs benefits needs to be taken into account. The more quality information that can be searched means that the resulting answer set is likely to be far more comprehensive and relevant. However, this is likely to increase costs. Low-cost options may lead to the risk of an incomplete search and key third-party patents may be missed, resulting in an increased risk of expensive litigation and potential damage to business. A search budget needs to be carefully considered when assessing the level of risk proportional to investment.

It should always be remembered that however comprehensive a search may be, there will be instances when not all relevant third-party patents are identified, and as such there can never be absolute certainty with regard to search results capturing all relevant patents. Consequently, as well as identifying third-party patents through comprehensive database searching, it is also important for the company, as part of its risk management strategy, to be aware of its competition. Attending meetings and monitoring third-party publications are useful means of maintaining awareness of competitor activity.

Assessment of third-party rights and dealing with the threat

A patent affords a grant of rights to exclude others, not a right to operate or commercialize. Protection afforded by a patent has a limited duration, normally 20 years from the date of filing, the protection is territorial, and a patent is determined by the scope of the granted claims. All of these aspects form important features when identifying potentially relevant third-party patents.

Prior to any detailed analysis, the status of any patent should be checked to see if the patentee has allowed it to lapse, to see if it has expired and to check whether or not it has been granted. At the same time, territorial scope should be determined to see if patent filings cover the territories of interest.

Determining the scope of a patent requires considerable experience and knowledge, since it is not always easy to interpret granted claims. When assessing third-party patents, the written specification and the examination history of a patent should also be taken into consideration to help with interpreting the granted claims. It is also worth bearing in mind that the claim scope of a granted patent may vary from territory to territory.

If, following analysis of a third-party patent, there is deemed to be a risk of infringement, an assessment of the validity of the claims should be the next stage. If the patent is flawed, the company may feel comfortable to ignore it on the basis that should it be sued it is confident of its ability to counter-claim for invalidity. However, this strategy carries the risk of costly litigation.

If the patent is still pending, simply monitoring through to grant and then challenging validity may help pre-empt any infringement suit. This strategy will incur costs, including further search and analysis costs to identify publications that question the validity of the pending claims, along with associated patent attorney fees to carry out the analysis. There is no guarantee that a challenge will prove successful and, accordingly, this approach needs to be weighed against alternative approaches that may be taken post-grant.

If a third-party patent is identified in which the claims pose an infringement threat and are considered valid, there are a number of strategies that the company can consider. One option is to cease those activities as the risk of infringement is too great; the company may, however, identify a way in which to 'work around' the claims. The earlier in the company's R&D process a third-party patent is identified, the greater the likelihood that it will be easier and cheaper to devise an alternative approach to work around third-party claims.

Turning the threat into an opportunity by acquiring the patent and making it part of the company's own portfolio may be an alternative option, as may be obtaining a licence under the claims. Any licence will most likely provide authorization from the patent holder for the company to use the patented subject matter for specified acts, in designated markets and for a specified period of time. The terms of such a licence will need to be negotiated carefully to ensure that the company's commercialization needs are best met. Ideally, an exclusive licence under the claims will be agreed, ensuring that no other parties are free to commercialize without risk of litigation. Failing that, a non-exclusive licence giving the company the freedom it needs to commercialize, but no exclusive protection, may be adequate for its needs and free it from any further threat.

In some instances the company may own a patent, the claims of which fall within the broad scope of a third-party patent. In this situation the third-party patent will dominate, but it may be that the company patent covers a specific improvement that the third party is unable to make use of, and, as such, it may be beneficial to both parties if a 'cross-licence' is negotiated. In such a scenario the two companies will exchange licences that enable each other to use certain patents owned by the other party.

Conclusion

Whatever approach is taken to minimize the possibility of facing potentially risky and expensive patent litigation, companies are well advised to start looking into the matter early on in the research and development process. As the company's products and services evolve, so the 'freedom to commercialize' must evolve too. Minor changes to a product or process may be sufficient to overcome third-party claims, and the earlier on in the process third-party issues are identified the easier it is likely to be to 'work around' these issues. Payment of a licensing fee to a patent owner may be sufficient to avoid costly disputes in the future.

In order to obtain a meaningful 'freedom to commercialize' patent search, the use of an experienced searcher is advisable, with the quality of the search more often than not dictating the quality of the results. Care needs to be taken in keeping a record of all searches and analyses, but attention needs to be paid not to create a negative record which could be used against the company during litigation proceedings. When assessing third-party patents it is vitally important to seek formal opinions only under careful patent attorney guidance. Such opinions should not be generally released to avoid breaking client–attorney privilege.

Nicola Baker-Munton founded Stratagem IPM in 1999. She is a Chartered UK Patent Attorney and European Patent Attorney with a joint honours degree in biology and biochemistry. With steady growth Strategem IPM has become the leading specialist company providing active strategic management of intellectual property portfolios from inception through development to market, and from academia through start-up to stock market listing.

Hannah Kendall is an IP Manager at Stratagem IPM. Hannah has experience of maintaining patent and agreement portfolios within the pharmaceutical industry. She has a background in synthetic organic chemistry, and has worked for a number of years within IP departments of pharmaceutical research sites. Hannah also has experience of patent and agreement database management.

Further details from Stratagem IPM: tel: 01223 550740;
web: http://www.stratagemipm.co.uk/

Risks, losses, liabilities and indemnities

Matthew R Hogg at Liberty International Underwriters discusses how to sustain innovation and intangible asset value through the use of IP insurance

You have the idea – the concept – a strategy. You perceive a market opportunity and have mustered finances, a team and a business model. Those surrounding you have stressed the need to drive home your differentiators; the competitive advantages. In the contemporary business, much of this can be found in your intellectual property (IP), whether it is the trade secret or know-how or the carefully calculated portfolio of current and prospective property rights framed from the laws of copyright, trade marks and patents, among others. The concept builds momentum.

As a fledging business emerges, its first tentative steps will be towards building resilience. More revenue brings investment in risk management and risk transfer. Less uncertainty, more stability. Such resilience has traditionally led to the purchasing of standard insurance products, honed from the practices of many hundreds of years: property, product and public liability and employer's liability insurance, often driven also by the legal necessity for coverage. However, the competitive advantages are all too often abandoned to the whim of the markets and the demands of the bankroller. Intellectual property insurance has been around for decades, yet the take-up in Europe has at best been limited to larger companies' professional indemnity coverage, without consideration of patent matters, or piecemeal standalone purchasing. At best, no survey has shown that more than 13 per cent of businesses have any form of patent insurance cover,[1] and in the author's opinion, any protection from patent litigation or the enforcement of patents is, in reality, limited to less than 1 per cent of businesses.

However, the IP of a business is critical to its ability to trade or, at the very least, provide the business with a solution to a barrier to entry, while bringing additional returns on investment and increased profit margins as detailed in this book. How many savvy businesses start from a tiny office with limited means or, indeed, the garage or garden shed? Not much of an asset base in such an entity other than its idea, which generates first seed capital, then VC funding, product sales and shareholder value. In fact, value has been assigned by academics to each freshly issued patent right of around $58,000 (in today's terms) per individual, prior to mass commercialization.[2] UK investments in products and services that are protected by intellectual property rights (IPR) have been calculated at £65 billion a year[3] and it is often said that around 70 per cent of typical company value lies in intangible assets. Now this sounds like an asset worth both protecting and leveraging.

Intellectual property insurance has a role to play in the protection of all stake-holders' interests when the innovation process is already in full swing. Its growth may have been hindered by inconsistency from insurance markets, lack of promotion, poor underwriting results and a turbulent 15 years in the global economy. Yet poor underwriting results probably actually signify a greater need for purchase than any other statistic brought to bear – two insurance companies very publicly stated that they lost $4,000 to $6,000 for every $1 of insurance premium received covering patent litigation. The products will forever have a rocky road while results are poor; there has been a historic trend of high premiums forced by poor results which has led to the uptake of such expensive insurance only by those businesses most at risk. It is called 'adverse selection' in the insurance industry.

In many other classes of insurance, laws and regulation have driven uptake. For many others, professional standards and the contracting of services have. It is in this latter scenario that we can see the development of a consistent, stable and responsible attitude from underwriters and buyers of intellectual property insurance. The economic climate of the past five years has certainly driven an increase in hold-harmless provisions among contracts where IP is licensed or sold, and, importantly, has even led to requests for identifiable insurance coverage. When more money is flushed into the market from banks, VCs and business angels in the forthcoming years, should they too not be pressing for 'security' on the most valuable assets of all? IP has been additionally used for loan collateral, monetization and securitization schemes, including pension funding, investment vehicles and bonds. It was estimated that 21 per cent of US-originated, secured syndicated loans during 1996–2005 were collateralized by intangibles, with such practice significantly increasing over time until the banking sector went into meltdown.[4] Would insurance of the intangible assets not attract a better rate? It could be argued that insurance should be compulsory for intangible assets.

Intellectual property insurance products

There are a number of intellectual property insurance products which stand alone to provide the most comprehensive protection for matters arising from IP value and litigation. Yet, absurdly, there remain only five or six significant insurers globally that focus on products for the small to mid-sized enterprise. The main insurances available are discussed below.

Intellectual property defence insurance

This is the bread and butter of the IP insurance market. This product supports the proposition that regardless of how innovative a business may be, and how carefully it may construct its own intellectual property protection programme, there are many, many other businesses with the same objectives which are watchful of maintaining and growing their market share. Additionally, it may make good business practice to stunt the growth of, or even financially bankrupt, the smaller business, by pursuing a less than robust infringement case and so prey on the financial insecurity of such businesses.

IP defence insurance looks to indemnify the policy owner from damages, settlements, legal fees and expenses arising from an alleged infringement of a third party's IP through its sale or distribution of products and services. The product is likely to insure for infringement of most if not all intellectual property matters, whether it be copyrights, trade marks and patents to registered designs, trade secrets or more obscure proprietary protections. Some products limit the insured's control of the defence and settlement more significantly than others and may only cover legal expenses.

Furthermore, these products often provide additional cover, such as claims by third parties disputing the insured's ownership of intellectual property, and so can cover invalidity matters, applications for a grant of compulsory ownership or claims from a current employee that he or she has ownership or joint title in the intellectual property. Other areas of extension include coverage of disputes among contracted parties over licensing or payment matters.

An IP defence policy can also be extended to provide cover to parties other than the insured, providing there is the requisite 'insurable interest' at law. Therefore it is common to see coverage provided for the directors and officers of a company. Additionally, the insurance can sit behind the indemnity and 'hold-harmless' provisions can be granted by the insured to business partners such as distributors, collaborators and customers for any threats or litigation they receive as a result of exploiting the insured's products or services.

Lest we forget, IPR are granted at a national level only at present and the legal interpretation of requirements for such rights, and the penalties for infringing, differ internationally, as do the quality and quantity of proprietary rights. Without a requirement of 'negligence' in disputes to assert an infringement action, the innocents can be as exposed to litigation as the pirates, bootleggers and knock-off merchants. Those businesses entering a new product or country market might tread carefully. The median damages award in the United States from 2006 to 2011 for a patent litigation was $4 million[5] which, according to another survey, would also have required an average legal costs spend of $2.8m around that period.[6] While the US litigation costs and expenses are clearly an outlier to any average around the world, IP litigation is notoriously expensive and time consuming, regardless of jurisdiction. It should also be noted, from survey evidence, that when comparing the United States to Europe, a worrying 28 per cent of European businesses had to defend at least one IP action in the past five years compared to an astronomical 50 per cent of US businesses.[7]

A word might also be said about the rise of non-practising entities (NPEs) (sometimes unfairly named 'patent trolls') at this juncture. Such businesses are common in the United States and on the rise in Europe. Many NPEs have made patent acquisitions from distressed businesses and sought to license such IP to businesses for a 'reasonable royalty'. The NPE is, by definition, not interested in selling a product or service but only to generate cash from the patents it owns. Coincidentally or not, the royalties requested for a licence are often less than the costs likely to be spent in litigation and so the defendant is minded to pay for a licence on what might be, on the whole, a weak-looking patent. The licensing arrangements of NPEs lend themselves to bringing actions relating to products and services that many businesses may exploit even if not directly sold, such as wi-fi, internet and telecommunications technology.

Intellectual property enforcement/abatement insurance

Unsurprisingly, this insurance product is designed to provide the insured with the financial means to bring an action against competitors it believes are infringing its intellectual property. Again, the breadth of the IP insured can be broad. The average small business, typically being cash poor, can struggle to enforce its 'differentiators' against opponents in its market. The presence of an enforcement policy can be used as a 'threat' to any potentially infringing parties as well as be called upon where required.

Historically, such insurance was readily available on a 'known' and 'unknown' basis. This means that an insured could purchase cover where there was clear knowledge of an infringing party. An insurance product would then be constructed following a thorough review of the likely litigation success and merits by underwriters for an upfront premium and a potential 'slice' of any damages awarded to the insured following the litigation. However, the learning process for many underwriters proved expensive and also increasingly uncompetitive to the contingent commission lawyers. Currently, the standard enforcement policies focus on an annually renewable insurance policy whereby the bringing of actions by the insured is likely to be only fortuitous. Indeed, much enforcement coverage is purchased in a package format with IP defence insurance.

Intellectual property value insurance

This is the most recent of insurance covers for IP exposures, yet by no means a recent concept. This product is safely 15 years old and looks to provide true cover to the value of IP assets either by way of insuring lost revenues and profit or as a fixed insured value. Additional cost of working, such as design-around costs, may also be covered. The value insured could also be derived from the R&D expenditure to create the IP, a monetized or securitized value, including loans and investments, or by some other method applied by a valuation expert, such as a royalty-based or market-forces calculation.

The preferred trigger typically purchased is for legal claims. Cover is provided where a legal claim is made against the insured alleging that any of the insured's IPR are invalid or that it has infringed the claimant's IPR, as well as for claims by employees for ownership of intellectual property that they have been involved in creating. Additionally, cover can be acquired for loss of revenue arising from injunctive actions against products and services of the insured.

Less common, but more likely to be of interest to those in the life sciences, pharmaceutical and defence sectors, are triggers arising from actions by governments and states. Cover is provided where any law, order, decree or regulation prevents or restricts the insured from enforcing or exploiting its IPR. This could occur, for example, where a competitor was granted identical IPR or where a government decided to cancel the insured's authority to export or import its product.

Concluding thoughts

As a practitioner, the author can safely say from experience that the purchase of IP insurance typically commences after a loss has been experienced rather than from a well-considered 'just in case' position. With the values, damage awards and costs surrounding IP being so high, it is surprising that all stakeholders, in innovative and non-innovative businesses alike, do not prioritize the purchase of some catastrophe-level cover.

It arguably makes sense to consider IP insurance to be more than just a 'liability' cover, but one that can protect the bottom line of a business by bolstering income, protecting market share or minimizing large-scale shock losses. Money may be at a premium for smaller businesses, but in providing greater risk management to intangibles by purchasing insurance, it will be rarely ill spent.

Notes

1 The 2011 Intellectual Property Survey Report, Marsh & Liberty International Underwriters, http://uk.marsh.com/NewsInsights/FeaturedContent/The2011IntellectualPropertySurveyReport.aspx

2 Serrano, CJ (2006) The Market for Intellectual Property: Evidence from the Transfer of Patents, University of Toronto and NBER, June.

3 Farooqui, S, Goodridge, P and Haskel, J (2011) The Role of Intellectual Property Rights in the UK Market Sector, July, Intellectual Property Office, London

4 Loumioti, M (2011) The Use of Intangible Assets as Loan Collateral, PhD thesis, University of California.

5 PricewaterhouseCoopers (2012) 2012 Patent Litigation Study, PwC, New York

6 AIPLA (2011) The American Intellectual Property Law Association Economic Survey, AIPLA, Arlington, VA

7 See note 1.

Matthew Hogg is Vice President at Liberty International Underwriters where he leads the Strategic Assets Division. The division underwrites specialist risks in the classes of intellectual property, reputation, cyber, privacy and non-material damage business interruption. He holds a degree in law, a Masters in Law & Economics and an Advanced Diploma in Insurance.

Further details: www.liueurope.com

An independent law firm,
challenging convention
and achieving great results
for its clients.

www.walkermorris.co.uk

Patrick Cantrill, Head of Intellectual Property
+44 (0)113 283 2591
patrick.cantrill@walkermorris.co.uk

WALKER
MORRIS

Options for taking action

Patrick Cantrill at Walker Morris reviews a series of changes that are making infringements easier to pursue

Intellectual property (IP) rights increasingly occupy centre stage in most commercial transactions. They serve as the glue for globalization – the means by which technology is protected and exchanged within and across borders. Their importance has accelerated as China, India and other developing nations emerge both as major manufacturing hubs and as consumer markets in their own right. In addition, IP systems need to remain relevant and fit for purpose. Accordingly, they need to adapt to the continuous challenge posed by new technologies, for example in life sciences, with regard to 3D printers and overlaying the ability of the internet to allow for data and trade to be exchanged and made with ever greater complexity and speed.

More affordable, effective remedies

The worldwide IP regime is a testament to what can be achieved by countries co-operating with each other. Through a string of international treaties and conventions there is enshrined the principle that states will, through their domestic courts and enforcement agencies, recognize the IP rights of nationals from other signatory states.

However, to have any meaning, the enforcement of IP rights has to be effective. Until relatively recently, the UK courts were characterized correctly like the Savoy Hotel – first class, but very expensive. However, in the past three years, there have been several developments which have had and will have a dramatic and beneficial impact on the remedies available in the UK and across Europe for the enforcement of patents and other IP rights. This chapter looks at a few of these developments.

The cost and inefficiencies of the current European patent system

Under the 1973 European Patent Convention (the EPC), there was introduced, by way of an alternative to national patents, a single filing procedure administered by the European Patent Office (the EPO) whose central office is based in Munich for patent applications across various European countries. Currently, all 27 member states of the European Union and 11 other European countries are members of the EPO.

However, single granted patents did not emerge under the EPC. Instead, after examination and the grant by the EPO, European patents are converted into a bundle of national, independent patent rights in those countries to where the patents are to be enforced. It is estimated by the European Commission that the cost of obtaining protection by means of a European patent across all 27 states of the EU is €36,000 (the majority of which goes on translation and national office fees). This figure and other assertions by the Commission as to the considerable cost and inconvenience of obtaining patents within Europe are hotly contested but, neverthe-less, it is indeed the case that the cost of obtaining a patent elsewhere is significantly less; for example, in the United States (population > 300 million) the cost is about €4,000 and for China (population >1.2 billion) it is about €1,500.

Another perceived problem with the EPC is that disputes as to the validity and alleged infringement of European patents are essentially left to be addressed at the national level by the courts of the designated countries. This has led on a few occa-sions to there being conflicting judgments between the national courts when they consider validity and infringement issues relating to the same European patent. Moreover, some national patent enforcement systems (eg Germany's) are bifurcated, that is, the infringement courts will not address issues of validity, whereas others, such as the UK with its highly specialized technically trained judges, will consider both issues together when handling disputes.

The proposed introduction of the unitary European patent

The EPC was not the 'one-stop shop' for which its original promoters had initially hoped, but now, with the publication in December 2012 of Regulation No. 1257/2012 ('the Regulation') and related developments, there is a clear intention to introduce by 2014/15 a truly harmonized patent system across all countries within the EU (other than Spain and Italy who have declined to join the new system). Accordingly, the Regulation aims to achieve for European patents the type of unitary effect that already exists for Community designs and trade marks.

The proposed introduction of the Unified Patent Court

The unified patent system will be supported by a specialized, streamlined Unified Patent Court (the UPC) which ultimately, after a transitional period, will have exclu-sive jurisdiction over all European patents.

There is no doubt that the move towards the unitary patent is a positive step for Europe. It is part of a wider acknowledgement that much of the rest of the world provides patent systems that are more efficient and cost-effective. However, its implementation is not guaranteed since it still awaits ratification by the member states, and it is likely that many patentees will take advantage of the transitional provisions which will allow them, for a period of some years, to declare that their European patents will not be treated as unified patents. Patentees may also wish to wait and see how the unified patents court will function and they may well be concerned about how a unified patent which is successfully attacked will be revoked across all 25 states which participate in the system.

There is therefore much about the proposed unified patent system which is unclear and incomplete. However, by any analysis it represents a very major development in the harmonization of both European patent law and European jurisprudence, and it is to be hoped that it will be ratified and brought into effect since it embodies the aims of the single market.

The Patents County Court (the PCC)

The PCC (misnamed as such because it adjudicates across a full spectrum of IP rights – not just patents) was established as long ago as 1990 but only now, under rules introduced in 2010 and 2011, has it finally emerged as a truly viable forum for the cost-effective resolution of IP disputes. The PCC is actively engaged in serving in the UK as a real alternative to the High Court for the type of relatively straightforward cases that, through a streamlined procedure, can be dealt with by trial lasting no more than two days. As a result, the PCC has dispelled the widely held belief that, when compared with the rest of Europe, although the UK courts delivered thorough, reasoned judgments, such remedies came at a price which was too high for most litigants, in particular for SMEs. Moreover, like the High Court, the PCC is not bifurcated; that is, it can handle both the infringement and validity issues of a dispute.

In the UK, and since the implementation of European Directive 2004/48, there is a general rule that the reasonable costs and other expenses associated with the dispute incurred by the successful party will normally be borne by the losing party. However, in the PCC, regardless of the outcome, the maximum that a party is required to pay to another party is capped at £50,000 up to and into a trial on liability plus an additional cap of £25,000 in respect of the costs for assessing damages. In addition to the cap on costs, there is a cap of £500,000 on the amount of the damages recoverable before the PCC.

What cases are suitable for the PCC?

To date, since its overhaul in 2010/11, the PCC has heard all manner of IP cases. In particular, providing a case can reasonably be heard in two days, the PCC seems to be sending out a message that it is more than capable of handling relatively complicated IP claims. Of course, in light of the damages cap, the PCC is usually seen as a forum for only low-value claims; but in the world of IP, injunctions usually speak louder than cash and rarely will the courts order an award in excess of £500,000.

What are the benefits of the PCC?

Although a party before the PCC is unlikely to recover more than half of its actual costs, the great benefit of the costs cap is that it provides a great amount of commercial certainty. To meet the needs of their clients, in particular the SMEs, and to bridge this gap of irrecoverable costs, IP practitioners in the UK have responded by standardizing many of their litigation services. As such, IP practitioners are increasingly prepared to offer their clients a range of fixed-fee arrangements when dealing with the PCC.

Whereas there will remain a number of UK disputes whose complexity and substance dictate that they should be heard in the High Court, the PCC has shown the rest of Europe that quality of justice does not need always to come with a expensive price tag.

The Jackson Reforms to civil procedure

The PCC foreshadowed many of the changes that are now to be introduced as from 1 April 2013 in the High Court as a result of the Jackson Reforms. Under these reforms, parties are expected to communicate with each other from an early stage on the conduct of the case, and this expectation coupled with active engagement by the court has resulted in parties narrowing the need for cross-examination, disclosure and experts. This has led to cases being heard expeditiously and/or being settled.

The Jackson Reforms are the single biggest overhaul to civil procedure in England and Wales for a generation. The main amendments are as follows.

Costs budgeting

At an early stage in the proceedings (shortly after the service of a defence), each party will need to disclose to the court, and the other parties, a detailed and structured estimate of the costs it is likely to incur in the litigation. Once submitted to the court (and there will be severe repercussions for non-compliance), the court can then approve or reject the budget. Once approved, the party is very committed to these estimates unless that party makes a successful application justifying at a later date why there needs to be a revision to its earlier figures.

All this will entail a considerable amount of forecasting by the parties and their legal teams. At the start of a complex IP litigation, it can often prove difficult to be very precise about damages and about costs going forward to trial, but nevertheless parties will need to engage with the process since the submission of wildly inaccurate or unreasonably high budgets will run the risk of either the estimates being rejected by the court or else being unrealistic for the particular litigation.

This radical shift to dealing early and openly with costs is good news for all litigants seeking to enforce IP rights, especially SMEs. Having an approved budget in place for both claimant and defendant, from an early stage in the proceedings, achieves the same level of certainty and business-friendly forecasting that is achieved today by the PCC.

Reform of conditional fee agreements (CFAs)

As part of the Jackson Reforms, CFAs are to be overhauled. Until these changes, so-called 'success fees', being the uplift applied to a legal team's fees in the event of a 'successful outcome', were recoverable from the unsuccessful litigant as part of the usual 'loser pays' rule.

Changes to after the event (ATE) insurance

Equally, as from 1 April 2013, the costs payable under ATE policies where a litigant has sought cover, for example, the risk of an adverse costs order being made against it if it does not in fact win at trial is no longer recoverable from the unsuccessful party. Instead, after implementation of the Jackson Reforms, the 'uplift' portion of a winning party's costs will be paid out of that party's pocket – not that of the losing party. In addition, the ATE premium will no longer be a cost recoverable from the unsuccessful litigant but will instead have to be paid by the successful litigant.

While some will clamour that making ATE premiums and 'no win, no fee' uplifts irrecoverable hinders access to justice, the reality is that most CFA and ATE arrangements have not in recent years been entered into in order to aid impecunious clients in cases where justice requires those cases be taken to trial, and the lawyer is willing to take on the risk.

The essence of IP rights is 'exclusivity' – the ability by the owner to prevent third parties from the area covered by his or her IP. Accordingly, the majority of IP cases are commenced not for damages but to obtain injunctions and/or to invalidate a right. Indeed, it is more often than not that at the commencement of an IP dispute, the claimant has little understanding of how much is likely to be awarded by way of damages should the claimant prove that the defendant has infringed its rights.

Patrick Cantrill is Head of the Intellectual Property Department at Walker Morris, the major commercial law firm based in Leeds. Walker Morris acts for corporations across the UK and overseas. Independent sources such as Legal 500 and Chambers often comment on the great experience and seamless, quality service provided by the large team of lawyers that comprise the IP Department. It has a particularly strong national and international reputation in the field of IP enforcement but in addition to litigation, the IP Department also offers advice and assistance on collaboration, licensing, merchandising, franchising etc and through its integrated unit of specialists, it provides a complete range of design and trade mark searching, prosecution and recordal services.

Tel: 0113 2832500; e-mail: patrick.cantrill@walkermorris.co.uk; web: www.walkermorris.co.uk

PART TEN
Early-stage ventures

From start-up to first round

For Adrian Burden of Key IQ Ltd and Mark Yeadon of Yeadon IP Ltd the period between starting up a business and winning the first round of investment is the opportunity to instil a company ethos of best practice for growth and the eventual exit

The first year or so of a new business is a hectic whirlwind of frenetic activity. It starts off as a blank canvas; a germ of an idea and a window of opportunity. But very soon it becomes an all-consuming activity taking over family life, eating into your sleep patterns and leaving little time to breathe during the day.

Investing such a large amount of time, energy and money into a new venture makes it all the more important that it should succeed. The first few months of activity are therefore crucial in laying the foundations on which the new business will grow. Ensuring that things remain organized in the early stages will pay dividends later when the operation has become larger and more complex.

Like a snowball rolling down a hill, the new business will gain momentum. As it grows, it will become harder to steer, and indeed the direction you set it off in is likely to be the general direction it follows thereafter. Once the first round of investment is secured, there will be little opportunity to make major changes to the business, and doing so will come with a costly overhead.

Therefore, making an effort early on can define the way your new company will operate in years to come. Below we have set out a few key points that should help you in these critical early stages of growing a fledgling business.

1. Build your IP on rock, not sand

Most new businesses, particularly in the knowledge economies, will rely on a good new idea to bring initial value. This is the basis of your intellectual property (IP). For technology-based business, this is often an invention that is later filed and defended as a patent. However, intellectual property extends to a clever design, written material including software code in the form of copyright, a branding idea embodied in a trade mark, or simply know-how that you will keep secret from others.

Often the first major round of funding, and any funding in between from friends, family and business angels, will rely on this IP having some present and future value. More importantly, you yourself must be convinced of its value, because maintaining and defending an IP portfolio soon becomes an expensive and time-consuming activity for a company.

Therefore, you should look critically at your invention or idea from the outset and do as much research around it as possible to fully understand what is new and what has been done before. You should become an expert on the landscape, appreciating why similar ideas succeeded or failed, and whether third parties may have rights to any aspects of your idea. These conflicting rights may affect your freedom to operate, perhaps requiring lengthy negotiations and costly licensing deals later. They may also greatly affect the value of your IP and hence your business when you try to raise future rounds of finance.

If you believe that your IP is novel and inventive in light of the prior art of which you are aware, look beyond your original idea and see if you can carve out an even larger area of protection. This could bring you much greater value in the future, and also open up new opportunities in which to diversify your business as it grows. For example, you should consider whether there may be applications for your technology in fields other than those in which you plan to exploit it at the moment.

Investors like defendable IP because it helps to protect the core of the business in which they are investing. But they are also suspicious of IP and will often engage experts to review it before investing. You therefore need to be up to date and fully conversant with all the developments in the field, and know what each of your competitors is doing and how this activity could impact your future business.

2. Start as you mean to go on

There is a great temptation as you start a new business to cut corners and race towards the distant finish line. However, you should see the growth of a new business as a marathon and not a sprint. In fact, it will be more like a challenging steeple-chase, so being systematic and process driven with all aspects of the company's activities from incorporation will greatly help in the future.

This does not mean getting bogged down in creating company bureaucracy, but it does mean keeping detailed records and structuring the business more like a corporation from the outset. In simple terms, think of the roles of the different departments in the future business (such as R&D, marketing, and sales) and organize files and paperwork in appropriate departmental directories or folders. This will mean that as you delegate new recruits to take on these roles in the future, the company history that is relevant to them is already in place, and the standard of best practice already set. It will also be easier to give them access to the information they need without letting them see everything about the business, or requiring you to reorganize the information.

You may be the only board member at the start, or you may be one of a handful of founding directors. Later, investors may join your company board, and so it is far better to have a track record of regular board meetings with board reports and minutes from the outset. Make it a monthly or bi-monthly activity so that you discipline yourself to look critically at the progress of the business on a regular basis, adjusting the strategy in a controlled manner. Having this activity in place will be highly attractive to investors coming in at the first round.

3. No skeletons in the closet

Investors do not like surprises, and as such they will undertake detailed research (due diligence) into your company before investing. This process will become more sophisticated as the size of the investment increases with future rounds, and should you become publicly listed, the process can be very onerous. Moreover, as a founding director, you will be required to sign all kinds of warrants that you are disclosing the truth, have been running your business legally and are not hiding evidence that could be detrimental to the value of the company.

A particularly relevant example would be failing to disclose a third-party patent that impinges on your own IP, creating future uncertainties in your own freedom to operate.

All of these problems can be mitigated by keeping detailed accounts of every problem and every success encountered during the running of the business. This is best done through regular disclosures in the board reports discussed in point 2 above. Having these reports and associated minutes as a historical account of the company will greatly help the due diligence process without you having to dredge your memory or worry that you've overlooked disclosing something material.

4. Where there's smoke, there are mirrors

Even as a small company, do not underestimate the power of generating a buzz to build interest in your new venture. This can be done inexpensively by using social networks like LinkedIn, Twitter and Facebook, as well as more traditional methods of press releases to newspapers, radio, and trade journals.

Having your successes in print or trending on the social networks will build credibility and increase the value of your brand and hence your company. Staff will like to be associated with a dynamic talked-about venture, and customers will be comforted that their choice to buy your products and services was a good one. All of this provides evidence to the future investor that your business has a growing value, and they too will want to be part of the success story.

As a company based on IP, you need to be careful not to disclose trade secrets or compromise your patent filings. It is also important not to tell lies, as apart from the obvious legal and branding implications, these false claims will be used as evidence against you by investors if and when things go wrong.

5. Eyes on the prize

The Achilles' heel of an innovative company is that its promoters tend to be easily distracted by another creative idea. There is nothing wrong with generating new IP to help the business, but be wary of the cost and time penalties of wandering from the path.

As a new business, you need to focus tirelessly on the main prize and a few smaller ones along the way. Be very sure about what you are aiming to achieve from the outset, and what the key milestones are to make this happen quickly and with the least expense. This approach is especially important in the lead-up to the first round of funding, as the margin for error is small and there are fewer guides working with you to help you stay on track.

Dr Adrian Burden is a serial entrepreneur and technologist, having worked in both academia and industry. He has a degree in natural sciences from the University of Cambridge and a DPhil. in materials science from the University of Oxford. He is currently Technical Director of Key IQ Ltd, a business and technology catalyst based in Malvern UK. He recently co-founded the Wyche Innovation Centre and the Malvern Festival of Innovation, both initiatives aimed at helping small businesses to grow and succeed.

Tel: 01684 252 201; e-mail: adrian.burden@key-iq.com; web: www.key-iq.com, www.wyche.in, www.festival-innovation.com

Dr Mark Yeadon is a Chartered UK and European patent attorney specializing in electronic and mechanical engineering and the physical sciences. He has a degree in engineering science from the University of Oxford and a PhD in materials engineering from the University of Birmingham. He is currently a director of Yeadon IP Limited, which specializes in the protection of intellectual property.

Tel: 0113 274 7475; e-mail: markyeadon@yeadonip.com;
web: www.yeadonip.com

Building and scaling a commercial platform

10.2

Mike Herd at the Sussex Innovation Centre reviews the process of clearing the way for an innovation to grow to its full potential

Scalability is the main pillar on which the success of a business is built. Any plan to build a commercial platform for an early-stage venture should focus on a sustainable strategy to scale the business – one that aims at every turn to streamline processes, effectively target end users, minimize roadblocks and bottlenecks, and build and maintain strong support networks.

Building a commercial platform via management development

The biggest gear shift involved in making the change from a start-up into a profitable business is in going from recognizing a niche that can be filled to actively and sustainably selling your product. When you've reached that point, there is a tendency for growth to plateau. Provided that the desire for continued growth exists, and that the problem is not one of ambition, the next challenge involves realizing your product's market potential. It is vital to recognize what is restricting growth, which is often not as simple as it sounds. There are several different factors which you'll have to consider carefully:

- People – do you have the right people to grow? It may seem obvious, but when a company has grown organically, sometimes you can easily miss the gaps in your collective knowledge or experience. Think about where you want your company to be. If you are to grow your business to 10 times its current size, what positions are you going to need to fill along the way? Which are the most vital?

- Structure – this is connected with the people you have at your disposal. Are you playing to everyone's strengths, or are there people doing jobs they're not suited to, simply because you don't have anyone else? While

you're thinking about taking on new staff, look closely at your chain of command. Ensure that everyone is in the right place to do their best work, most effectively.

- Systems – are you doing everything as simply as you can, or are you wasting time and money by repeating the same processes? Examine your typical process when you take a new order or court a new client – are there things that should be formalized? Can you work from templates rather than treating each piece of work as a new and individual project?

- Focus – when growth begins to stagnate, it is often because you are failing to focus on where the growth opportunity lies. Take the time to understand your market, research the sectors where your innovation is currently being used and learn where your clients' problems lie. It's better to sell the perfect product to a smaller market than to try to sell an imperfect product to a larger one.

To formalize this top-down approach, let us examine two different routes to management development – incubation and investment.

Incubation

At the Sussex Innovation Centre, an example of a small business successfully negotiating the path from product demand to growth is the story of Oban Multilingual SEO.

Oban provides search engine optimization services to enhance the profile of international companies. It can target a wide range of specific local markets, using tailored language, content and approach.

Oban had reached one of the most difficult and crucial periods in a company's development. While it had found that there was a demand for its product, opportunities for growth were hampered by a variety of factors. The level of demand for its service was beginning to outweigh its capability of meeting it, individual team members were building up too large a workload to handle on their own, yet it remained impractical to recruit new specialist staff. Oban needed to avoid falling into the trap of narrowing focus towards the company's core services, at the expense of working on the business's future strategy – the commercial platform upon which it would be built.

The Centre engaged Oban in its 'super incubation' process – a period of intensive accelerated growth support – which saw it use members of the support team as interim managers, to facilitate growth professionally without financial burden. In short, we put our team around the entrepreneur.

Working closely with this support structure, the expanded team devised a strategy to scale the business, doubling revenue while developing the market knowledge, management skills, business processes and delivery resources required for future growth. In 12 months, working with our team, Oban more than doubled its revenue. It also increased its profit, established scalable processes and was able to recruit permanent key personnel to replace the interim team. Oban is now one of the leaders in its sector.

> It's very difficult to invite people from different fields into your business – in effect, what you're asking them to do is to rip it up and start again – but it helps you to recognize a need for balance. Everything works systematically, to simplify your business model.
> (Greig Holbrook, MD, Oban Multilingual SEO)

Business incubation is about planning for strategic growth, rather than letting growth occur organically and (often) inefficiently. It should challenge your assumptions about production, financing, sales and marketing, recognize which skills you already possess, and focus your attention on your target market.

Investment

As Greig Holbrook describes above, perhaps the hardest part of managing your business's growth is stepping back from what has been, up until now, a deeply personal relationship. It's important to recognize that your brand can no longer be you and you alone. It's time to focus on the potential of the idea, rather than the potential of the person.

Securing investment can often provide the impetus for that to happen. Introducing an active angel investor into the mix, one who takes a role in shaping the way the business is run, can have a similar effect in helping to redefine your strategy, as well as giving you access to valuable experience and business savvy.

IRIS Connect uses highly sophisticated audio-visual capture systems and web-enabled software to deliver professional development for educational and corporate clients. With the help of the Centre, it was matched with an experienced investor who takes an active interest in the development of the company, and as a result it has seen very rapid growth in the education technology market:

> Without that investment of resources and experience, we would have struggled to realize the growth and market penetration we now have. The investor saw the potential of our service, and has helped IRIS Connect on its path towards working in over 400 schools in England, as well as having a growing presence in Europe and Australasia.
> (Graham Newell, Director, IRIS Connect)

Capital investment can also be a necessary part of bringing a new technology to market. The technical requirements of a project can take it beyond the reach of its original developers, and greater financial backing, or even a licensing agreement, can sometimes be required to make large-scale manufacturing a possibility (see Case Study: EP Sensors). Whatever the reason, you will need to prove the value of the investment to suitors, which will again mean demonstrating that the business model, with their support, is scalable.

But value isn't just a measure of what profit you can make for potential investors. You can find value in everything your company does, from the capacity of your innovation to improving your clients' offering and increasing their profits, to the market knowledge and unique insight that you can provide.

Building a commercial platform with the support of big business

Recognizing this second kind of value in your business can often be the foundation upon which your commercial platform is built. Two recent examples of award-winning companies from the Innovation Centre that demonstrate different ways to utilize the support of big business are the online and mobile tuition service Maths Doctor, and the manufacturers of electric vehicle charging technology, Elektromotive. In the first case, the company's value was as an acquisition, while in the second, the relationship with big business became that of a 'customer mentor'.

CASE STUDY　EP Sensors – facilitating commercialization

What if you hold the patent for an innovation, but setting up a business in order to commercialize that innovation is not the right course for you? That was the dilemma faced by Professor Robert Prance and his research team at the University of Sussex when they developed an electric potential sensor (EPS) capable of accurately measuring the potential of electric fields at the microvolt level.

Professor Prance and his team recognized that this innovation held multiple commercial applications (from material, military and medical technologies, to geophysics and aerospace engineering), but lacked the market knowledge and business acumen to leverage the patented technology, meaning that previous attempts at commercialization had failed.

For the Sussex Innovation Centre and the University's enterprise panel, the first step was market research, in order to recognize applications for the technology that were close to market – applications where there was a tangible benefit, or savings to be made, over existing solutions.

By taking the innovation out of its academic environment and into a commercial setting, the Centre helped to engage with businesses across a range of sectors as part of this market research. By understanding intimately the processes where similar technology was currently in use, the support team realized that there was an opportunity in the market for home medical care, as a way of simply performing an electrocardiogram without a medical professional present.

Out of these discussions came the recognition that miniaturization was a key factor in getting the technology to market. This led to conversations with the microchip manufacturer Plessey Semiconductors, which procured a full licence to manufacture and market the technology. Plessey continues to work collaboratively with Professor Prance and his team to further develop the EPS.

Just as relationships with a corporate network can be utilized to upscale an existing business, they can be of tremendous help in facilitating the commercial prospects of innovation.

Acquisition

Sometimes, when the strength of a business is in its core services, all that is required for growth is financial and logistical help. If the company's model is demonstrably scalable, but it lacks the reach needed in order to build upon its commercial successes, then being bought out by the right partner is a business decision worth considering. In Maths Doctor's case, the support team learnt that a major UK publishing house was planning to build a portfolio of e-learning facilities to support its educational output.

Maths Doctor saw the opportunities for growth that a larger company's brand, funding, marketing and support would provide it. It could offer the value of a service that was already proven to be an operational success, and it made sense for both parties that Maths Doctor be folded into the publisher's digital offering. The buyout was completed in October 2012, and the business has since seen the benefit of increased resources for sales staff:

> Since the acquisition, we have been able to focus internally on our strengths, without everything else that was necessary for our development falling by the wayside. With the added tools and impetus that were needed for growth, Maths Doctor is on track to see revenue increase fourfold over the next nine months.
>
> (Simon Walsh, MD, Maths Doctor Ltd)

Customer mentors

In some cases the introduction of new technology requires the input of resources beyond that available to an early-stage business. This can be as much about credibility as money or human resources.

Building a strong relationship with one of the big players in your sector can be the catalyst for increasing your value in the marketplace. Partnering for added credibility increases your prospects for finding business, and if your work is innovative in its field it will provide value to these market-leading companies. For instance, a large national energy provider that was keen to become more involved in the emerging clean energy market was the ideal partner for the Centre to introduce to Elektromotive, which had developed a universal electric car charging technology. What was holding the commercialization of the innovation back was the ability to convince local authorities that it was an infrastructure worth investing in.

It was vital for Elektromotive's growth that it realized the value of the market insight that it could provide, and the competitive advantage that a close relationship with big business could afford it. In discussing the sector with Elektromotive, the provider was able to visualize this emerging opportunity from a new perspective.

The growth of the electric car market was hampered by the lack of infrastructure to support it. What was needed was readily available charging station technology, which could be provided by Elektromotive. Unless charging stations in public places became a more common sight, there would be limited consumer interest in electric cars, and consequently, limited quantities of energy would be used for this purpose.

The mutual benefit to both businesses was obvious. They sponsored some of the initial installations, and that helped give us both credibility and visibility. With their confidence and support, we have seen the development of a nationwide charging station network over the past decade, with Elektromotive involved every step of the way.

(Calvey Taylor-Haw, MD, Elektromotive Ltd)

In Elektromotive's case, what was holding the company back from scaling up its operation and developing a commercial platform was customer confidence – an issue which partnering for credibility went a long way towards resolving.

Mike Herd has been the Director at the Sussex Innovation Centre, a technology business incubator, since 1997. The Centre, based at the University of Sussex, provides tailored accommodation and assistance to over 100 early-stage technology companies and research commercialization projects, and has developed a wide range of specialist entrepreneurial support initiatives. The Centre has a high profile nationally, an excellent track record and is frequently cited as an example of best practice. Mike was named Sussex Businessman of the Year in November 2000, was the National Achievement in Business Incubation Award in 2007 and in 2013 received the Queen's Award for Enterprise Promotion, in recognition of his ongoing efforts to foster, promote and support entrepreneurship.

Tel: 01273 704 400; e-mail: mike@sinc.co.uk; web: www.sinc.co.uk

Ideas in the incubator

David Gill at St John's Innovation Centre in Cambridge discusses what early-stage ventures can expect to learn in an incubator

Users rarely beat a path to the door of the inventor. The move from a focus on technology to solving customer problems is the hard part of innovation.

Market focus is often a key discipline instilled in tenants by incubators, especially tenants from a tech background, who might otherwise fixate on technical originality at the expense of customer need. Early-stage firms and novice entrepreneurs in particular tend to need assistance with both marketing and innovation, and over the past dozen years in the UK, business incubation has emerged as an effective forum for combining help with both.

From necessity to opportunity

The first recognizable incubator was created in 1959 in Batavia in up-state New York, a classic example of a crisis creating an opportunity: closure of an 850,000 sq ft multi-storey Massey-Ferguson factory left unemployment rates at 20 per cent and an empty building, unlettable to a single occupant.

Entrepreneur Joe Mancuso created the Batavia Industrial Center (BIC) by sub-dividing the site, providing shared office services, assistance with capital-raising and business advice – amenities that established corporations take for granted but which small firms struggle for. BIC generated numerous spin-offs, providing grow-on space for expanding tenants – a critical need of successful incubators to this day.

The Batavia example was taken up in the UK a generation later, with the opening in 1987 of the St John's Innovation Centre, owned by St John's College in Cambridge. In 1997, research conducted by Malcolm Buckler of HM Treasury identified 42 named incubators in Britain (25 extant, others in formation) and led to the creation of UK Business Incubation, the professional association for the industry, which today has around 160 members. The European Business Network includes some 150 Business and Innovation Centres across 42 countries and the National Business Incubator Association based in Ohio has about 1,900 members worldwide.

Defining business incubation

While no single template applies to all variants (adaptation to circumstances is critical to success), business incubation can be defined as: *a flexible combination of people, processes and premises designed to accelerate ambitious firms through key development stages.*

What this means in practice was implicit in the Batavia experiment 50 years ago: a combination of shared premises and services, with a centre management team to provide advice and contacts; formal and informal training programmes; guidance in becoming investment-ready; 'warm' introductions to advisers, investors, new staff and potential customers. In addition to providing presentable premises for client and investor meetings, the incubator is also frequently a 'good address' for early-stage firms, especially if its entry criteria add credibility to tenants in the eyes of investors and customers.

Ownership (public, private, academic) and business model (for profit, community interest) differ widely, but at heart incubators supply the key needs of ambitious firms by: taking the burden of premises issues off their shoulders; and providing them with tools and contacts to accelerate their growth.

It follows that time spent in an incubator should be intensive and finite: if many firms begin incubation with just two or three founders, their goal should be to leave within perhaps three to five years once they are large and strong enough to justify having their own 'front door'. Incubators assist with the 'natural pursuit by entrepreneurs of opportunities without regard to resources they currently control', but soon the internal locus of control of founders should lead them to move on.

Incubators or incubation?

Fashions afflict incubation as other sectors. In the United States, after a wave of dot.com popularity, incubators were often seen as 'homes for sick dogs' providing little more than 'heat, light and dial tone'. Nowadays in American usage 'incubator' may mean a seed fund with premises attached – an unusual arrangement in Europe. In the UK:

- In the noughties, following a spate of construction of new centres led by public sources, capacity (availability of physical units of accommodation) began to outstrip capability (people and programmes to advise growth firms).

- The pendulum then began to swing away from the 'edifice complex', with *incubation* (mentoring, training) seen as more important than *incubators* (physical premises). This overlooked the physical advantages of incubators, including the common practice of providing short, flexible leases: small firms cannot commit to the 15- or 25-year lease (with upward-only rent reviews) common for commercial lettings, and many will pay higher rent in exchange for the right to move on at short notice – typically one or three months.

- More recently, a consensus has emerged that incubation is often more effective when based in a dedicated building, which acts as 'clubhouse' for varied coaching and training activities and also facilitates peer-to-peer learning, a key feature of incubation. Premises and programmes can be configured to work together; home-working is least helpful when teams are undergoing intense formative stages.

Accelerators: old wine in new bottles?

Accelerator programmes are a specific subset of incubation not necessarily linked to a particular location. Inspired by successful schemes in the United States (Y Combinator, angelpad, Techstars), they have proliferated in Europe in the past five years. As with incubators, no one template applies to all models but characteristic features include the following:

1 A rigorous selection process for acceptance on to the programme, securing a manageable cohort of 20 to 50 companies. Some accelerators are sector or theme specific (social media, internet of things), others focused on stage of development or commercial potential. Since accelerators seek to engage only with the best companies most likely to succeed in the short term, the question arises whether supply of programmes in Europe will soon exceed the supply of quality candidate firms.

2 Time-limited, often 'boot camp'-style duration (perhaps six weeks to four months), with a combination of lectures for all participants, individual team mentoring and time spent revisiting the business plan (often having to pivot, or adjust direction quickly) and seeking out early-adopter customers.

3 Some accelerators in Europe cover the majority of their costs through government grants or private sponsorship, but the US model favours remuneration of the organizers (often experienced entrepreneurs turned investors) in the form of shares in participant firms, with many accelerators stipulating a fixed equity percentage (3–6 per cent). This investment may also provide just enough cash for the founders to survive on the programme.

4 Accelerators often conclude with cohort companies pitching to panels of professional investors, the success of the programme depending on its long-run ability to secure funding for participants. Given the dearth of venture funding in Europe, it is unclear how well a model based on attaining substantial equity investment will translate from its Californian origins over the longer term.

In reality, accelerators are a potentially useful subset of the wider incubation process, which in almost every sector (except apps?) will likely take years rather than the months allowed by accelerator 'boot camps'. Properly structured, accelerators and 'clubhouse' incubation complement each other – as do incubators and science parks (designed for larger research-based firms), and incubators and hives of hot-desking entrepreneurship such as Google Campus in East London or ideaSpace Enterprise Accelerator in Cambridge (aimed at start-ups).

Schemes and markets

Examples of the advantages to entrepreneurs of joining an incubator include accelerated access to internationalization and managing intellectual property:

- One of the responsibilities of incubator managers is to keep abreast of government and other schemes to assist growth firms in a way that founders themselves find difficult given the number and complexity of such programmes. For instance, incubators have a valuable signposting role for the publications and services provided by the Intellectual Property Office (IPO). Patents matter to innovators because they enable inventors to 'keep other people off their lawn'. Incubators use their convening power to organize regular training sessions with intellectual property advisers for cohorts of tenants.

- As with the IPO, so with the Technology Strategy Board (TSB). Especially in tech sectors, incubators help guide tenants to identify and apply for grants (SMART awards, for instance) and other assistance through competitive tender. Grants are a complex and specialist area that can be daunting for entrepreneurs; incubators will most likely provide experts to advise on availability, suitability and process.

- Incubators can also be expected to work closely with agencies facilitating trade, such as UK Trade & Investment (UKTI) or the UK–India Business Council (UKIBC). Furthermore, many incubators belong to international organizations and as a result build up useful networks of like-minded contacts in key overseas geographies, even hosting study or trade delegations from partner organizations abroad.

- As a result, the incubator management is well placed to seek advice on behalf of tenants from overseas partners on establishing a presence abroad. A vital lesson from highly innovative clusters is the need for high-potential start-ups to build internationalism into their corporate DNA from the outset, and witnessing other companies in an incubator operate in this way subliminally inspires the next generation.

- The 'good address' principle also applies for tenants seeking to export or set up a new office. Working out of an established incubator can lend credibility to young firms with great products but few resources or employees.

- Some incubators also participate in reciprocal 'soft landing' schemes, enabling tenants in one country to be hosted in an incubator in another for a limited number of days at low cost while exploratory commercial discussions take place, assisted by the host incubator.

The bottom line

Incubators tend to be run by experienced teams with credibility arising from a track record of building successful businesses. The team helps accelerate the progress of ambitious entrepreneurs by acting as a 'translator' or facilitator for tenants between different worlds – academia and commerce, grants and investment, the UK and export markets. 'If you want to be first class, first join a class': joining the right incubator can tip the balance quickly towards higher achievement for motivated entrepreneurs. But as every school knows, each success is ultimately that of the student – or tenant.

St John's Innovation Centre (SJIC) is a property-based incubator designed for knowledge-intensive enterprises in their early stages. It offers flexible accommodation alongside assistance with growing and running a business, especially the commercial exploitation of technology. Founded by St John's College, Cambridge, in 1987, SJIC is an EU-accredited Business and Innovation Centre (BIC) and a founder member of UK Business Incubation.

David Gill was appointed Managing Director of the St John's Innovation Centre in October 2008. He previously set up and ran the Innovation & Technology Unit at HSBC Bank in London (1997–2004), before serving as an executive director of ETCapital Ltd, a venture firm focused on early-stage, technology-based investments. A Sloan Fellow at the Stanford Graduate School of Business in California (2005), David is currently an Academic Collaborator at the University of Cambridge Institute for Manufacturing, a non-executive director of UK Business Incubation Ltd and a member of the Department for Business Access to Finance Expert Group.

BIC: www.ebn.eu; UK Business Incubation: www.ukbi.co.uk

Finding the right revenue model for your IP

Sarah Boxall at Boxall IPM weighs up the strategic alternatives in commercializing an innovation

When constructing and managing an intellectual property (IP) portfolio, consideration should always be given to the commercial end goal for the product(s) protected by the portfolio. This enables the IP to be tailored to achieve maximum return on investment.

There are three basic commercial end-points that influence IP decisions:

1 Keep the product development and sale in-house with direct exploitation of IP.
2 License the product with indirect exploitation of IP.
3 Divest the product and IP.

A decision on a preferred route is best taken early in the life cycle of a product as the decision enables efficient management of the IP portfolio protecting the product, as well as control of expenditure on the portfolio. Ultimately, the decision is driven by financial considerations, in particular when cash is most needed.

1. Keep the product in-house

For a cash-rich company, keeping a product and its IP in-house is the best option as control can be maintained on everything from patent strategy to marketing and branding. However, this is an expensive option in the short, medium and long term.

IP is an evolving creature and, as a product/service develops, the IP needs to keep pace. Development and refinement of a product or service usually brings new ideas and creations into play and so new IP arises. Similarly, as products and services move on, old services and products fall out of use and so the IP loses its fundamental value to an organization. However, such IP may be of interest or even essential to a third party and so should not be written off.

A positive outcome from this position is that more consideration can be given to whether the IP is worth registering or whether common law rights, trade secrets and confidentiality should be relied upon. The bottom line is whether the financial return on the product covers the cost of IP registration.

2. License the product

Licensing provides flexibility to divide an IP and product portfolio to suit a company's needs, both for the licensor and the licensee. Licensing also provides an income stream that can be tailored to suit the cash needs of a company.

For example, a small enterprise is likely to need up-front cash to fund R&D of new and existing products. Therefore, a licence deal that is weighted towards a larger up-front lump sum payment is desirable, with lower downstream milestone and royalty payments. A company with more financial backing may be looking for a more long-term revenue stream and so higher royalties become an important factor, with lower up-front and milestone payments.

Other considerations with licensing include how much control the licensor wishes to keep over the portfolio. An exclusive licence enables a single licensee to exploit the IP rights, to the exclusion of the licensor. This could be considered a halfway house to total divestment, allowing the licensor to be a party only to enforcement of the rights.

For some companies, the need to be able to continue R&D in a particular field or territory is important and so a sole or non-exclusive licence is preferable. A sole licence allows a single licensee while a non-exclusive licence allows multiple licence holders. When negotiating the first licence for a portfolio, consideration needs to be given to future commercial plans for the licensor as it may be desirable to have, for example, an exclusive licensee in one field worldwide and non-exclusive licensees in single territories or regions across a broader field of use.

Cross-licenses are a useful tool when parties wish to use each other's IP to advance a collaboration or partnership, or even to settle a litigation issue. In such a case, financial considerations play a smaller role in deciding which licence option is most suitable.

3. Divest the product

If a product and its associated IP portfolio are no longer of commercial interest to a company, or a company needs to raise funds, then divestment is an option. Obviously, careful consideration needs to be taken to make sure that the product and IP really are no longer of commercial interest.

The IP portfolio should be constructed with a view to divestment at a particular stage in product development. Again, taking a decision on when a portfolio is to be divested, as well as identifying potential acquirers, early in the product process is important to maximize return on investment in the portfolio.

IP should, more likely than not, be registered to provide tangible assets to which a financial value may be applied. More nebulous IP, such as know-how and trade secrets, is harder to identify with precision and it is also harder to estimate its value. However, such rights should always be included in any divested package.

Filing strategies should also be aligned with the territorial landscape of any potential acquiring partner. If your company's commercial interests are in Europe and the United States but your nearest competitor and most likely acquirer of product and rights is most active in South America, it is a sensible investment to ensure that IP is protected in countries that are of likely commercial interest to both parties.

There is also value in studying the behaviour of a potential acquirer so that your IP portfolio and product are an easy fit with the potential acquirer. For example, if the potential acquirer is aggressive in its marketing and litigation, patent and trade mark strategies should be similarly aggressive.

IP portfolio decisions are also influenced by when the portfolio is likely to be divested. If pre-product launch, the portfolio will be focused on patent rights having sufficient breadth to provide an acquirer with maximum scope for choosing the right product. If post-product launch, the portfolio will have more emphasis on trade marks, patent term extensions, data exclusivity and non-registerable IP rights.

Whatever revenue path is chosen, IP should be integrated into a business plan. A strong, focused, well-managed intellectual property portfolio provides market exclusivity, and planned and full exploitation provides a return on investment.

Dr Sarah Boxall is a Chartered UK and European Patent Attorney and US Patent Agent at Boxall IPM Ltd. Boxall IPM is a boutique IP firm offering strategic management of IP portfolios, as well as a range of IP services from patent and trade mark drafting and prosecution to commercial advice and negotiations. The company has a particular interest in biotechnology, health care and the life sciences.

Tel: 01304 615226; e-mail: sarah.boxall@boxallipm.com; web: www.boxallipm.com

tech city · open source · android · global protection · strategic guidance · competitive advantage · cloud computing · patent box · start-ups · shoreditch · javascript · iOS · big data · software · ruby on rails · NoSQL · technology · innovation · attract funding · leverage R&D · apps · patents · growth · IP portfolio

rational
INTELLECTUAL PROPERTY

Patent and Trade Mark Attorneys
Software Protection Specialists

www.rationalip.com | +44 20 7504 1066 | 81 Rivington Street, London, EC2A 3AY

Leveraging IP for tech start-ups

Intelligent allocation of resources into intellectual property can be immensely remunerative, says Gerard Chandrahasen of Rational IP Ltd

One of the most important considerations for companies when considering intellectual property (IP) is aligning the intellectual property strategy with the business strategy. Start-ups need to be careful in allocating their resources. An ill-advised investment in intellectual property at too early a stage in business development can undermine success. However, intelligent allocation of resources into intellectual property can be immensely remunerative.

Technology start-ups have three core areas of value: people, product and IP. Generally, to grow quickly tech start-ups must access investment. This can come in the form of a 'friends and family' round, an angel round, or, later, a VC round. Of course, some fortunate start-ups can self-fund their expansion using revenue. For the rest, investment in intellectual property should be based in an effort to attract and secure investment.

Investors are interested in the addressable market for your product or service. A large or profitable market is generally necessary before investors will commit to a funding round. The corollary of this is that investors are interested in the competition for that market, and consequently, in any barriers to entry to that market for competitors.

Intellectual property can form a barrier to entry because it provides a monopoly right that can be used to prevent others from copying your brand (in the case of trade marks), your designs (in the case of copyright and registered design) and your ideas (in the case of patents).

Maximizing value from your intellectual property

To create successful companies, entrepreneurs and CEOs must have a fundamental understanding of the narrative of the company: its purpose, its value and its goals.

To be valuable, intellectual property must be aligned with this narrative. For example, if the story of your business is the development of innovative technology relating to payments where the United States is a major market and VISA or MasterCard are key competitors, then the business may want to apply for several patents protecting core aspects of that technology in the United States. The IP strategy can then be explained to investors, customers and acquisition targets as:

> We have developed new payment technology which will revolutionize the payments sector. Opportunities for acquisition or licensing reside within major credit card companies. We have applied for several patents in the United States covering our core technology. These potential monopoly rights prevent duplication of our technology and aim to create a licensing bidding war among potential acquirers.

To effectively align IP with the narrative of the company, an understanding of the purposes of IP is necessary. There are several uses to which IP can be put during the life of a company:

1. Attract investment

Early-stage investors look for companies that are attractive to later investment, and late-stage investment, particularly series B or C rounds, are often predicated on your company holding a strong IP portfolio.

Therefore, constructing an IP portfolio can encourage investment from these early-stage investors.

2. Competitor deterrence

While your brand reputation is becoming established in the market, the creation and use of a similar brand by a competitor could divert potential customers. A registered trade mark for your brand establishes your priority rights to that brand.

The deployment of unique technology will often attract imitators looking to capitalize on the impact of your innovation in the market. A pending or granted patent may help to indicate to competitors that the concepts underlying your technology are not just novel and inventive, but proprietary.

3. Defensive – first to invent

Many other companies utilize the patent system to secure monopoly rights in innovations. This can place you at a disadvantage even if you were the original creator of the innovation. A patent once granted is presumed to be valid and it can be difficult, expensive and time consuming to revoke a patent. Accordingly, it may be prudent to apply for patents for those innovations you consider to be core to your business. Particular attention should be given to this issue if you sell into the United States. Companies within the United States seek patents at a greater frequency than the UK, and your company being based outside the United States is no defence to patent infringement.

Additionally, some companies, known as non-practising entities or 'patent trolls', are in the business of threatening companies with patent infringement. Your earlier patents covering the same innovation can be used to undermine this threat.

4. Defensive – cross-licence

In a crowded field, you may be accused of infringing the IP rights of another company. In this situation, it can be useful to have secured your own patent portfolio, because it may be that the accusing company is infringing your patent rights.

A threat of counter-suit can encourage the other side to negotiate a cross-licensing arrangement, which gives you the right to use its IP in exchange for its right to use your IP.

5. Tax breaks

In the UK, from 1 April 2013, corporations which pay tax within the UK can place worldwide profits from products incorporating a UK or European granted patent into a Patent Box. The corporate tax rate for these profits is effectively halved.

6. Improve exit

IP is an asset much like any other part of your business. Building IP assets during the life of the company is, therefore, a prudent action that will increase the value of the company for trade sale or IPO.

Dispelling common myths

As well as understanding the purposes of IP, it is also important to understand common misconceptions about IP that may be raised by potential investors, partners, customers and acquirers.

By being prepared for these misconceptions, you can ensure that your IP retains its value in their perception.

1. IP is expensive to defend

Generally IP is never attacked unless you use it offensively and, even then, most IP disputes are settled well before court. IP should be best considered as a means to force the other side to the negotiating table, rather than a blunt legal instrument.

2. Software can't be patented

Novel and inventive concepts that reside within innovative software can be patented in the United States, and can even be patented in the UK and Europe if the concepts relate to technical solutions to technical problems.

3. IP is expensive to obtain

Any investment in IP should be considered with a keen eye on return on investment (ROI). In any event, development of any IP strategy will focus on maximization of value within a budget.

4. Patents have no value because they can be designed around

Well-drafted patents can prove to be difficult to design around, because they are crafted with these attempts in mind.

5. The software field moves too quickly, so patents aren't valuable

Many key concepts within software do not change completely but evolve or develop. Well-drafted patents protect concepts in a way that accommodates this evolution.

6. Patents take a long time to grant

This is not actually a misconception. In the United States, patents can take six years to grant. In Europe, seven years is not uncommon. The UK is somewhat faster at about three years.

However, a patent obtains much of its value at the date it is filed rather than the date it is granted, because damages can often be obtained for infringement of any subsequently granted patent back to the date that the pending patent is first published. Therefore, other companies are careful not to develop technology covered by a pending patent.

7. IP is more valuable for big companies

Intellectual property investment is an arena of diminishing returns, which benefits small companies. Furthermore, in any litigation, owing to deep pockets, large companies have the most to lose, which encourages them to negotiate an early resolution to any infringement allegation.

Summary

Intellectual property is a key interest for a company at all stages of its life cycle, and tech start-ups, in particular, have much to gain by careful investment in a protection strategy.

Gerard Chandrahasen is a Chartered and European Patent Attorney and Intellectual Property Solicitor at Rational IP Limited. He has a background in computer science and has advised companies from Mind Candy to Hewlett-Packard on intellectual property issues.

Further details: tel: 020 7504 1066; e-mail: gerard@rationalip.com; web: www.rationalip.com

PART ELEVEN
IP fit for purpose

Value-for-money IP

Matthew Smith at Mewburn Ellis discusses how to budget without budging

Most businesses generate intellectual property (IP). Identifying what it is, and harnessing it to increase business profitability, can be costly. In the current economic environment, many companies are having to reconsider their IP strategy in view of those costs.

'Value for money' is therefore of great importance now – but when has it not been? A well-thought-out IP strategy gives value for money without a need to compromise too greatly on strength and flexibility. That is true no matter the prevailing economic wind.

The foundations

Like any structure, a good IP portfolio is based on good foundations. A solid place to start is identifying the 'cornerstones' on which your business is built: strong protection of those is vital.

So, you must ask yourself: why does (or will) my company have the edge over my competition? Be specific: a general answer such as 'our better quality product' or 'we are more well known' will not be useful. Why is your product better quality? Why are you more well known? Are there technical features which make your product work better? Is your logo particularly recognizable? In particular, identify any trends that appear. Perhaps multiple products share common technical features, or a striking appearance is common across a product range.

Looked at differently, ask yourself: what do (or will) I need to stop other people doing if my company is going to retain its advantage and success? Those are probably the things on which an IP strategy should focus.

Of course, avaricious though it sounds, 'commercial success' is to an extent based on revenue. A company's most 'successful' products are often those that bring in the most revenue. There is little point focusing on IP surrounding a product or service that is only ever going to find a small market if, in doing so, the budget for less 'exciting' but more monetarily important products or services is reduced.

By identifying the commercial cornerstones of your company's success, present or future, you can focus on priorities for IP protection. By doing this, unnecessary expenditure on protection which is not critical can be avoided.

The roles of IP

IP can play two very different roles in a commercial setting: attractive and repulsive. More and more, a strong IP portfolio is used as an attractive force when companies seek investment – investors are very aware of the importance of IP, and although they may be attracted by 'good science', they also (of course) need to think about 'good business'. The absence of an appropriate IP strategy can be a deal-breaker.

Equally, the traditional role of IP as a 'keep off the grass' sign to competitors remains. The ability to exclude competitors is an important one. It can be used for market preservation or as a bargaining tool.

Recently, some countries' governments have introduced legislation which adds a third role for certain types of IP: as a tool for reducing taxation. These legislations (often called a 'Patent Box' or the like) seek to encourage innovation by giving tax breaks to companies with relevant IP rights.

IP strategy must therefore take account of these roles.

Before you start building – ownership

Before rushing ahead, it's worth taking some time to consider the ownership of the relevant IP. Laws relating to IP ownership are by no means straightforward, and often businesses fall into the trap of thinking that, if they paid for the development, they must own the product. Often that is the case, but not always.

Particular problems can arise, for example, where a subcontractor or consultant is used, or where there is collaboration between companies. It is always best to have agreements in place at an early stage (preferably before work begins), which set out ownership of any IP generated.

It is generally easier to sort out issues of ownership sooner rather than later. The longer one waits, the more likely it is that key evidence will be mislaid, for example, or that the level of investments by different companies will make matters more contentious. It is therefore prudent to determine at an early stage the identity of any individuals who have contributed to development of the IP, followed by a check to make sure that the necessary rights have passed from those individuals to the business.

How to build

In constructing an IP portfolio, a wide range of building blocks is available. Each has different uses. Each has different associated costs. Even the ways in which they are obtained vary widely.

Some IP rights come into existence automatically (for example copyright in the UK). Stronger 'registered' rights, such as patents, registered trade marks and registered designs, must be specifically applied for. Sometimes, keeping something as a 'trade secret' can be just as effective.

For any product or service, various rights covering different aspects can make up the protective IP tapestry. Patents cover innovative technical features, while designs protect the appearance of a product. Trade marks protect things like slogans and logos which help customers identify the origin of a given product or service.

So, a product might be protected by way of a patent covering a technical aspect of the mechanism, a registered design covering the look of the product, trade marks covering the manufacturer's logo and the name of the product.

Of course, with costs in mind each piece of the tapestry must be considered. Patents are expensive, but can protect a technical idea which applies to many different products. Copyright is free to obtain in the UK (since it is automatic), but is more difficult to enforce successfully.

Where to build

IP rights are territorial. The more territories in which you want protection, the more IP rights will be needed. The more IP rights that are wanted, the higher costs will be.

Most, if not all, businesses cannot afford to pursue every possible type of protection in every possible country. Therefore they must adopt an approach whereby protection is sought in some countries and not others. Typically, protection is sought in large or strategically important markets and, where they are well defined, countries where competitors operate (for example to manufacture their products).

This approach cannot keep competitors off the market entirely. However, if a competitor's only route is to set up new manufacturing facilities and sell in small markets, they may be significantly discouraged. By picking off major markets with targeted IP protection, then, a business may still be able to make healthy profits while accepting that in smaller markets they must share the spoils.

Timing and costs

Like comedy, a lot of IP strategy is about timing. Unfortunately, that is generally where the similarities end.

The time at which IP rights are applied for can be very important. It is particularly so for patents: it is important that the first applications are filed before the invention for which protection is sought is made public. This is because the question of whether or not protection is granted is decided based on what was known to the public at the time the application was made. Further, registered IP rights in most countries are granted on a 'first come, first served' basis.

With this in mind, there can be understandable concern: must important decisions on which countries and rights are wanted be made before any filing is done? Delay might be very disadvantageous in a competitive field. Fortunately, systems exist that enable the most costly decisions to be delayed significantly.

Taking patents as an example, it is usual that the first application is filed at a local patent office (such as the UK Intellectual Property Office). The date of that first filing is called the 'priority date'. Applications for the same invention can then be filed in other countries. If they are filed within 12 months of the priority date, they are treated as if they had been filed on the priority date.

Things can be pushed out still further. An 'international patent application' can be filed. That acts as a bundle of patent applications covering nearly every country in the world. Only after two and a half years from the priority date does it split down into separate patent applications for individual countries or regions. The applications for countries which are wanted are kept, and the others left to expire.

Where applications covering an entire geographical region are available (for example in Europe), things may be delayed still further, with selection of individual countries within the region coming still later in the procedure.

Therefore, it is often possible to delay until a time when the project has either taken off or failed, allowing a better-informed decision to be made about which (if any) countries are wanted.

Keeping up with the Joneses

Developing your own IP portfolio is obviously worthwhile. Therefore it should come as no surprise that your competitors will be doing the same with their own portfolios – and that might impact on you in just the same ways as you hope your own portfolio will impact on them!

Therefore, a complete IP strategy will not only look inward, at your company's activity, but also outward, at your competitors'. That might involve, for example, periodically reviewing their filings for registered IP rights. That can give hints as to their new product developments, and allow you to start working to avoid any potential infringement of a competitor's rights or on strategies to attack their portfolio.

Building your own IP portfolio is only one part of the overall strategy. To keep on top of things, vigilance is required. Are new IP registrations needed for a particular product or development? Can previous registrations be dropped? What is the competition up to, and how will that affect you?

Build your IP portfolio carefully and strongly, and it can prove a powerful commercial force offering excellent value for money. Build it unwisely, and loss of money, rights and commercial position are all very possible.

Matthew Smith is a Patent Attorney at Mewburn Ellis LLP, one of Europe's premier IP firms, with over 60 patent and trade mark attorneys and technical specialists, covering the full range of intellectual property issues, including patents (in all technology areas), trade marks, designs, copyright and related matters.

Matthew has a degree in chemistry from the University of Oxford. He joined Mewburn Ellis in 2006, qualifying as a Chartered Patent Attorney and European Patent Attorney in 2010. His work is mainly in the chemical and pharmaceutical fields.

Further details are available from Mewburn Ellis LLP, 33 Gutter Lane, London EC2V 8AS; tel: +44 (0)20 7776 5300; e-mail: matthew.smith@mewburn.com; web: www.mewburn.com

A combination of rights

Dr Sarah Boxall at Boxall IPM discusses the layers of protection that can sit round an idea

Intellectual property (IP) needs to provide exclusivity for a product so that the product is able to compete in the marketplace for the life of the product, as well as provide a return on investment in the product. The most efficient way to identify IP is to look at the product as a whole and to hang IP onto the appropriate parts.

The first, basic question is how does the product work? Patents protect technical subject matter, such as apparatus, methods and processes, and (bio)chemical compositions. To obtain a patent, an invention must be new, inventive and applicable on an industrial scale. In return for disclosing full details of a patentable invention, a national government provides 20 years of exclusivity that enables the patent holder to stop others from exploiting that invention, provided that annual renewal fees are paid.

While patents are the most obvious form of IP for technical features, there is much knowledge and know-how that goes into the development and production of a product that is able to compete successfully in the marketplace. Know-how, trade secrets and confidential information add value to an IP portfolio and the product itself. However, these non-registerable rights need careful management to ensure that they stay secret. Regular education of a workforce is imperative to minimize the likelihood of sensitive information being publicized.

If the product includes computer code, then such code will (generally) be protected by copyright: most jurisdictions in the world do not allow the patenting of software, with the United States being the most high-profile exception. Within the European Union, the Computer Programs Directive controls the legal protection of computer programs under copyright law and provides exclusivity for life of the author plus 70 years for computer code.

Any results or technical information that is held in a database will also attract IP in the form of database rights. A database right is considered to be a property right, comparable to but distinct from copyright, that exists to recognize the investment that is made in compiling a database, even when this does not involve the 'creative' aspect that is reflected by copyright. Database rights last for 15 years. However, each time a database is substantially modified, a new set of rights are created for that database. Owners have the right to object to the copying of substantial parts of their database, even if data are extracted and reconstructed piecemeal.

Clinical data for pharmaceutical products automatically attract data exclusivity, preventing a third party from launching a copycat product using the innovator's clinical data. In the EU, clinical trial data exclusivity provides at least 10 years of exclusivity, which can be extremely valuable when other IP, namely patents, has expired.

Once IP around the technical side of a product has been identified, the next stage is to look at non-technical and non-functional features and any arising IP.

Designs encompass shape, feel, lines, contours, textures, colour combinations, materials and ornamentation, that is, features that are 'pleasing to the eye'. There are two types of design rights available: registered rights and unregistered rights. However, the criteria for attracting design protection are the same for both types of rights, in that a design must be novel or original and have an individual character. A registered design is entitled to up to 25 years of protection from the date of filing on payment of renewal fees every five years, while unregistered rights attract 15 years of protection from the end of the year in which the design is recorded in a document or article or 10 years from date on which the design was first offered for sale or hire.

Copyright may reside in, for example, instructions for use and/or assembly, drawings, technical plans and specifications. Copyright is a common law right that arises automatically on creation of an original work and protects works such as literary, dramatic, musical or artistic creations, both published and unpublished, against copying by others. In most of the world, the default length of copyright is the life of the author plus either 50 or 70 years.

Whether or not there are technical features in a product, a product will almost always be marketed under a brand, and a strong brand is invaluable as the battle for customers intensifies day by day. Brands are protected by trade marks and serve as a badge of origin that identifies services or goods as arising from a particular provider. A trade mark must be capable of distinguishing products or services and must be distinctive. For example, the word 'computer' could not be used as a trade mark for computers because a) it is not a distinctive word and b) it describes the product to which it is applied. The best trade marks are those using made-up words, such as Kodak®. However, trade mark protection is also available for colour combinations, sounds, smells and logos. As with designs, both registered (®) and unregistered rights (™) are available. Registered rights provide an absolute right to stop others using the same or a similar mark for the same or similar goods and/or services, while the much higher hurdle of confusion and passing off is required for unregistered rights. Registered trade marks have an indefinite term provided the rights are renewed every 10 years.

When thinking about branding and trade marks, domain names must not be forgotten as the power of the internet and its global importance continue to grow. The restriction on generic top-level domain names (gTLD) was abolished on 12 January 2012, so companies and organizations are now able to choose essentially arbitrary top-level internet domains, including domains using non-Latin characters (such as Cyrillic, Arabic, Chinese).

IP rights set one entity apart from another and are the basis from which wealth realization and commerce occur, as well as adding investment and trade value to an organization. To that end, the generation of a portfolio of IP for a product using as many rights on offer as possible not only presents a complex hurdle to a competitor but, most importantly, adds significant value to the product and, in turn, the commercializing company.

Dr Sarah Boxall is a Chartered UK and European Patent Attorney and US Patent Agent at Boxall IPM Ltd. Boxall IPM is a boutique IP firm offering strategic management of IP portfolios, as well as a range of IP services from patent and trade mark drafting and prosecution to commercial advice and negotiations. The company has a particular interest in biotechnology, health care and the life sciences.

Tel: 01304 615226; e-mail: sarah.boxall@boxallipm.com;
web: www.boxallipm.com

Broad or narrow

If you cannot look into the future, how do you determine the scope of your patent for an innovative idea? Ilya Kazi at Mathys & Squire recommends taking a commercial approach

To determine the ideal scope of a patent, one needs to take an idea, look forward 20 years to anticipate all developments in technology, and determine everything a business or any of its competitors or partners might wish to do around the idea within the life of the patent.

To ensure that it will be valid, one then needs to subtract all prior art available in any form anywhere on earth, factor in the varying standards in each jurisdiction regarding the assessment of obviousness and patentability, and formulate a set of claims taking into account varying requirements for unity of invention.

Unfortunately, notwithstanding expansion of online searching and a wealth of technology commentators and trends reports, current technology does not permit one to look reliably into the future nor to form a complete picture of available art within a finite budget.

So, given constraints of imperfect knowledge and finite resources, what should one do? Having some idea of the background art, a common simplistic starting point is to start with a broad claim that is barely defensible over the art one is certain exists.

Such an approach is academically attractive and it is not *wrong* as it is generally impossible to go back and seek broader protection later. However, if insufficient thought is given to realistic defensible fall-back positions, the patent application may turn into a balloon that simply bursts under pressure when the main claim is knocked out. In addition, in certain commercial situations this simplistic approach may also not prove optimal, however, for certain commercial situations if it leads to greater costs or delays in prosecution than can be tolerated.

Thus, in the author's view, producing optimal IP protection for a growing business should be viewed as an engineering or architecture process in its own right with multiple strands.

Strategic planning

A deep understanding of the technology, from what it is to how it might evolve, is important, but not enough. Knowledge of a business and its plans and potential markets is another key element, as is a view of likely competitors and threats. Some of this, such as analysing the art and the invention, is a science. Gaining a feel for a business and its likely operating environment is more of an art. However, IP strategy is neither a science nor an art but a business; it must be put together in a manner which makes commercial sense, which means the cost must be related to the potential value to the business.

One should not be satisfied with not knowing enough about the business plans to take this into account when drafting claims. Seeking patent protection implicitly involves a decision that the initial filing expenditure is justified, and this should be challenged and projected forward.

The IP needs of a well-funded organization that is actively licensing technology, from a major high-technology manufacturer with large numbers of innovations, to a latecomer to a technology area, a low-technology manufacturer in a competitive low-margin field, or a technology incubator or a start-up with funding constraints, all differ. After acting for all of the above, I know that, although the optimum approach to IP strategy for a given innovation varies for each type of entity, it must also be remembered that one may evolve into another over time.

Despite differing needs, one thing that is common to all is that there should be, at some level, an analysis of the broadest possible *claims* that one might try. Emphasis is placed on the plural as it is rare that an invention is so simple or its application so limited that there is only one element or revenue stream to protect.

A given innovation may generate subsequent opportunities for potential services, markets for derivative or disposable/recyclable products or accessories, or alternative applications in other fields. For example, an innovation in a printer head nozzle may potentially have opened up a market in printing alternative substrates such as T-shirts, made viable a customized web-based service, a market for refills and have applications in medicine or drug dispensing.

Prior art

Strategic analysis intrinsically requires some knowledge of the prior art. Searching for it is an open-ended and unsatisfying task as it can only yield negative results.

The resources allocated to searching should thus be commensurate with the nature and value of a venture. Where this is heavily dependent on patent protection for viability, a greater level of confidence in the likely scope of protection available may be required and extensive searching may be justified.

In many cases, however, given a basic indication that there is likely to be something worth protecting, resources are better expended on constructing fall-back positions, taking a general background picture and an educated guess based on judgement and experience as to what is likely to turn up.

Although prior art searching is generally unsatisfying and freedom to operate searching has a different emphasis, there can be some synergies in search strategy. For an entrant to an unfamiliar market, searching to gain both competitor intelligence and a better knowledge of the art to guide future IP strategy may be valuable.

Framing claims

When framing claims, an important issue to consider is the extent to which an idea may be applied to fields outside the core field and the amount of resource allocated to secondary claims or claims at the margins.

For an active licensor, an ambitious strategy may be appropriate. For a start-up, claiming fields widely outside any realistic business may expose an application to attack from art which might not otherwise have come into play. If an applicant has implicitly admitted that other fields are related, retrenching subsequently may leave an examiner pursuing an obviousness attack based on art outside the field.

For inventions which are at the margins of patentability, particularly software innovations, patentability issues may be exacerbated by over-ambitious claiming. Moreover, given ever-increasing claims fees and more restrictive approaches to division and number of claims allowable, patent prosecution costs become a serious consideration.

In practice, owing to procedural and financial constraints, the examination process is non-conservative. Starting too broad with the plan of narrowing to a more realistic claim may not get the same end result as starting with something closer to the more realistic claim might have done.

An overly ambitious or academic strategy may mean that a start-up spends more on prosecution than can be justified and may end up, owing to financial constraints, obtaining no protection, rather than more quickly and effectively obtaining protection which is practically useful. Even for a larger organization, all budgets are finite. Over-zealous protection of one innovation may impact adversely on budget available to protect another innovation, or to enforce or license protection.

While one should always consider the broadest claims potentially available, it does not necessarily follow that one should always file starting with the broadest conceivable claim.

In some cases, basis for the broadest claims might be included in the form of additional statements of invention or clear statements positively teaching alternatives or in later claims. This particularly applies in software cases where a broader claim may be allowable in one jurisdiction but not another. If a tactical decision is made to run for home with the first application, the option can be retained of fighting a bigger battle another day while the core business, protected by a quickly granted and credible patent, is generating revenue to justify and fund the fight.

In some business models, a multi-track approach can be beneficial, providing an extra layer of protection for relatively little additional cost. Targeted claims focused on the current product can be pursued in selected jurisdictions, with broader claims being prosecuted in parallel, over a longer timescale. The fast and cost-effective grant of a focused patent based on such claims can enable a company to take advantage of provisions such as the Patent Box tax arrangements in the UK or may enable action to be taken against competitors more quickly. Such early, focused patents can also increase investor confidence and increase the likelihood of licensing deals and the potential revenues from such deals.

While an optimal strategy requires careful professional judgement to formulate, some basic steps are set out below:

1 Identify all innovative components of an idea or solution.
2 Identify all possible revenue streams.
3 Identify all possible competitor approaches/alternative business solutions.
4 Consider application to fields outside core business.
5 In the light of steps 2–4, revisit the first step to see if there is further potential for protection of products or process.
6 Estimate market geographical extent and financial value.
7 Project own business plans to capture market.
8 Project partnering/licensing opportunities to capture further market.
9 Project appropriate IP budget.
10 Assess level of knowledge of art and competitors.
11 If appropriate, search to fill gaps in knowledge.
12 Consider patentability issues.
13 Prioritize claims and protection.

Conclusion

The correct approach to IP strategy requires an understanding not only of the technology but of the business environment in which the technology is likely to evolve over the coming couple of decades.

Identifying broad protection which might be sought is one part of the challenge. However, formulating a prosecution strategy which takes into account the costs and challenges in each jurisdiction and evolution of the business, and builds this into an initial application, generally gives a better and more cost-effective end result.

Ilya Kazi is a Partner in the major UK-based IP firm Mathys & Squire which has offices in London, Manchester, Cambridge, Reading and York. Ilya has represented clients in over 2,000 cases before the European Patent Office and has received personal commendations in leading directories such as the Legal 500 and has been named by *Intellectual Asset Management* as one of the world's top IP strategists. He acts for clients ranging from start-ups and UK SMEs to major multinationals, specializing in complex software and IT, clean tech and medical device technology and providing strategic advice on IP to growing businesses.

Tel: +44 207 830 0000; e-mail: ikazi@mathys-squire.com; web: www.mathys-squire.com

Patent exclusions

John Hardwick at Hardwick & Co discusses why patent applications can fail

Every new enterprise starts with a new idea. Some ideas just 'spring into the mind'. Other ideas are the result of extended work. Yet other ideas come from employees, partners and consultants. Whatever the source of the idea, the innovator will wish to protect it, if possible, against use by others. One form of protection is to file a patent application for the idea.

Nearly everything is patentable. The idea simply needs to find an expression (embodiment) that is new and has an inventive step. There is no need for a prototype to exist before a patent application is filed. The embodiment explained in the patent application merely has to be capable of working.

There can be a snag for a few ideas. The new idea might not be acceptable subject matter for a patent to be granted. If a patent application were to be prepared and filed, the patent examiner would eventually reject the application.

There are lots of things that the Patent Office considers to be 'excluded matter'. For excluded matter, whatever the merits of the idea, whether it be new or involves a creative and inventive step, it's very subject matter means that a patent can never be granted for that idea.

What is excluded? It is quite a list. Software, business methods, mathematical methods, scientific discoveries, methods of performing a mental act and methods of treatment of the human or animal body are deemed, in Europe and the UK, to be unacceptable 'excluded' matter.

The list of excluded matter covers a very large area of human endeavour. In the case of software, most modern products involve a considerable software element. If you open up a modern calculator, for example, all you find apart from the screen and buttons is a processor chip that contains software that does all of the work. The world is full of computer devices talking to one another almost non-stop. How can software not be patentable?

An aspect of software very prevalent in the modern day is the graphical user interface (GUI) used in the human interface for nearly every computer application. This can prove difficult to patent in the UK and Europe since it is 'software doing just what you would expect software to do'. GUIs are more readily patentable in the United States.

Business methods simply are not patentable in the UK or Europe. Very few countries in the world allow business methods to be patented. However, the United States is a notable exception and offers a large market.

Scientific discoveries are the bread and butter of the modern world. Without scientific discoveries our survival would be uncertain and our lives would be impoverished. How can scientific discoveries not be patentable? There is a way!

Hardwick & Co

Exxapatent

IP Attorneys

Tel-Fax +44 (0)208 751 6182
Email mail@exxapatent.com

Patents Trademarks Registered Designs Free Initial Consultation:
Firm Quotes Reasonable Charges: Card and Invoice Payment

From the simple to the most complex
National And International
Electronics Physics Mechanical Garments Oil Industry Software
Business Methods Internet Optics Communications Consumer Goods
Mathematical Printers Bank Machines Antennas Fibre Optics
Satellites Memories IC Fabrication Plastics Materials Methods
Assistance Advice Preparation Prosecution Renewal Fee Payment
Address for Service Patent Registration
EPA CIPA OHIM IPReg

Website www.exxapatent.com

Bay Cottage, 455 Hatton Road, Hatton Cross, Bedfont TW14 9QP GB
Tel +44 (0)208 751 6182 Mobile +44 (0)798 492 1867 Fax +44 (0)208 751 6182.
Internet VoIP Phone 044 (0)20 7193 0526
Skype johnfrederickhardwick (exxapatent ® is a registered trademark)

Methods of performing a mental act may be a little more problematical. However, keep it in mind that a mental act can be computerized to be executed by a processor. The processor can be incorporated into an apparatus to provide a patentable invention.

Exclusion of methods for treatment of the human or animal body seems to exclude a great deal of beneficial improvements to the human and animal condition. There is also an embargo against methods of medical diagnosis that require intrusion into the surface of the body. This can also be overcome!

Embody the idea

An embodiment is simply an apparatus that is used in a patent application to describe something including the idea that has the possibility of working. Patent offices only feel comfortable when they allow patents for 'things'. The 'things' are real objects. Objects can also include systems of many parts working together. The 'things' are 'items of kit'. Just think 'things' to know what you can and cannot patent. Patent offices are comfortable patenting 'items of kit'.

Even if you have a 'thing' you might like to patent, it has to fulfil two conditions before a patent can be granted:

- The first condition is fairly straightforward. The 'thing' must not have been made before. That is fairly easy to establish one way or the other. A search can establish earlier patent documents, books and other material that shows how things have been done before. If it has not been done before, in exactly the same way that you propose to do that thing, then the newness (novelty) hurdle has been cleared.

- The second condition for a patent to be granted is not so easy to establish. Your embodiment must exhibit an inventive step (sometimes called a technical effect or improvement). An inventive step depends upon alleged knowledge of 'the skilled man' or 'one skilled in the art', who is a legal myth used in patent examination to decide whether or not a patent application can be granted. In whatever field the invention lies, the skilled man is presumed be highly experienced and to know all about those things that have been done in the field of the invention right up to the day the patent application is filed. However, the skilled man is defined as being totally without inventive ability. The skilled man knows a range of applicable solutions, but nothing more. Different patent offices may argue different levels of inventive ability in the skilled man at different times. However, it is fair to say that the skilled man is largely unimaginative. If the skilled man, in order to solve the same problem you set out to solve, by applying one or more of his own solutions, is able to arrive at your claimed result, then the claimed material is obvious and so lacks an inventive step. However, if the skilled man is unable to arrive at your solution by applying known solutions, then the claim has an inventive step. Much of the patent examination process involves arguments about inventive step. Believe it or not, the notion of the 'skilled man' makes it much easier to patent excluded material.

Software

Software is not excluded 'in itself'. This does not mean that software is precluded from being part of an apparatus or system, merely that the software cannot have a patent granted for 'doing just what you would expect software to do anyway'. You can, however, have a patent granted for a new and inventive apparatus/system that employs a software-driven element as one of its component parts. A software-driven element can be interpreted as 'a processor, that when loaded with the software, behaves as a component part of the apparatus system'.

Mathematical methods

A mathematical method can be expressed in executable software. A processor running that software can become part of an apparatus that is both new and inventive.

Let me give you an example. Three-dimensional landscape mapping using images taken from ground level is of cartographical and military interest. The mathematical method of interpreting a small number of photographic images to construct a 3D landscape of the viewed area was found patentable by the European Patent Office. The mathematical method was new, the claim claimed an apparatus using a functional part employing the mathematical method, and the skilled man had no previous knowledge of the mathematical method ever having been applied, more or less automatically meaning that an inventive step (technical advantage or improvement) existed.

As another example, a novel statistical method was employed in gathering data from sensors for determining fuel–air mixture ratios in an internal combustion electrical generator motor. Once again, the statistical method was expressed in software that became part of a new apparatus whose inventive step was almost guaranteed by virtue of the skilled man never having seen the statistical method before the patent application was filed.

Scientific discoveries

A scientific discovery, with a few exceptions, can nearly always be turned into an apparatus that exploits that discovery.

As an example, a discovery concerning a chemical reaction can be turned into a plant to exploit that chemical reaction. An historic example of such a piece of plant was to be found in the Haber process for converting atmospheric nitrogen into ammonia that formed the backbone to British munitions nitrate manufactured during the First World War. You just have to use your imagination. The transformation from 'scientific discovery' to 'thing' is usually quite straightforward. Indeed, many chemical patents might be considered 'discoveries'.

Performance of a mental act

Performance of a mental act bears a close similarity with a mathematical method. Both can be expressed in a computer program that can then be employed in a processor for the processor to become part of a greater inventive apparatus.

There are many examples of mental acts that might be of use in a practical situation. Almost by definition, a mental act that is somehow an invention is likely to be new. An apparatus that performs a useful task using the new mental act would potentially be new and unknown to the skilled man.

Treatment of the human or animal body

This is possibly the best example of why reading the words in the legislation and not expanding upon their meaning is important. It is only methods of treatment that are excluded. Any apparatus is not excluded.

The patent world is awash with a whole host of treatment apparatus ranging from improved asthma inhalers and extending to therapeutic radiation machines, improved wound dressings, single-use purpose-constructed surgical instruments, endoscopes, monitoring machines of all kinds and treatment machines of all kinds, including dialysis machines, artificial spleens, automatic resuscitators and assisted breathing apparatus. It is absolutely clear that only the method is excluded. Remotely controllable and/or automatic machines for performing surgery are also patentable. The method of treating the human body itself may not be patentable, but the apparatus is.

Invasive medical diagnosis

This really means any method that involves breaching the various surfaces of the human or animal body. Diagnosis need not be invasive of the body. Many parameters can be measured or estimated by external scrutiny; for example, blood flow, blood oxygenation, breathing, body scans and blood vessel tracking can all be done without bodily invasion. No samples are required.

Apparatus that analyses a sample drawn from the human or animal body is also patentable. Such apparatus can include, for example, blood cell counting apparatus, blood sugar analysing devices and gastric analysing devices that can be swallowed and tracked.

All manner of optical viewing equipment, insertable into the human or animal body, is also patentable. No breaching of a pre-existing surface in the body is required. Once again, it is the apparatus that is patentable, not the method.

Business methods

So far as business methods are concerned, the European Patent Office has even rejected a new 'one-armed bandit' mechanism for lacking invention because its effect was to 'maintain the interest of the individual gambler'. This was considered by the European Patent Office as not being a 'technical' effect, instead being a 'business effect' rendering the invention a business method and thereby lacking the required technical improvement. The subject matter was excluded despite the description being entirely technical apart from this one small point. The UK Patent Office rejects applications on the same grounds.

If you cannot get around the excluded matter objection in the UK and Europe, it may be possible to utilize the US Patent Office to obtain a business method patent. Business methods are definitely not patentable in the UK or Europe. However, if an apparatus connected with the business method uses a new and inventive technical approach, for example a protocol, or message exchange, the apparatus may itself be patentable.

That apart, a business method is patentable in the United States, provided, once again, it is not already known and is inventive. You can prepare and file a UK patent application that can be used within the priority year to file a US business method application.

The US Patent Office puts out a set of examination guidelines for business methods that includes: a transformation of data that provides a business advantage; and embodiment in a system or apparatus where transformations, decisions and assessments are predominantly made by the system or apparatus rather than by human agency.

You can see from the US Patent Office examination guidelines that it is not possible to escape 'things'. The US business method might better be described as a 'business method apparatus'. Of course, in most business methods the 'apparatus' is a system involving two or more cooperative parts.

Graphical user interfaces

A GUI might be considered as 'software doing just what you would expect software to do anyway'. To the European mind, it is! However, looking back at the 'one-armed bandit' case (described above), which was rejected in Europe, provides insight into what is acceptable in the United States. While a strict technical interpretation of inventive step is enforced in Europe and the UK, the United States will allow such criteria as ease of use, convenience of use and human participation improvement to be considered as an inventive improvement. GUIs enjoy a much easier passage through the USPTO (the United States Patent and Trademark Office) than they ever experience in the UK or Europe. Who can forget the Amazon 'one-click shopping' patent in the United States? That patent was for a system. So, even in the United States, patentability of embodiment of 'things' cannot be escaped.

Summary

There are very few things that are not patentable provided they are new and have an inventive step. Just think 'apparatus embodiment'.

John Hardwick is the owner of Hardwick & Co, an international patent and trademark attorney firm offering all types of patent and trademark protection in all areas of IP and specializing in control systems, electrical and electronic engineering, physics, telecommunications software and business methods. Previously, John Hardwick was Senior European Patent Counsel for Unisys Corporation and in private practice in the London area in the Hi Tech area.

Further details: tel: +44 (0)208 751 6182;
e-mail: exxapatent.com@btinernet.com; web: www.exxapatent.com

IP offshoring

Christian Bunke at Basck reviews changing patterns in how IP is being managed

The intellectual property (IP) industry is inherently a conservative industry, with many IP firms and law firms having long traditions of delivering a full service offering. At the same time, the pace of innovation, strategic decision making and need for efficiency improvements is ever increasing. Add to this the fact that the global number of patent filings increased by 7.7 per cent, China having a 29.9 per cent and India an 11.1 per cent growth per year (CAGR) increase between 2009 and 2011.[1] This overview of IP services offshoring shows that today it is now more a matter of working with the best optimized organizational structure and finding talent rather than transaction cost that is of key importance. With the growth in IP filings now coming from Asia (93 per cent of Asian filings coming from China, Japan and South Korea), many of these offshored IP services offerings will allow best practice and access to top talent located in Asia, further strengthening their IP position.

Traditionally, there has always been a question of when things would be out-sourced to the external counsel or when one would build an in-house team to handle the work from administration through to commercialization. In the 2000s, administrative tasks of the IP value chain were commoditized faster than ever before. The additional pressures of IP departments becoming profit centres rather than cost centres resulted in a need to access the right skills of, for example, licensing and commercial exploitation of IP in an efficient and cost-effective way.

The offshoring wave

In the 1990s, there was a wave of services that were being offshored. This was occurring at the same time as ever-increasing globalization and the so-called information boom, which utilized the powers of remote working and the internet, leading to services providers such as Capgemini and Accenture offering offshoring of IT, financial and HR services to developing countries in Central Europe and Asia. It has been said and speculated that advanced IP and Legal offshoring was about 15 years behind software and FSA. So are we at that point in time now? In the early 2000s, multinationals such as GE and Philips and service providers such as Pangea3 (Thomson Reuters), Intellevate (CPA Global) and Evalueserve (for sale at \$250m[2]) set up offshored IP services offered mainly to the US and European markets.

Initially IP admin and cost focused

Labour arbitrage, access to large talent pools and the emergence of electronic record keeping using software enabled offshoring of IP functions. Offshoring IP services became a proven business model offering patent search services, IP admin, and paralegals through transactional engagements at competitive cost. GE and Philips also set up captive IP centres, moving to the next stage of development, with multi-shore set-up well established by the mid-2000s. It was a time when IP firms started losing this business to offshore companies and work earlier outsourced became offshored. Most multinationals, initially from the United States and then followed by the EU and Asia, used and tried offshoring of IP services and the skills, and the quality of the work of patent searchers, patent engineers and paralegals rapidly improved. Also, the big law and IP firms started working with offshore service providers, sometimes by setting up their own offshore teams within the service provider, enabling them to maintain profit margins as services became more commoditized.

Flexibility and access to talent

The global financial crisis in 2007 opened a new door of opportunity for the IP offshoring industry owing to increased cost-cutting pressures. Services such as licensing support and more advanced commercialization-focused work started to be offshored owing to lower transaction cost but also to the advantage of working with different time zones. Also, increasing litigation activities led to support work and, for example, product to patent claim mapping being done offshore. The flexibility of having a component of offshoring in your IP organizational structure was attractive after the experiences of needing to cut costs rapidly during the recession. More companies started to use dedicated teams offshore to further lower cost and secure the technology, skills and know-how developed by the people working for them. Multishoring was the best practice and some multinationals have people from the offshore team onshore, in-house, to improve the work flow, communication and cultural understanding.

Top quality work

Taking India as an example, this development has resulted in there being several thousand IP specialists who have worked with mainly patent services for up to 10 years. This means that the IP specialists have now built up considerable knowledge and know-how, and hiding behind an excuse of quality concerns is not valid today. Also, the work is moving up the value chain of IP services, covering, for example, patent prosecution, drafting and more advanced commercialization work. For all of us working in the world of innovation, the IP services industry has passed through Gartner's stages of expectations to be at the end of the slope of enlightenment. With the right people, the quality is as good as or better than locally outsourced work, which changes the market dynamics and now allows services to be moving up the value chain. Yes, there are and have always been some cases of moving IP services back onshore as the cost advantage disappears, but then you are forgetting the access to talent and time zone advantage as services higher up the value chain are being offered.

Conclusion

There is no one size fits all, but IP teams with some offshore component are today being used for work across the whole IP value chain. The use of different time zones and organizational flexibility is key to getting the best out of any IP team of professionals. The decision to have an offshore capability is now an organizational drive to best service level rather than one of cost.

Notes

1 WIPO, 2012

2 *India Times*, 10 December 2012 (http://articles.economictimes.indiatimes.com/ 2012-12-10/news/35726637_1_evalueserve-promoters-marc-vollenweider)

Christian Bunke is the Founder and Managing Director of Basck, an IP consultancy firm with offices in the UK, Nordics and India. Basck works with some of Europe's leading start-ups and SMEs on IP strategy, patenting prosecution and brokering. The team of technical PhDs, Patent Attorneys and experienced business professionals make Basck a leading IP commercialization partner.

Tel: +44(0)7884052079; e-mail: christian@basck.com; Twitter: BasckIPR; web: www.basck.com

PART TWELVE
International rights

Feel like you're in over your head?
Here's how to stay on top of everything.

You can start by reading the article on protecting IP internationally, written by Murgitroyd Director of Patents Wendy Crosby. Then call her at +44 (0)20 7153 1255 for your free initial consultation – and preserve the ideas you've worked so hard to create.

Mention the Innovation Handbook and we will file your UK patent application for £1,000.

MURGITROYD & ©OMPANY
EUROPEAN PATENT AND TRADE MARK ATTORNEYS

UK | USA | FRANCE | GERMANY | ITALY | IRELAND | FINLAND

murgitroyd.com

Launching innovation in emerging countries

Wendy Crosby at Murgitroyd considers the questions to ask about IP when expanding in new economic powers such as China, India and Brazil

For companies that develop innovative products or innovative solutions to local problems, important aspects of their business strategy will be how to launch their products in new territories and how to protect their products from copying by local competitors. The strategy may include filing a patent application in the new territory to protect the product. In most countries, a patent application must be filed before any details of the product have been released to the public, for example by sale of the product or even by releasing marketing material such as flyers or press releases, and therefore there can be only a short time available for companies to put in place the geographic protection that they need to cover the launch of a product in a number of countries. Typically, a company will file a patent application in the UK to protect the product, which provides a 12-month window within which to file corresponding patent applications in other countries into which they may, in time, wish to expand. It is possible to file an international patent application which effectively increases this 12-month window by a further 18 months, but it is important that companies begin strategic planning as early as possible in the product lifetime to ensure that they cover the most important markets.

Emerging territories

The emerging territories, which include countries such as China, India and Brazil, are regional economic powerhouses with large populations and resource bases but, significantly, they are now also being viewed as promising markets in their own right as they are showing sustained economic development and a growing aspirational population. Therefore these countries now represent a significant opportunity for companies with innovative products to open up new trade channels for their products to supplement sales from more traditional domestic markets.

Business issues

There are many local factors which companies have to consider when devising a strategy for launching a product in a new territory. Understanding the local market, business culture, the needs and requirements of your potential new customers and having a clear grasp of local industry and business regulations are issues that are crucial to the success of any product launch, particularly in one of the emerging territories where the local infrastructure may still be catching up to the rapid pace of development of the country.

Companies may establish their own local base within the country or alternatively may prefer to form a joint venture with a local agent to provide a local base for the product launch. However, with the latter approach, it is important to formalize and manage the relationship with local agents to ensure that this is mutually beneficial and that the company objectives are being met, which may mean that staff and financial resources are spread thinly across a number of such ventures in different countries.

IP issues

Some products are specifically designed for use in a select number of countries, due, for example, to different geological properties of the regions where oil and gas deposits are found, and companies should consider carefully the geographic protection needed for each project. This can result in a company needing to maintain a number of different IP strategies depending upon the type of operation in which a tool will be used, the geographic area of use and also the local IP framework in force in those countries and so it is important to consider carefully the geographic protection needed for your different inventions.

When building an international IP portfolio a company should consider, at an early stage, how it will police the local market for unauthorized copies, as delay in taking action could lead to limitations in the remedies available to it. If you have a local base in the country you may be able to build up market awareness by directly monitoring the local business community, but if you are supplying products from outwith the country and have no local presence, this can be more problematic. One way in which to establish a local network monitoring the activities of competitors is to license local firms to manufacture your products in exchange for royalty payments.

Significant strides have been taken in recent years in some emerging countries such as China to strengthen the IP framework and to improve the processes for enforcing IP protection against competitors that copy the innovative parts of your products. Many companies now see protecting their innovation in China as a crucial step in launching their products in that country.

In Brazil, there is an historic backlog of patent applications awaiting examination and there is typically a delay of around 6–8 years from filing a patent application to the first indication from the patent office of whether protection is likely to be granted, which can lead to lengthy delays in securing local protection for innovative products. It is possible to speed up the prosecution of your patent applications in Brazil if you become aware of a competitor that is copying your products, so it is important to maintain an active watch on what competitors are doing.

However, it may be that the product in question has a shelf-life of only around 3–5 years and therefore a different approach to IP protection may have to be considered.

Registered designs

If your products only have a relatively short shelf-life or embody incremental modifications over time, particularly in relation to the appearance of the product, then the protection afforded by design rights and more specifically registered designs may be a more cost-effective alternative to patents, which typically involve a lengthy and more expensive prosecution process. In Brazil, for example, the process of registration of a design may be as short as six months compared to of many years for a patent application.

Also, as registered designs typically follow a much shorter prosecution cycle, this strategy provides a means for protecting the shape of the products very quickly while the patent application covering the way in which the product works is still being prosecuted. This can provide a way of claiming damages from competitors that fall foul of your registered design, particularly in the early years of your product life while your patent is still in the prosecution stage when patent infringement damages are not typically available.

For products that relate to the core technology of your company, combining the protection from both patents and registered designs is highly recommended. This provides separate and distinct rights that can each be enforced against competitors if their products incorporate the same features or look very similar to your own products, and so are useful in ring-fencing your innovations.

Trade marks

While protecting the innovative aspects of a product prior to launch in a new territory is important, companies should not lose sight of the fact that the branding of the product, and typically the trade mark under which the product will be sold in that territory, is another very import aspect of their business.

Choosing the right trade mark can mean the difference between success and failure of a global product launch strategy, particularly in countries where the trade mark has to be translated into the local language. When choosing a trade mark, a company should have an eye already on the possible territories in which it may, in time, wish to launch, and ensure that the trade mark is appropriate for all of these territories. For example, your chosen trade mark may be absolutely fine in English but when translated into Spanish for sale in Mexico it may either be offensive or translate into a word that is entirely unsuitable for your product. A prime example is the trade mark NOVA for cars which has no meaning in English but in Spanish the words 'no va' translate as 'it does not go', which is not particularly useful given the products with which the trade mark was to be associated.

Similarly, your chosen trade mark may not be pronounceable in the local language of some countries and this can have a detrimental effect on the sale of the product. Translation issues can be particularly relevant in China where trade marks can be protected either in the local language English translation or alternatively in the local language character form (transliteration), where each character of the trade mark is phonetically similar to the English syllable it represents but has a distinct meaning. As an example, the simple Chinese transliteration of MURGITROYD is 茂知权 which phonetically sounds like **mao** zhi chuan and which means **strong/ robust** intellectual property.

Therefore, if China is an important market for your company it is worth ensuring that your chosen trade mark is acceptable and you select the best version in the transliterated form to portray the characteristics of your company to the Chinese public before you exhaust your advertising budget having local brochures and advertising literature prepared.

Alternatively, you may be pushed into changing your global brand owing to conflict problems in one country that might have been avoidable with a little foresight. If you are anticipating a global market for your product with a business strategy built upon introducing the product in a number of different countries, it is also advisable to have trade mark searches conducted at least in the main markets of interest to you before launching your products in those countries to ensure that your chosen trade mark is clear for use and doesn't infringe some other company's rights. If the searches reveal a conflicting trade mark in your main market, it may be better to consider rethinking your chosen trade mark rather than be faced with launching the product under two different trade marks in different territories with the resulting marketing issues that arise from such a situation.

Summary

Launching and protecting innovation in a new territory, especially one of the emerging territories such as Brazil, China or India, requires a global strategy that deals with the many, varied and often specific local business and legal issues which arise, often due to the rapid nature of the development within the country despite a more limited local infrastructure. Having a good understanding of the product, the local market and the relevant product legislation, and a plan in place to manage the expansion of the business into each new territory and to monitor competitor activity so as to be in a position to take action at the appropriate time, is crucial to the successful international launch of an innovative product.

Wendy Crosby is a Patent Attorney and Director of Murgitroyd, a global firm of intellectual property attorneys specializing in the provision of services in the patent, trade mark, design and copyright fields. The firm has 15 offices world-wide located across the UK, United States, Germany, France, Italy, Ireland and Finland. The firm works with a range of clients across a variety of commercial sectors, including life sciences, chemistry, pharmaceuticals, engineering, ICT and energy.

Please contact Wendy to discuss ways in which you could maximize the value of your intellectual property: tel: +44 (0)1224 706616; e-mail: wendy.crosby@murgitroyd.com; web: murgitroyd.com

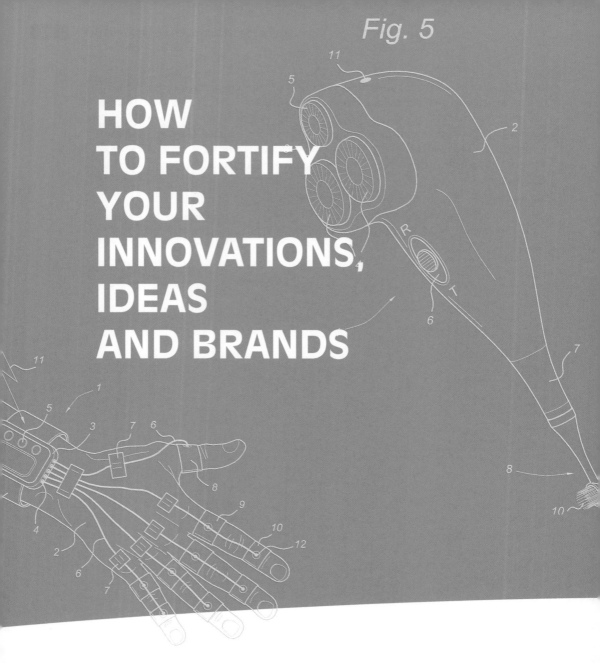

Fig. 5

HOW TO FORTIFY YOUR INNOVATIONS, IDEAS AND BRANDS

As you may have noticed, recently we launched a new name and new look. These two changes should tell you we are perfectly ready for the future. In this future, innovations, ideas and brands will determine even more whether a company will be successful. Therefore, protecting and fortifying these innovations, ideas and trademarks has become pivotal. We use the following ingredients: innovation, expertise, passion, teamwork, creativity and experience. It is exactly what we have been doing for the past 125 years. For more information, you are most welcome to visit us at www.nlo.nl

NEDERLANDSCH OCTROOIBUREAU

European Patent & Trademark attorneys

www.nlo.nl

The EU's unitary patent

What does it mean for your innovations? Hans Hutter at Nederlandsch

Octrooibureau considers the strategic implications of a major shake-up

in European IP

After many years of intense debates, small victories and mainly serious disappointments, at last the European Parliament has approved a unitary patent package that will definitely change the European patent landscape over time. The package consists of three pillars: a unitary patent system, translation arrangements and a Unified Patent Court (see box for more details).

In March 2011, 25 out of 27 EU member states set up a programme for 'enhanced cooperation' to arrive at such a unitary patent package. Italy and Spain opposed this enhanced cooperation because they wanted an important role for their national languages in the unitary system.

In the meantime, 24 out of the 27 Union member states have signed the agreement. However, Spain and Italy have filed lawsuits against the decision to start a unitary patent system. It is difficult to predict the outcome of these legal proceedings; however, it is hard to believe that the new system will eventually fail owing to lack of legal basis. The political will to get the new system up and running is strong. In the optimistic scenario, it will enter into force in 2014. So, every manager of an innovative industry, be it inside or outside Europe, should become familiar with the basics of the new system and make strategic decisions as soon as possible.

In principle, the situation seems clear. If all Union member states joined, the new system would cover a territory of more than 500 million people. That is far more than the United States, which has about 310 million inhabitants. Even if Spain and Italy (and maybe Poland) do not join, an area of more than 350 million people will still be covered. What is more attractive than to have a patent valid in such a huge area that you can use against your competitors in a single lawsuit? As usual, the devil is in the detail.

The new unitary patent system

The new system has three pillars, as follows.

Unitary patent

The unitary patent is a special form of a European patent granted by the European Patent Office. It will be valid in those member states that have decided to join (currently 24 out of 27 EU member states have signed but not yet ratified). The unitary patent will have, in principle, identical scope everywhere in all participating countries. And it will be a single unit of property. This will also hold for licensing, infringement and nullity.

Renewal fees will no longer have to be paid to the national governments of the states in which the patent is valid, but to the European Patent Office. The level of the renewal fees is expected to be equal to about the average of the combined renewal fees of five to six member states.

Translation arrangements

- The application may be filed in either English, German or French.

- At the time of grant, all claims should be made available in all three official languages of the EPC: English, German and French.

- During a transitional period of 12 years at most, a patent that is granted in German or French should be translated into English in full. And, if the patent is granted in English, during that period, the proprietor should translate the granted patent into one other official language of the Union.

Single patent court

The new court system has, in principle, a straightforward structure: it will have a court of first instance and a court of appeal, whereas questions relating to interpretation of the new legal system may be referred to the European Court of Justice.

Its implementation is less straightforward. The court of first instance will be organized as follows:

- any participating state may set up its own local division; or

- any participating state may decide to set up a regional division together with one or more other participating states; or

- any participating state may decide to refer any future unitary patent case to a central division. The central division will be in Paris, with specialist branches in Munich (mechanical) and London (chemistry/pharmaceutical/life sciences).

The new court system will also have jurisdiction over non-unitary European patents and those that have been granted in the past and are still valid. However, there is a transitional period that may last a long time:

- For seven (extendable up to 14) years, any enforcement and/or invalidation action can still be initiated before national courts.

- During that time, owners of European patents granted, or applications pending, before entry into force can opt out of the unified patent court system.

Entering into force

It is hoped that the new system will enter into force in 2014. However, it will not begin until 13 contracting states have ratified the agreement on the unified patent court, provided that the UK, France and Germany are among them.

Basic change

The new unitary patent will become available alongside all current patents in Europe, that is, national patents obtained either via a national route, via the PCT system or via the current European system. So, in the future there will be old-style European patents and new-style unitary European patents.

The old-style European patents remain available for all those 40 member states of the European Patent Convention (EPC) that are not member states of the EU, such as Switzerland and Turkey, but also for those EU member states that do not sign/ratify the agreement. Currently, we may assume that countries like Spain, Italy and Poland will not do so. Finally, an applicant may continue to validate a granted European patent only in its chosen unitary patent member states.

Which choice to make will depend on strategic considerations, including the market for a particular product, the vulnerability of a single unitary patent, litigation options, and costs.

Strategic choices

The new system will have, no doubt, a serious impact on the way companies have to think about obtaining a European patent. A typical way of deciding which route to follow in the near future may be as follows.

Existing patent portfolio

All existing European patents remain a bundle of individual national patents. The only tricky consequence of the new unitary patent arrangement is that the unified patent court system is also applicable to all presently valid European patents and all European patents granted on current pending patent applications in the unitary patent member states. You can avoid these legal consequences by filing a request to opt out of the unified patent court system. For those companies that wish to be cautious with their existing patents and patent applications, we recommend filing such a request as soon as the system comes into operation.

Note that the unified patent court will not, of course, have jurisdiction over European patents valid in countries that are not unitary patent member states, such as Switzerland and Turkey.

Transitional period of seven (or more) years

Assuming that you wish to file one or more patent applications relating to a certain product, questions to ask are:

1 Do I want to have protection in a large European territory?
2 Do I like the ease of administration relating to a unitary patent?
3 Do I care about the risk of losing the unitary patent in one single lawsuit?
4 Do I wish to keep options open to abandon my European patent in individual member states after a few years to save maintenance costs?

In answering these questions, you may consider the following situations. There are two extreme cases:

- 'Large European patent', that is, you wish to have protection in, for example, 10 or more unitary patent member states and maybe a few more EPC member states. Then, from a cost perspective, you would decide to validate the patent as a unitary patent and individually in other EPC member states. However, the unitary patent is a single entity of property and the may be revoked by a single court decision for the whole territory of all unitary patent member states. If you think this is too dangerous, you have to validate the granted patent individually in all desired countries and directly file a request with the competent authorities to opt out of the unitary patent court system, which can be done at least seven years after the agreement enters into force.

- 'Small European patent', that is, you wish to have protection in only a small number of European countries. You have, basically, two options. Either you file national patent applications in those individual European countries to avoid any risk arising from the new system, or you file a European patent application which, after grant, is validated only in the desired small number of countries. To avoid the risk of losing the European patent in a single court decision, you may then decide to opt out of the unified patent court system.

A more difficult decision may be needed if you wish to have protection in, say, 5 to 10 European countries, of which, for instance, four countries are unitary patent member states. In view of the expected renewal fee for the unitary patent, there will be no cost benefit in using the unitary patent route. Depending on the case at hand, you will have to decide either to treat this as a 'small European patent' or to upgrade it into a 'large European patent'.

Gradual change

The new system may provide benefits to applicants. Patent proprietors who wish to cover a large market will have cost advantages and may attack competitors in a single lawsuit as far as the unitary patent member states are concerned. To avoid the risk of losing the unitary patent in one go, you can validate only in individual European countries and opt out of the legal consequences for at least seven years. And if you still wish to attack a competitor with a single lawsuit, you can simply opt in again during this period.

After the transitional period, the situation will be different, but in the next few years, you can strategically 'play' with your patent portfolio to ensure that the consequences are occurring only gradually, certainly for the most important European patents.

Hans Hutter is a partner of Nederlandsch Octrooibureau. He is a Dutch and European Patent Attorney. He has drafted and prosecuted patent applications in the field of semiconductor technology, smart cards, lithography machines, telecommunications, and navigation systems. He specializes in the field of patenting software-related inventions and has drafted several articles in this area. In recent years he has been involved in major complex litigation and advice cases relating to CD-R, DVD-R, MP3 and JPEG. Hans holds a PhD in the history of science and technology from Eindhoven University of Technology (1988).

Nederlandsch Octrooibureau is one of the leading intellectual property firms in the Netherlands. The firm was established in 1888 and now has about 40 consultants in the field of patents, trade marks, designs and licence contracts. These consultants serve major clients in countries both within and outside Europe to protect their intellectual property in Europe.

Contact Hans Hutter: tel: +31 70 3312505 or +31 621 105 115 (mobile); e-mail: hutter@octrooibureau.nl

Why file in the United States first?

There are seven good reasons why a US patent will put you in a strong competitive position, says John Moetteli of Da Vinci Partners LLC

With respect to patent strategy, patent attorneys best advise their clients by suggesting that they start their patent filing in the jurisdiction of the most commercial importance to them, whether due to the market the country represents or because of the presence of competitors or potential licensees.[1] The practice of merely filing locally without any justification other than tradition often fails to serve the client's best interests. Why? Because failing to do so may cause commercial damage to the client.

What your US competition doesn't want you to know about US patent law

Few Europe-based companies are aware that despite recent changes in US patent law, filing their patent applications in the United States is often the best filing strategy, particularly in cases where at least one competitor is located there.

Recent changes in the national security laws of major European countries (the UK, Germany and Italy, for example) allow freedom of choice of country for their resident's first (ie priority) patent filing. You now have the choice of filing first in the country of the most commercial importance to you as determined by the market in that country or by the presence of competitors or potential licensees.[2] With the exception of Russian and perhaps French residents, European applicants are free to file their first, priority application anywhere they choose, provided that the technology does not involve a local state secret. The country of choice for the first filing is often the United States.

This is because the United States has a homogeneous consuming population many times larger than even the largest European country, and its patent law, despite recent harmonization, remains substantially different from European patent law. Because of this and other differences, the choice of where to file first can have a more than negligible effect on the value and usefulness of your patent portfolio. Therefore, the decision of where to file your patent applications first should be taken after careful deliberation in light of your goals and the commercial potential of the invention.

Taking the correct first step is important, because where you have competitors in the United States, failing to file early there may needlessly increase the expense of acting against those US-based competitors. For example, failure to file early in the United States may ultimately subject you to an expensive interference action or a patent infringement suit, something you might have otherwise been able to avoid.

What's more, filing first in the United States makes good business sense. The United States has a developed patent system (more than 200 years old) which, in many ways, has helped shape the laws of many other industrialized nations. This developed patent system helps reduce uncertainties which increase the risks of litigation. Still further, the United States remains a dominant force in international commerce and if a client is forced (because of budget constraints for example) to choose one single national patent to have in its portfolio, most clients choose a US patent.[3]

For these and other reasons listed below, your US patent rights are probably the most flexible and powerful tools for monetizing an invention, and are in fact the only patents useful against a potential licensee or infringer residing in the United States. A company patent counsel's failure to communicate the advantages of filing in the United States is the strategic equivalent to a chess instructor failing to tell his or her student that the queen is allowed to move in all directions as far as the way is clear. Winning at the game of intellectual property is difficult enough without being handicapped by ignorance of the rules of the game. The game is global now and clients expect to be informed of the basic rules affecting their international patent strategy.

Here is an ordered listing of some of the most important reasons supporting a patent strategy that begins with an early US filing:

1 First and most important: Provided you do not file any applications foreign to the United States and you request non-publication of the US application in a timely manner, your US application is kept secret and never published by the US Patent Office unless it is granted.[4] No other country allows you this option. On the contrary, essentially all other countries require publication of your application at 18 months from the earliest priority date. Because of this mandatory publication, preserving trade secret rights as well as patent rights is simply not possible outside the United States. Therefore, by filing in the United States and not filing elsewhere, those who practise a secret process need not relinquish trade secret protection until you are convinced that the patent protection obtained in the United States will protect you more effectively than merely maintaining the secrecy of the technology. This is particularly important for companies outside the United States because the first commercial user defence (introduced with the America Invents Act) only applies to inventions practised by the first user *in the United States*. Consequently, if you manufacture outside the United States, filing a US application with a non-publication request is essentially the only 'insurance' you can take out against competitors that might otherwise obtain and assert their patent against you for what you would consider is your secret invention. In other words, if you rely only on trade secret protection and do not file a US patent application, it is possible that a competitor could obtain a patent on the process you've been using freely for years to make your product and

so threaten to stop you from importing your products made by this process into the United States.

2 You may file a US patent application in any language. If you file a US provisional application, a translation will only become due when a deadline for filing the translation is set by the US Patent Office, which will, at the earliest, be more than a year and, at the latest, more than 36 months after your priority filing date. This means that there is no handicap in using a US provisional application as a matter of practice to reserve your priority date.

3 Where you have a patent application pending on the basic technology, patent applications filed for incremental improvements stand the best chance of being patentable in the United States. US patent law offers the filing of what is called a 'continuation-in-part' or 'CIP' application, which is entitled to rely on the filing date of an earlier application with respect to subject matter common to both applications. Such a mechanism to file an application for an incremental improvement is unique to US patent law. This means that, in the United States, you can receive a patent on an increment of improvement to the earlier filed invention which would not be patentable in Europe or other significant jurisdictions such as Japan or China. Consequently, if you judge your incremental improvement not to be patentable under your home country patent law in view of your prior pending application on the basic technology (because the prior application is considered prior art to the improvement), the only significant jurisdiction in which you can still obtain a patent is the United States. In such a case, you should file first and perhaps only in the United States.

4 Effectively filing earlier in the United States means that a US examiner examining your competitor's patent application will be able to consider your application as prior art earlier than if you file later in the United States. Unfortunately, a US patent examiner can only cite (as prior art against a US patent application of a competitor) your European (or other non-US) patent application as of its publication date. Fortunately, once you've filed your US application, the US patent examiner can cite it to block third-party filings filed after your earliest priority date, which of course is significantly earlier than the 18-month publication date. Consequently, where no separate US applications are filed, PCT applications designating the United States should be filed because such PCT filings are considered US national filings and so have prior art effect as of their earliest claimed priority date. In addition, filing a US application and requesting early publication better ensures that US examiners are able to find and so consider your application as prior art vis-à-vis competitor filings earlier in prosecution of your competitor's patent application, well before your competitor's application grants. By catching the eye of the US examiner early, again, before your competitor's application grants, more and less expensive tools (some costing as little as a few hundred dollars) are available to you to challenge your competitor's application. On the other hand, challenging after grant involves expensive court litigation or post-grant procedures for which the filing fee alone can amount to US $30,000 or more.

5 Because the United States represents the largest domestic market for a broad range of products and services and because the likelihood is high that if any patent in your portfolio is litigated, it will be litigated in the United States, the US market is arguably your most important single market. Further, the size of the US market and the fact that a single patent covers this market means that, on a per capita consumer basis, the United States is by far the least expensive jurisdiction in which to obtain patent protection.[5] A US patent typically costs half that of a European patent, yet covers a comparable market. Further, renewal fees are only due every 3.5 years, not yearly as in Europe. This means that if the US market is most important to you, and you later decide not to file anywhere but in the United States, starting with the United States is the least costly alternative, one which avoids aborted filings while preserving all your options.

6 Formal (non-provisional) US patent applications are generally filed in English, the language of computer science, information technology, business and law. English is an official language of many other industrialized nations around the world, such as the UK, India, Ireland, Australia, Canada, New Zealand and Singapore. Further, Japan and Switzerland (to name a few) permit initial filing in English, subject, in some cases, to the submission of a translation at a later date. In addition, patent rights in Germany, Switzerland, France, the UK, the Netherlands, Denmark, Sweden, Luxembourg, Monaco, Slovenia, Iceland, Latvia, Liechtenstein and Croatia can be protected via a later English-language European patent application, without further translation costs, thanks to the London Agreement.[6] Therefore, a patent application drafted in English first can be prosecuted through grant in many important jurisdictions without translation and so is less likely to suffer from losses in meaning due to translation in these important regions.

7 Fortunately, the European Patent Office and the patent offices of all industrialized countries of the world consider a US patent filing a valid priority filing for their own purposes, thereby serving to reserve rights in these countries as of the US priority filing date. This means that a US filing provides all the priority benefits that a local filing can provide.

Conclusions

If you wish to minimize litigation risk, maximize licensing value, and you are not a resident of France or Russia, you should be advised of the advantages of filing your patent applications in the United States first. If the claimed invention is a commercially valuable and patentable technology with applications in the United States, then ignoring these advantages may lead to diminished value of your IP portfolio or to increased litigation risk and related costs. What's more, if you file first in the United States, you will no longer operate at a disadvantage vis-à-vis your US-based competitors.

Notes

1 Where such a choice is permitted under national law, discussed below.

2 Where such a choice is permitted under national law.

3 Companies and institutions that, from the public record, do this include: IBM Rüschlikon, Logitech, the University of Geneva, HUG, the EPFL, and many large Swiss chemical and pharma companies, for example, to mention just a few.

4 35 USC §102(a)(2) and §102(b)(1) Exceptions, new law March 2013.

5 The licensing value of a US patent is therefore probably much greater than any other national patent.

6 See http://www.epo.org/law-practice/legal-texts/london-agreement.html for further information.

John Moetteli is an International Patent Attorney and Managing Attorney of Da Vinci Partners LLC, an IP firm in Switzerland specializing in preparing and filing US and European patent applications for globally minded clients. He has spoken on the subject of intellectual property at NASA, INTA Trademark Roundtables, the Association of International Business Lawyers in Geneva, NanoEurope, the University of St Gallen, the University of Neuchâtel, the University of Constance, the Swiss Patent Office and at IMD in Lausanne, as well as other institutions. Besides his more than 20 years' total IP experience, Mr Moetteli has more than 15 years' experience filing US patent applications directly from Europe. Note that although this chapter is subject to copyright © 2009–2013, the author does not object to reproduction and redistribution of this chapter provided it is copied and distributed in its entirety, including footnotes and credits.

Further information from Da Vinci Partners LLC: www.davincipartners.com

PART THIRTEEN
Innovation finance

HIGHBURY

Maximising the value in your innovation

We work with you to recognise, protect, value and commercialise your creations

What we do:
Business development & market research
Pre-partnering due diligence
Technology, product and company valuation
Technology transfer and licensing
Deal negotiation and implementation

We run workshops for entrepreneurs, transferring our IP skills to your community

Christi Mitchell T: 01462436894 M: 07973224804 E: Christi@highburyltd.com

www.highburyltd.com

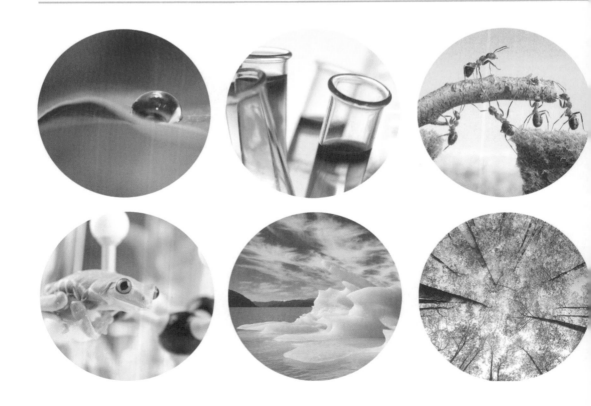

Valuation of ideas and early-stage technology

Sky high? Rock bottom? Christi Mitchell at Highbury steers a path towards putting a robust value on an idea

During the 13 years that we have worked with intellectual property (IP) and devised our own model for early-stage technology valuation (we have worked far longer with technology commercialization), we have seen a number of outrageous valuations; more recently, with the explosion of a technology-based drive to arrive at significant financial values, we have seen individuals caught up on the wrong side of the law through the use of inappropriate IP values.

This is a serious and complicated subject that must be treated analytically and realistically – this is a tough call. Reports suggest that over 49 per cent of companies which enter into negotiation with another party for the sale or licensing of their technology have not had the technology in question independently valued. This has implications all round for all parties participating in the innovation process, and it is difficult to understand how one can seriously negotiate a deal in the absence of a considered valuation. Further, third parties, the revenue services and other agencies are taking a keener interest on the basis of such valuations.

Ideas reside within the head of the creator. These ideas must be captured or reduced to practice before value can be realistically attributed to them. Ideas alone are generally considered to be valueless – a controversial point! Value is subjective and will be altered by a variety of different interpretations, even among those who work with and fully understand that technology.

The valuer needs to understand why the organization requires a valuation. Reasons can include: for a licensing negotiation, to raise bank or venture capital (VC) funding, to sell, to include within the annual accounts, to calculate share values, for commercial due diligence, to help create financial forecasts or as a tax requirement.

The concepts of valuation and pricing are similar and often used interchangeably. Valuation represents the development of a model that represents an asset's intrinsic worth under a defined set of assumptions.

Pricing represents the integration of both buyer and seller perceptions of value to develop a price at which a deal can be done. In other words, the formulation of a specific mix of deal terms and payments in which both sides believe they are better off for agreeing to a deal.

Your technology may have a greater or lesser value than your business. Sometimes the technology is robust and has multiple applications, all of which are not necessarily exploited by the business. Many technologies will have no value.

There are three valuation models that are most commonly used by businesses and valuers. These are:

1 market approach – benchmarking similar deals;
2 income approach – used only for a commercialized product;
3 cost approach – possible for a new technology.

Then, we have our approach: a risk-adjusted mix of the above.

The market approach – based on a comparable transaction

The free market economy principle states that, in competitive markets, supply and demand will drive the price of goods to a point of equilibrium. Value is determined by analysing comparable intangible asset transactions which have occurred recently in similar markets. Finding such similar deals within recent time frames can prove impossible. This is not a valuation method that can be easily applied alone to early-stage technology valuation, because there are unlikely to be comparable deals. We are also faced with the challenge that very few 'done deals' are fully reported.

The income approach – based on anticipation

This model assumes that cash flow will be generated by commercializing the technology. The valuation approaches can be developed from three perspectives:

1 Risk-adjusted cash flows. Here, anticipated cash flow (inflation adjusted) takes into account all known risk factors that are likely to affect the generation of the anticipated income. In other words, risk-adjusted profits or revenue from the project minus costs/net investment in the project are used to build the cash flow forecasts. The model builds in adjustments for perceived risks. These risks could be: regulatory, competitors, patent infringement, loss of know-how, lack of participation of an inventor, market lifespan, time taken to reach market, securing finance etc. Also considered is the length of time income can be anticipated. Duration is dependent upon the demand, industry sector, competitive technology strength (emerging and existing) and other factors. For example, a software technology may have a lifespan of 1–5 years while a pharmaceutical technology could have a lifespan equal to that of the patent. This method can seldom be used alone for the valuation of an early-stage technology that has no market history.

2 Discounted cash flow (DCF) and the income method. A projection of future net cash flows (unadjusted for risks) is prepared as detailed above from commercializing the technology over the lifetime of the technology. These projections are then 'discounted' by the time value of money and the risk associated with the asset/invention ('discounted rate') to achieve a net present value (NPV) of the IP asset. A venture capitalist (VC) considering an investment in an early-stage technology may deem 50 per cent, or more, a reasonable discount rate; this is one reason why you must identify why you need to have a valuation carried out. Valuation for a VC has a very different basis from that for a licensing negotiation or technology sale.

3 Cost approach – generally used for early-stage technology. This approach is based on the principle of economic and technical substitution and concentrates on the cost of technology development or the cost of re-creating the technology. These costs could include patents, R&D, staff, consumables etc.

Our technology valuation model

Our model includes the three methods described above, where the greatest emphasis is on the analysis of risk and potential reward.

Cash flows will be calculated for each of the items included here under due diligence (this list is fluid and will depend on the type of technology under review). We create a series of risk-adjusted snapshots that come together to create an overall valuation model. This is a time-consuming process and will be subjective, but we consider that it creates a more useful value, where all the key components can be understood and discussed in a commercial negotiation and where individual adjustments can be made as the risk profile changes. For instance, the risk associated with IP will alter when the patent is granted for a key market sector or once certain regulatory milestones have been achieved.

Due diligence

The starting point for the technology valuation will be due diligence. The information gathered will help create the valuation building blocks, indicating the potential risks and rewards.

Key considerations for due diligence are:

● Commercial:
  – Who are the competitors, what is their added advantage, what are they in the process of developing?
  – Has confidentiality been maintained?
  – Where are the markets geographically – ease of access?
  – Is the technology too early for the market?

- What is the state of this industry: contracting, expanding or static?
- Is there government legislation that will hinder or help market entry and sales?
- Is this a short-life industry (software) or a long-life industry (pharmaceutical)?
- What is your unique competitive advantage?

- Intellectual property:
  - What types of IP are included: trade marks, established brands, registered designs, design rights, copyright, trade secrets/know-how, patents etc?
  - Are there unidentified ownership issues (can ownership be proven)?
  - Have the patents been examined – what is the outcome?
  - How likely are patent challenges and could these result in the patent not being granted?
  - Is the invention truly novel?
  - Can the patent be put into industrial practice?
  - How robust are the patent claims?
  - Has the patent been filed in key markets?
  - Can the product be easily copied or reinvented?

- Technical validity:
  - Can the idea be executed (are the required skills available)?
  - What is the level of potential technology failure?
  - Is this technology unproven outside the laboratory or workshop?
  - Have the research results been made to look a little more positive than they should?
  - Are the key researchers/inventors accessible?
  - Who has access to the know-how?
  - What are the regulatory hurdles and do they create unpredictability?

- Financial:
  - What will the market look like over time – forecasts?
  - Is the 'take to market chain' too cumbersome and expensive – what are the time frames and costs (may include prototype development and trials)?
  - What are the regulatory costs?
  - What are the potential financial margins/profit?
  - Are the finances available to bring the product to market (or to a stage of partnering/commercialization)?

A priority in ensuring that the technology value is captured and protected requires a sound analysis of fundamental issues impacting the value, and a valuation process enables the technology participants to attempt to work in unison to achieve their combined goal.

Recognizing the value of your IP allows you to manage the IP, to take decisions related to the commercialization of the IP and so to leverage the IP and achieve financial reward.

There is no doubt we are in challenging times. Innovative thought is needed to arrive at new products and concepts that will drive the markets of tomorrow, and the way we approach valuing and protecting these new opportunities must be carefully considered for this new environment.

Christi Mitchell, Intellectual Property (IP) Director, founded Highbury Ltd 14 years ago as an independent business development company specializing in international product and technology licensing and commercialization across a range of technical fields. Christi's academic background includes human genetics, molecular biology and business. She has over 25 years' worldwide IP, technology and product collaboration experience specializing in the life sciences and healthcare sectors. Highbury Ltd also specializes in raising start-up funding, in social enterprise roll-out and replication, and in patent, trade mark and IP portfolio development, management and valuation.

How to pitch to investors

David Gill at St John's Innovation Centre in Cambridge follows 10 rules in making an early-stage venture ready for investment

In an incubator, the task of preparing a pitch to investors is one of the fundamental tasks. Many centres run regular training classes, supplemented by intensive one-to-one coaching for firms likely to benefit from a final 'cramming' session before the 'exam' of presenting live to appropriate investors. This may even extend beyond generic 'investment readiness' to specific 'deal readiness' – preparing candidate companies to cover the deal requirements of particular business angel groups or venture funds.

Investment readiness means working with the entrepreneurial team first on knocking the fundamental proposition into shape, then on expressing the proposal in a way that is compelling to potential investors and in tune with their criteria:

1 Opportunity: to justify receiving the rare commodity that is risk funding, a proposal will need to show that it 'solves a point of pain' for a significant potential market (think of supplying life-scientists with reagents on an industrial scale, or producing low-cost, platform-agnostic smart meters); or at least has found a way of delighting consumers that they had not expected (no one 'needs' social networks, but millions will pay – directly or indirectly – to use them).

2 Business model: the entrepreneurs must identify the best way of 'productizing' – reproducing the product or service flawlessly and efficiently thousands of times over – and 'monetizing' – extracting financial value out of innovation. A gap in the market is not the same as a market in the gap.

3 Market pull vs technology push: many entrepreneurs focus on the originality of the idea or the craft behind the underlying technology. But neither customers nor investors share those priorities. Their focus is on how well the product solves a problem and how the venture can capture value created.

4 Entrepreneurs must research the preferences of venture funds and business angels (high-net-worth private individuals who generally take a hands-on approach to the companies they invest in). Do they invest in that sector? In that amount?

5 Timing and exit: external investors require an exit for the monies they commit to new ventures, usually in the form of a trade sale of investee companies. Has such an exit been identified, how realistic is it and when will it happen? Most venture funds are time-limited, lasting a maximum of 10 years. How close to expiry is the fund you are courting? If it is already in its 7th year out of 10, will its lifespan expire before you are ready?

6 While a full-scale business plan setting out operational and legal details may not be required until potential investors are interested enough to start detailed investigation (or 'due diligence'), to capture their initial attention entrepreneurs must perfect their 'elevator pitch'. This (imaginary) scenario envisages what an entrepreneur should say to his or her ideal investors if they walked into the lift and rode to the top floor with him or her. Such a pitch will last no more than one to three minutes at most.

7 With both the oral elevator pitch and the written executive summary, the first few sentences must grab the audience's attention – 'gasp and grasp'. Good investors are inundated with proposals, so standing out from the crowd means being able to convey straight off why *this* proposal really is transformative and able to scale.

8 All material must be presented so that the essential areas are covered in a logical way – efficiently: if it need not be in, it should not be in. This may sound obvious, but at a live pitch the rules matter: if the start-up team only has three minutes to speak and has not wowed the audience or set out the 'ask' (such as a request for 'an investment of £500,000 for a 30 per cent equity stake, with an exit by means of a trade sale to XYZ Inc or OPQ Ltd in year six') by the time the whistle blows, it will have no second chance.

9 Valuation: for early-stage firms commonly found in business incubators, textbook valuation techniques are unlikely to apply because the historic data (turnover, profits) will be lacking. Valuation is then a matter of negotiation: at what point will both investor and entrepreneur feel each is likely to be suitably rewarded if success comes knocking in five or seven years' time? This will likely mean that the founders stay as majority owners and that early-round investors acquire a stake that will remain meaningful if later-round investors dilute them (say between 15 and 35 per cent).

10 Pivoting: most new ventures will need to change direction quickly while staying grounded in what they have learnt, often several times before identifying the killer formula. This is *not* jumping randomly from one plan to another but a variation of the evolutionary pattern of selecting then amplifying the strongest candidate (product, business model, customer) out of diverse options. Shrewd investors know this and appreciate entrepreneurs demonstrating how their original idea has already mutated in contact with the market; it will likely adapt further.

St John's Innovation Centre (SJIC) is a property-based incubator designed for knowledge-intensive enterprises in their early stages. It offers flexible accommodation alongside assistance with growing and running a business, especially the commercial exploitation of technology. Founded by St John's College, Cambridge, in 1987, SJIC is an EU-accredited Business and Innovation Centre (BIC) and a founder member of UK Business Incubation.

David Gill was appointed Managing Director of the St John's Innovation Centre in October 2008. He previously set up and ran the Innovation & Technology Unit at HSBC Bank in London (1997–2004), before serving as an executive director of ETCapital Ltd, a venture firm focused on early-stage, technology-based investments. A Sloan Fellow at the Stanford Graduate School of Business in California (2005), David is currently an Academic Collaborator at the University of Cambridge Institute for Manufacturing, a non-executive director of UK Business Incubation Ltd and a member of the Department for Business Access to Finance Expert Group.

BIC: www.ebn.eu; UK Business Incubation: www.ukbi.co.uk

Crowdfunding

Nigel Walker at the Technology Strategy Board reviews the emergence of crowdfunding as a genuinely alternative source of finance

The first stage in the (mythical) 'finance escalator' is often described as investment from 'FFF' – friends, family and fools. Is crowdfunding – particularly equity based – just a way to help fools part with their money into start-ups? Or is it a valuable financial innovation offering a genuine alternative to more traditional forms of investment?

Crowdfunding is a hot topic at the moment, attracting lots of attention and not a little hype. The Pebble Watch project on Kickstarter, for example, attracted $1m in its first 24 hours, raising almost $10.3m from some 69,000 backers, each committing between $115 (pre-orders for a single watch worth $150) and $10,000 (for 31 'mega-distributors' pre-ordering 100). This is an extreme example of the power of 'the crowd', where a large number of individuals come together online and provide small amounts of finance to a project, organization, company or cause. Kickstarter statistics in April 2013 show that nearly 100,000 projects have been launched, raising nearly $500 million, with 28 projects having raised over $1m. It's not just a US phenomenon, though, and sites and projects are launching all around the world. Nesta has written a useful report into the phenomenon (available at http://www.nesta.org.uk/home1/assets/features/crowding_in) where it has tried to size the market, concluding that, in 2011, crowdfunders raised $1.5 billion, mostly in the United States, to finance over a million projects, ranging from start-ups to community projects, and from new video games to scientific research.

Nesta's report categorized the four main sorts of crowdfunding: donation, reward based, lending and equity. In business lending and risk capital it estimates a potential market size over the next three years of £7.5bn and £0.2bn respectively, assuming that crowdfunding addresses 10 per cent of the market.

The UK crowdfunding market is small, but growing fast. Nesta expects that over the course of 2012, UK crowdfunders will have deployed double the £120 million they invested in 2011. In the UK already, sites such as Crowdcube and Seedrs have raised over £6.7m and £1m respectively in equity investments, while Zopa and Funding Circle have raised £250m and £120m respectively in debt finance. That certainly sounds like a genuinely alternative source of finance.

What are some of the factors to consider when using crowdfunding?

As with any investment, it is vital to understand the motivation of those offering funding. In the case of crowdfunding, where there are different classes of 'supporters', it is necessary to consider whether they are simply backing a cause ('art for art's sake' or social impact), buying products or looking for a purely financial return on investment in businesses and projects. Crowdfunding can be a great way to combine these motivations, though, in a way that more traditional forms of investment are unable to do. The examples of the many early-stage product ideas such as the Pebble Watch or the 'Run Zombies Run!' game show how offering an early release in exchange for a donation can permit the entrepreneur to assess demand and start to develop a customer base. Demonstration, again, that markets are what businesses need, whereas money is what people think they want.

Making the investment pitch crystal clear and very easy to understand is just as important in crowdfunding as in presenting to business angels or venture capitalists. The business model must be well articulated. It is critical to show not just the features of the product or service, but the benefits that it brings to customers – benefits that they will be prepared to pay for. As with any investment pitch, it is imperative to demonstrate that this addressable market is large and growing if a potential financial return is to be expected. The sector involved can make a significant difference here: the capital needs and time-frame for delivery of a biosciences idea may be entirely different from those of a digital start-up. One of the key concerns of regulators and potential investors revolves around the needs for follow-on funding – a topic that sophisticated angel investors will be very aware of (probably from past painful experience), but which newcomers to the investment world may overlook in their enthusiasm for a 'cool' idea.

The offering structure is not just an arcane topic for capital markets professionals and corporate finance advisers to worry about. Those raising finance through online platforms need to consider this carefully, as it may have real implications on the ability to raise future capital when the business shifts from 'start up' to 'scale up'. Getting the wrong valuation early on may impact the next round of investment. Another important facet of the offering structure can be how shares are held: while it may be important for an equity investor to hold ordinary shares directly (potentially impacting tax incentives such as the ability to take advantage of the Seed Enterprise Investment Scheme, for example), having a very large number of small individual shareholders may be considered unworkable to a follow-on investor concerned about ensuring alignment of interests when it comes to further capital raising or exit. There is no substitute for professional expert advice on complex topics of this nature.

One of the key reasons for entrepreneurs to approach angel or venture capital investors is not just for their money, but also for the added value that the right investor can bring to the development and implementation of a growth plan. Crowdfunding, with its large number of small investors, may miss this, so it is vital for the entrepreneur to find another way to access the experience, contacts and wisdom that can help them grow. Mixing investment from business angels and the crowd may be the right way to do this, or alternatively these attributes may be found in non-executive directors.

All the main crowdfunding platforms have tips on how to complete a successful campaign and there are many online blogs to supplement this advice. In addition to the points noted above, two features are perhaps specific to crowdfunding, given its online nature: first, understanding the digital culture and use of networks to draw attention to the offer; and second, creating momentum – data are now showing that the tipping point for success is getting pledges of around 40 per cent of the target amount.

Nesta's report also identifies a number of key factors necessary for the UK crowd-funding market to thrive: ensuring equality will motivate early adopters to engage without excluding others; 'proportionate' regulation (developed by early engage-ment between platform operators and regulators) will allow the underlying plat-forms (and the value they capture) to be kept in the UK; developing and 'curating' communities will pay off with successful fundraising campaigns; and developing the right standards and use of data for disclosure will reduce risk and allow the market to grow. The issue of investor protection is currently a real source of debate. On one side are those who point out the imbalance between regulation of small investments in equity online and of online gambling, arguing for a significant relaxation of the UK regulatory regime for unlisted equity investments. Others take a more pragmatic view, focusing on a subset of the 'crowd' that has the means and the experience to invest – the traditional high-net-worth or sophisticated investors catered to by the angel investment market. It is interesting to note that, while they may have different strategies for their own regulatory approval and the way they approach potential investors, the main crowdfunding platforms in the UK have joined together to form the UK Crowdfunding Association. This represents a sensible response to a funda-mental issue for the development of the market.

At an event held by the Biosciences Knowledge Transfer Network in late 2012, there was an animated, but very useful discussion about the future of crowdfunding. The comparison between placing £10 either as an online bet or as a crowd share purchase was made, to argue for relaxed regulation. Two experienced investors high-lighted how they would look at that investment decision: not as a single £10 transac-tion, but as a series of perhaps four investments of £2.50 made over a period of time to meet the capital needs of the growing business. Maybe understanding investment at that level of fundamental detail is what differentiates between an alternative – and complementary – market and a way for fools to lose their money?

Nigel Walker leads on Access to Finance activities at the Technology Strategy Board, the UK's innovation agency. Its goal is to accelerate economic growth by stimulating and supporting business-led innovation. Sponsored by the Department for Business, Innovation and Skills (BIS), the Technology Strategy Board brings together business, research and the public sector, supporting and accelerating the development of innovative products and services to meet market needs, tackle major societal challenges and help build the future economy.

Tel: 01793 442700; e-mail: nigel.walker@tsb.gov.uk; Twitter: @NigelWalker7; web: www.innovateuk.org

The UK: a competitive location for IP

For companies creating intellectual property, the UK's tax system is

the business, argues Alastair Wilson at Tait Walker

Companies who are investing in innovation and the development of new intellectual property (IP) should make sure they are aware of the range of tax reliefs and incentives available in the UK. These tax reliefs and incentives are intended to be used to encourage investment and job creation by companies, and the value of the reliefs and incentives provided via the UK's corporate tax system is now more than £2.5bn annually.

As a result of changes made over the past decade, the UK is now seen as one of the leading global locations for businesses that create and own intellectual property. Not only has the UK now got the lowest corporate tax rate of any of the G7 countries (and one of the lowest in the G20), but recent changes in the UK's tax reliefs have seen a number of multinational companies choosing to make substantial investment in new R&D facilities in the UK.

The process of improving the UK's competitiveness has accelerated in recent years as the coalition government has addressed concerns voiced by the business community that the UK needed to be more attractive for companies and in particular that the UK needed to compete effectively with nearby countries such as the Republic of Ireland and the Netherlands. In addition, the government asked the inventor James Dyson to prepare a report considering the effectiveness of tax incentives as a mechanism to encourage innovation. The Dyson Report was then used to shape how the UK's tax system could be used as a catalyst for growth by innovative businesses.

The UK's corporate tax system now includes valuable incentives in the form of enhanced tax reliefs for companies carrying out R&D in the UK and additional tax reliefs for companies generating income from patents which are developed and held in the UK. New tax reliefs are also being implemented for companies developing new creative sector products such as computer games and high-end television and animation programmes.

The tax incentives for companies carrying out R&D include enhanced tax deductions for SMEs at up to 225 per cent of the expenditure on the R&D; in the event that the company is not profitable, the tax relief can instead be surrendered for a tax

It's not rocket science.

Did you know that...

- UK companies claim more than £1bn a year in R&D Tax Reliefs?
- A new Tax Relief for income from Patents comes into force on 1 April 2013?
- A new Tax Relief for video games development comes into force on 1 April 2013?

If your business is designing, engineering, manufacturing or developing new products or software we can help you reduce the cost of the development.

Our specialist IP Taxes team can help your business with:

- R&D Tax Relief claims
- Patent Box claims
- Creative Sector Tax Relief

Plus much more, find out today!

If you want to understand more about how we can help your business reduce the cost of developing intellectual property, e-mail me at: alastair.wilson@taitwalker.co.uk

 **TAIT WALKER**
CHARTERED ACCOUNTANTS

www.taitwalker.co.uk

credit which is paid in cash. The payable tax credit can provide a cash rebate of up to approximately 25 per cent of the expenditure on R&D. For large companies an enhanced tax deduction is also available and again for loss-making companies the relief can be surrendered for a cash credit of approximately 8 per cent of the qualifying expenditure.

The R&D tax incentives are now claimed by a broad range of companies in the UK and making claims on an annual basis is becoming part of the financing agenda for companies across the UK's manufacturing, engineering, pharmaceutical and software industries. At the same time as considering grant funding for new projects, companies are increasingly factoring the R&D tax incentives into their project costings as they become used to claiming the incentives. For large companies new provisions are being enacted which will allow companies to recognize the tax incentives in their accounts in a similar manner to a grant, which will enable project teams to identify clearly the benefit of the incentives to their project.

The tax incentives for companies carrying out R&D in the UK together result in an overall annual benefit in excess of £1.5bn being provided via the tax system. However, the take-up rate within UK companies is still comparatively low when compared to the percentage of companies claiming similar incentives in other countries such as Australia or Canada where there are long-established R&D tax incentives programmes. The UK's tax authority, HM Revenue & Customs, is proactively trying to increase awareness of the tax incentives available so that the percentage of companies that claim the benefit of the incentives is increased.

For companies that create new IP which is then patented, the UK has now introduced provisions called Patent Box which give the profit generated from the patents a 10 per cent tax rate, which is half the UK's lowest current corporate tax rate. The profit which can be included within the special 10 per cent rate can include the profit from sales of patented products, income from licence fees generated by licensing the IP and also income derived by using a patented tool in the manufacturing process.

The Patent Box provisions are expected to be worth an additional £1.5bn annually to companies in the UK in the form of reduced taxes. The enactment of the provisions has been stated by a number of multinational companies as a key factor in their decision to locate in the UK.

The most recent addition to the UK's tax reliefs for companies creating IP are the Creative Sector Tax Reliefs which can be claimed by companies producing certain television programmes, animation or computer games. The Creative Sector Tax Reliefs can provide a benefit equivalent to up to 20 per cent of the cost of the project. These new reliefs have been introduced as a response to tax incentives which are provided in countries such as Canada and France and which had been causing companies in the creative industries to move away from the UK. The games sector in particular had been badly affected by the lack of any tax incentives and once the new relief is approved by the EU the games development industry is expecting the sector to grow strongly on the back of the new reliefs.

It is possible for companies to claim several of the tax reliefs and incentives at the same time; for example, it is possible for companies to claim the R&D tax reliefs on new development work while also claiming the Patent Box reliefs on income derived from developed and patented IP. The effect of the provisions is intended to encourage new investment in the development of IP and R&D facilities, along with the retention of the IP in the UK. By encouraging companies to claim the reliefs, the UK's tax authorities accept that overall corporate tax receipts from companies will reduce, but at the same time the receipts from payroll taxes from new job creation should increase to compensate.

The amount of benefit that companies can receive using these tax reliefs can be substantial. For example, many Formula 1 teams are based in the UK and, for example, Williams F1 benefited by approximately £3.8m in each of 2010 and 2011.

The tax reliefs and incentives can be a form of state aid and so the benefit can be restricted where grants have also been received on the same project. Unlike some grants, the tax reliefs are claimed during or after the activity on projects rather than in advance of the project. Compared to a grant, the cash-flow benefit could therefore be later than a grant of an equivalent amount.

However, unlike most UK grants, the tax reliefs are not subject to a competitive bidding process, so a company which has confirmed it is carrying out a qualifying activity will know it is entitled to claim the benefit of the incentive rather than hoping it will be awarded the benefit. To gain the maximum benefit of the tax reliefs and to understand when the benefit will be received, companies should consider the impact of the tax reliefs at the same time as applying for grants towards innovative projects.

Alastair Wilson is a partner in Tait Walker LLP which is the North East of England's largest independent accountancy firm. He has advised innovative companies on the tax reliefs available in the UK for more than 15 years and in particular since the inception of the UK's R&D tax relief regime in 2000. Since then he has helped a large number of companies to maximize the tax reliefs and incentives available from the costs incurred on the IP they have created.

Further details: www.taitwalker.co.uk

Tax relief for R&D

Why do so many small companies let money go begging when they find new uses for science and technology in their everyday operations, asks Barry Jefferd at George Hay

The government has been keen to encourage technological innovation. It sees technology as a UK success but wants to push further. It sees that one way of doing this is by incentivizing businesses through the tax system.

Research and Development (R&D) Tax Relief

It may be surprising to note that this relief was first introduced for small/medium enterprises (SMEs) on 1 April 2000, with the scheme extended to large companies two years later. Many businesses have used it to help fund significant expenditure on R&D.

Yet the government considers (and my experience confirms this) that it is a valuable relief that is under-claimed, and millions of pounds go begging. In fact, they actually employ tax inspectors to go out and talk to businesses to encourage them to claim.

What is it?

R&D relief rewards expenditure on research *or* development where a project seeks to achieve an advance in science or technology. It has been suggested that the word 'Research' in the title confuses matters as in reality it is development expenditure that is rewarded.

At first reading you would no doubt imagine a large research unit where highly qualified scientists pore over test tubes trying to find the new 'ultimate' solution which will be featured in science journals throughout the land. While there is no doubt that this does qualify, you do not need to set your sights so high.

For example, a composite company we acted for received a contract for an unusual order. It was difficult to work out how it could be achieved. It was too complex for the current set-up and the technology was not publicly available. Over a short period of time, the company's engineers created prototypes and devised a way to carry out the contract. This technological advance qualified for R&D Tax Relief.

In another case, one of our clients developed specialist safety gloves. For the particular industry this client worked in, normal safety covers would not have sufficed. Trial and error and 'development' led to a new coating being used – this was R&D.

I would suggest that most companies with any tooling or development process would be able to find some R&D that actually would qualify. The technology may have been used by a competitor or another business; however, if that advanced technology is not in the public domain then trying to develop it yourself is R&D. It has been suggested that if you cannot find how to do it via a search engine, it must be new development.

R&D can also extend to computer software.

Amount of relief

There are two schemes in the UK, the SME scheme and the Large Company Scheme. The definition of an SME is somewhat surprising, and may be considered generous. It is a company with fewer than 500 employees and either turnover of less than €100m *or* gross assets of less than €86m. This means that most companies will qualify as SMEs. The rate of relief for SMEs is 225 per cent and for large companies it is 130 per cent.

What does this mean?

Using the SME scheme, if a business spends, say, £10,000 on qualifying R&D then it can deduct £10,000 × 225 per cent ie £22,500 against its taxable profits for the year. For its published accounts only the £10,000 will be a deduction; for its corporation tax return the deduction will be £22,500. This £22,500 will then save tax at the company's rate of corporation tax. Given the aim to reduce the rate of corporation tax to 20 per cent, this will save £4,500 in tax, so as a summary:

Spend £10,000 on R&D and receive a tax deduction of £4,500.

With a 130 per cent uplift for large companies, the saving would be £2,600 or higher if their rate of corporation tax is higher than 20 per cent.

It is appreciated that not all companies make profits, so therefore there would be no tax to pay; what then is the point of the deduction? In that case, if the company wants to, it can sell its enhanced R&D – the £22,500 – to HM Revenue & Customs (HMRC). As a consequence of the early claim, HMRC will only repay at 11 per cent, which is £2,475, but it will be cash in the bank.

Whether or not to make the early claim depends on how quickly the company thinks it will become profitable. For large companies no early sale of R&D relief is possible.

So what are these qualifying costs?

Staff costs	It will be necessary to work out how much time an individual spends on R&D and non-R&D activities.
Director's time	It will be necessary to work out how much time a director spends on R&D compared to non-R&D activity. HMRC will not usually allow 100 per cent of director's time as some time must be spent running the company.
Software or consumable items	Anything directly attributable (or reasonably apportioned) to R&D.
Payment to subcontractors	Generally only available to SMEs and again must be on R&D work. Only 65 per cent of subcontracted costs are allowable for R&D as obviously the charge would include a 'profit' element from the subcontractor.
Directly attributable overheads	For example, light and heat, power.

Is it that easy?

The important point is to ensure that you keep appropriate records. Once the R&D activity has been defined, ensure that appropriate records are kept, so, for example, that the company can clearly demonstrate that the consumables are used directly for R&D. For staff costs, it is not necessary for staff to actually complete project time sheets, but if they do not, how are you able to prove to HMRC that your apportionment of such costs is reasonable?

The R&D could take years

As long as you are continuously looking to develop a product, it does not matter how long it takes. I had one client where we claimed R&D relief on the same project for eight years.

It does not even matter if the project fails and your development is in vain. Some commentators suggest that the failure to complete demonstrates clearly that the project must have been one of trying to advance technology. Failure certainly avoids the need to look carefully at where R&D stops and marketing starts. This is always a grey area, as the latter does not qualify and is something that HMRC will always look at closely.

Conclusion

I have worked with our clients, ensuring that they have procedures in place to make a valid claim. The biggest barrier that I come across is trying to tease out from my clients that they actually do R&D. Time and again I see expenditure in accounts which indicates that R&D could be present, yet it is only after much interrogating by me that the client finally identifies the project, usually with 'I didn't realize that counted as R&D'.

Remember that you only need to satisfy HMRC by making a valid claim under the Taxes Act; you are not stating that your R&D is worthy of a Nobel Prize.

Barry Jefferd is a Chartered Accountant and Chartered Tax Adviser and is a Tax Partner in George Hay Chartered Accountants, a firm with offices in Huntingdon, Biggleswade and Letchworth. Barry advises clients on various tax planning matters, including making claims for R&D Tax Relief. He also advises other accountants on this subject.

Tel: 01480 426500; e-mail: barry.jefferd@georgehay.co.uk

MHA MacIntyre Hudson

GLOBAL EXPERTISE · NATIONAL EXPERIENCE · LOCAL EXCELLENCE®

Chartered Accountants, Tax and Business Advisers

When it comes to business we're here to support and guide you.

With extensive experience of R&D tax credit claims and Patent Box relief, we will advise and support you every step of the way.

For more information contact
Patrick King on 01494 441 226 or email
patrick.king@mhllp.co.uk

MHA MacIntyre Hudson
31 Castle Street
High Wycombe
HP13 6RU

www.macintyrehudson.co.uk

The Patent Box

Rates of returns on innovations in technology are set to improve under

a new incentive. Patrick King at MHA MacIntyre Hudson explains how it works

The UK's Patent Box regime finally came into force on 1 April 2013, after lengthy consultations with interested parties, and is of potentially huge importance to any innovative company.

The purpose of this chapter is not to explain all the complexities and intricacies of the legislation (there are many), but rather to explain why it has been introduced, what its benefits are, how a company might qualify and some of the main areas for consideration both practically and from a planning perspective.

1. The background

The UK has had a steadily more advantageous regime for R&D expenditure for over 10 years now in the form of R&D Tax Credits. These offer up to a 225 per cent deduction for tax purposes for any qualifying R&D expenditure, and in loss-making companies this can be surrendered for a cash payment from the government. Very advantageous though these reliefs are, they are only available up to the point that the product is developed and no relief was generally available thereafter.

As a result of this, the government believed that many companies were choosing to move their high-value production of the finished innovative products overseas to more favourable tax jurisdictions. This caused a loss to the UK exchequer not only of the corporation tax (CT) on the profits those companies could make, but also of the employment (and related taxes) that went with it.

Patent Box (PB) was introduced to incentivize innovative companies to retain production in the UK by offering the carrot of an advantageous effective tax rate of 10 per cent on qualifying profits. It is hoped that this relief will not only cause companies to stay in the UK but also tempt others to move valuable intellectual property (IP) back to this country. If successful, the cost to the exchequer should in the fullness of time be repaid by an increase in the profits subjected to UK CT, and increased employment taxes.[1]

2. How to qualify

PB is only available to companies and relates to profits arising from qualifying patents and certain plant variety and breeders' rights. A qualifying patent means one issued by the UK Patent Office, a European patent or a patent issued by certain specified European Economic Area (EEA) states. Patents issued by anywhere else, the United States, Canada etc, will not qualify. The company must also have been involved in developing the patent or its applications. The patent does not need to be owned, as an exclusive licence over a patent will also qualify. There was some criticism that the UK chose only to include patents for the relief rather than other forms of IP, but to counter this the rules regarding what profits qualify have deliberately been set quite wide (see section 3 below).

Having established that it has qualifying patents, the company must next elect into the regime, but before doing so it should check that it will indeed have a PB profit. If the calculation rules result in a loss for PB purposes, it would probably be best to remain outside the box as such losses will be ring-fenced and in effect given tax relief at only 10 per cent. The regime allows a company to opt out of the box having elected in, but there is then a five-year wait before it can again elect in. Care is therefore needed.

3. What types of income qualify?

Five types of income can be included as relevant intellectual property income (RIPI), as follows:

(i)   income from the sale of a patented item or 'products incorporating it';

(ii)   income from licensing the patent (ie royalties);

(iii) the outright sale of the patent rights;

(iv)   notional royalties;

(v)   infringement income.

Of these, (i), (iv) and (v) warrant some further explanation as follows:

(i)   The interesting point here is that the qualifying income is not only that directly related to the patented product itself but also the whole item within which the patented item is designed to be incorporated. An example that HMRC gave is of a patented printer cartridge being sold in or with the (non-patented) printer with which it is designed to work. The patented item needs to fulfil a real useful function within the overall product or relief will be denied, and it has to be incorporated within the product rather than just used in it. For example, a patented DVD will not make a non-patented DVD player qualify.

(iv)   Where a company has a patented invention which is not incorporated in anything sold but, for example, is used in a machine to increase the productivity of the company's products, a notional royalty can be charged.

The notional royalty should be calculated on OECD transfer pricing guidelines as if the company charged itself an arm's-length royalty for the use of the patented device.

(v) If a patent is infringed and the patent owner successfully sues for compensation, the compensation will be within PB.

4. How to calculate relevant intellectual property profits (RIPP)

The calculations needed to arrive at RIPP are somewhat complex and shall be covered only in the briefest overview in this chapter. The HMRC guidance referred to in (i) above is very useful in working out how to carry out these computations.

In summary, there are two methods of calculation: the pro rata method and the streaming method. As the names suggest, the pro rata method seeks to pro rata profits based on the proportion of RIPI to total gross income (TGI), whereas the streaming method seeks to apportion costs more directly to the qualifying and non-qualifying income streams.

Having established the amount of qualifying profit, it is then necessary to make certain deductions for what are described as 'routine return items'. There are six types of costs (such as rent, rates and staff costs) which are each deemed to give rise to part of the overall profit at a notional rate of 10 per cent. Once deducted, this leaves the qualifying residual profit (QRP).

Having calculated the QRP it is then necessary to deduct a 'marketing assets return'. This is intended to remove the element of profit related to the brand, trade marks and other marketing assets the company may have. Again transfer pricing methodology is required, although there is a small claims procedure (less than £1m) where a notional 25 per cent of QRP is deducted.

Once the marketing assets adjustment is made, the company is left with its RIPP or RP (relevant profit), which is inserted into the fraction $RP \times \left(\frac{MR - IPR}{MR}\right)$, where MR is the main rate of CT and IPR is the IP rate of CT (ie 10 per cent). The product of this equation is a figure which is inserted into the company's tax computation as a deduction. The result of the deduction is that an effective rate of 10 per cent is applied to the RP.

5. Practical considerations and planning issues

Companies which innovate should review their IP to ensure that they obtain patents where possible to bring more income within PB. Patents already owned should be reviewed and any qualifying ones identified. Accounting systems should be reviewed to ensure easy availability of the income details relating to qualifying and non-qualifying items and the routine return items should be carefully reviewed. Marketing assets should be identified, but in many cases if the company sells to business or is engaged in a regulated market, HMRC may well accept that little or no adjustment is required. Where sales are to private customers, the marketing assets return could be significant for a well-established business.

Where a group of companies is involved, it is common for one company to hold the patents which are then utilized by other companies in the group. It is important that licences which meet the exclusivity tests in the legislation are in place, as otherwise the trading companies' income will not benefit from PB. Also, the patent holding company needs to 'actively manage' its patents in order that any patent income it receives will qualify.

Example of group licensing/patent ownership

An electronics manufacturing company (Man Co) owns several patents. Man Co sells about half its products to customers overseas and half to a group company (Sales Co) which then sells to customers in the UK. The result of this structure is that sales by Man Co are largely covered by PB but sales by Sales Co are not. A solution to this problem might be to assign some patents to Sales Co and then exclusively license the manufacturing company to develop, manufacture and sell the products. With care it should be possible for Man Co to continue qualifying as before (by virtue of having exclusive licences) and for Sales Co also to qualify by virtue of its ownership of the patents.

Summary

To conclude, PB offers an attractive tax benefit for companies owning or licensing qualifying patents, but the complexities of the rules mean that advance planning is essential. There are many practical as well as technical matters to consider, and companies should review their IP urgently to ensure that they maximize their benefit.

Note

1 The PB regime legislation can be found in new part 8A of CTA 2010 having been introduced by Schedule 2 of FA 2012. Extensive and helpful HMRC guidance is available in the HMRC manual at CIRD 200100-260000.

Patrick King is a Tax Partner and Head of the Technology Sector Group at chartered accountants and business advisers, MHA MacIntyre Hudson.

Further details: www.macintyrehudson.co.uk

INDEX

outsourcing innovation (and) 87–89
  benefits: cost; expertise; skills and capability;
      speed to market; unfettered thinking
      88
  questions to ask yourself on clear objectives;
      cost; cultural fit; IP; trust 87–88
OVO Innovation 100

Parker, R 84
the Patent Box (PB) (and) 125, 247, 254, 263,
      323–26
  background to 323
  calculating relevant intellectual property
      profits (RIPP) 325
  corporation tax 77–78
  due diligence 71
  group licensing/patent ownership (example)
      326
  practical considerations and planning issues
      325–26
  provisions 315
  qualifying for 324
  regimes 125–26
  types of income qualifying for 324–25
patent exclusions (and) 265–72
  business methods 265, 270
  embodiments/conditions for patent grant
      267
  graphical user interfaces (GUIs) 270
  invasive medical diagnosis 269
  mathematical methods 268
  performance of a mental act 269
  scientific discoveries 268
  the 'skilled man' 267, 268
  software 247, 257, 268
  treatment of human or animal body 269
patent landscaping benefits 199–202
  avoidance of potentially expensive litigious or
      defensive action 202
  avoidance of potentially expensive mistakes
      200
  identify current and future competitors
      200
  identify gaps in your R&D 201
  identify patents as seminal discoveries or as
      incremental improvements 201
  improve your licensing strategy 201
  learn what competitors are working on
      200
  learn whose innovations could be licensed to
      your benefit 202
  see rapidity of new innovation in your space
      200–201
  visualise most densely and sparsely populated
      patent areas 202
Patent & Licensing Exchange 71

patent markets 71–72
  non-practising entities (NPEs)
  Ocean Tomo 71
Patent Office (UK) 270, 274, 324
Patent Seekers 199–202
patent(s) (and) 93, 254, 257, 324–25
      see also freedom to commercialize and
      the Patent Box
  assessment of third-party rights/dealing with
      threat 205–06
  choice of country for first (priority) filing
      291
  cost and inefficiencies of current European
      system for 215–16
  determining scope of see determining scope of
      patents
  EEA 324
  European Common Patent 71
  filing for 69–70, 255–56
  filing in the US see subject entry
  global increase in filings 273
  granting 248
  and graphical user interfaces (GUIs) 265,
      270
  identification of third-party 203, 205
  infringement of 246
  international patent applications 256
  Jackson Reforms to civil procedure
      218–19
    changes to after the event (ATE) insurance
      219
    costs budgeting 218
    reform of conditional fee agreements
      (CFAs) 219
  myths about 247–48
  Patents County Court (PCC) see subject entry
  pools and standards 78
  proposed introduction of the Unified Patent
      Court 216–17
  protection 103, 119
  software 247, 265
  trolls 71, 75–76, 211
  unitary patent (EU) see subject entry
Patents County Court (PCC) 217–18
  benefits of 218
  cases suitable for 217
Pharma 110–11, 165, 167, 170
Philips 273
Phillips, J 100
The Pirbright Institute 117–20
portals facilitating access to databases of expertise
      140
Prabhu, J 72
PraxisUnico 83–86
Prigogine, I 48
prior art 262

INDEX OF ADVERTISERS